FREE MOVEMENT

FREE MOVEMENT

Ethical issues in the transnational migration of people and of money

edited by

Brian Barry
and
Robert E. Goodin

**HARVESTER
WHEATSHEAF**

New York   London   Toronto   Sydney   Tokyo   Singapore

First published 1992 by
Harvester Wheatsheaf,
Campus 400, Maylands Avenue,
Hemel Hempstead,
Hertfordshire, HP2 7 EZ
A division of
Simon & Schuster International Group

Typeset in 10/12pt Sabon
by Keyboard Services, Luton

Printed and bound in Great Britain by
BPCC Wheatons Ltd, Exeter

British Library Cataloguing in Publication Data

Free movement: Ethical issues in the
transnational migration of people and of money.
I. Barry, Brian II. Goodin, Robert E.
325.01

ISBN 0–7450–1152–7

1 2 3 4 5   95 94 93 92

This book is dedicated to Elena Gomez Valera
who teaches the children of immigrant families
in Los Angeles

Contents

Notes on the contributors

Brian Barry is Professor of Political Science at the London School of Economics, and sometime editor of both *Ethics* and the *British Journal of Political Science*. He is a Fellow of the British Academy and of the American Academy of Arts and Sciences. His publications include *Political Argument* (1965; second ed. 1991), *Sociologists, Economists and Democracy* (1970; second ed. 1978), *The Liberal Theory of Justice* (1973) and *Theories of Justice* (1989). *Power, Democracy, and Justice*, his collected essays, was published in 1989. A paperback edition in two volumes appeared in 1991, volume 1 entitled *Democracy and Power* and volume 2 (containing new material) *Liberty and Justice*.

Chris Brown is Lecturer in Politics and International Relations at the University of Kent in Canterbury, England. His interests are largely focused on the theory of international relations and international political economy. He has published articles in the *Review of International Studies*, *Millennium* and a number of other journals. His book *International Relations Theory: New normative approaches* will be published by Harvester Wheatsheaf in 1992.

Joseph H. Carens is Associate Professor of Political Science at the University of Toronto. He is author of *Equality, Moral Incentives and the Market* and various articles on political and social theory. He is currently working on a new book, *Immigration and Political Community*.

Ann Dummett is an independent consultant advising the Commission for Racial Equality in London on its European policies. She is the author of *A Portrait of English Racism* and of several works on nationality and immigration law including (in collaboration with Andrew Nicol) *Subjects, Citizens, Aliens and Others.*

John Finnis is Professor of Law and Legal Philosophy in the University of Oxford and Fellow of University College there. He is a Fellow of the British Academy and author of *Natural Law and Natural Rights* (written while working at the University of Malawi) and other books, and co-author of *Nuclear Deterrence, Morality and Realism.*

Robert E. Goodin is now Professor of Philosophy in the Research School of Social Sciences at the Australian National University, having spent the previous decade teaching government at the University of Essex. He is author of, most recently, *Motivating Political Morality* (1992) and is founding editor of the new *Journal of Political Philosophy*, commencing publication from Blackwell in 1993.

David C. Hendrickson is Associate Professor of Political Science at Colorado College. He is the author of two books on American defence policy and three books with Robert W. Tucker: *The Imperial Temptation: The new world order and America's purpose* (1992), *Empire of Liberty: The statecraft of Thomas Jefferson* (1990), and *The Fall of the First British Empire: Origins of the War of American Independence* (1982).

Kurt Hübner is a Research Assistant at the Institute for Political Science at the Free University of Berlin and a member of the advisory board for *PROKLA*. His recent publications include: *Alternative Wirtschaftsplitik jenseits des Keynesianismus* (with E. Altvater and M. Stanger, 1983); *Die Armut der Nationen* (with E. Altvater, J. Lorentzen and R. Rojas, 1987); *Theorie der Regulation – Eine kritische Rekonstruktion eines neuen Ansatzes der Politischen Ökonomie* (1989); and articles on the theories of crises and economic and trade union policy.

Deepak Lal is Professor of Political Economy at University College, London and James Coleman Professor of International Development Studies at the University of California, Los Angeles. He has been Research Administrator at the World Bank, and a consultant to numerous international organizations and governments in developing countries. His books include: *Appraising Foreign Investment in Developing Countries, The Poverty of Development Economics, The Hindu Equilibrium* and a number of other books and articles on public policy and development.

I. M. D. Little is sometime Professor of Economics in the University of Oxford, and an Emeritus Fellow of Nuffield College, Oxford. He is author of many books, among them *A Critique of Welfare Economics* (1950; second ed. 1957), *Economic Development: Theory, policy and international relations* (1982), with T. Scitovsky and M. H. Scott, *Industry and Trade in Some Developing Countries* (1970) and, with J. A. Mirrlees, *Project Appraisal and Planning* (1974).

Terry Nardin is Professor of Political Science at the University of Wisconsin, Milwaukee. He is author of *Law, Morality, and the Relations of States* (1983) and editor, with David R. Mapel, of *Traditions of International Ethics* (1992).

Onora O'Neill is Professor of Philosophy at the University of Essex. Her contribution to this volume was written while she was a Fellow at the Wissenschaftskolleg zu Berlin in 1989–90. In 1992 she will become Principal of Newnham College, Cambridge. She is author of *Faces of Hunger: An essay on poverty, development and justice* (1986) and *Constructions of Reason: Explorations of Kant's practical philosophy* (1989).

Philippe Van Parijs is Professor of Economic and Social Ethics at the Université Catholique de Louvain. He is the author of *Evolutionary Explanation in the Social Sciences* (1981), *Le Modèle économique et ses rivaux* (1990), *Qu'est-ce qu'une société juste?* (1991) and a forthcoming collection of essays on Marxism and the editor of *Arguing for Basic Income* (1992).

Hillel Steiner is Senior Lecturer in Political Philosophy at the University of Manchester. He is the author of various papers on liberty, rights and justice in philosophy, economics and politics in journals, and is currently completing a book entitled *An Essay on Rights*.

Susan Strange is Emeritus Professor of International Relations at the London School of Economics and Professor of International Relations at the European University Institute in Florence. Her books include *Casino Capitalism* (1986), *States and Markets* (1989), and (with John Stopford) *Rival States, Rival Firms* (1991).

Paul J. Weithman is Assistant Professor of Philosophy at the University of Notre Dame. He has published articles in *Philosophy and Public Affairs*, the *Journal of the History of Philosophy*, and other professional journals.

James Woodward is Associate Professor of Philosophy at the California Institute of Technology. His interests include philosophy of science as well as social and political philosophy.

The Ethikon Institute

The articles which comprise this book were written for a conference organized at Mont Saint Michel, France in September, 1989 by The Ethikon Institute in collaboration with The California Institute of Technology. The Ethikon Institute was established to promote mutual understanding and greater tolerance among peoples of different moral traditions. Focusing on issues of broad public concern, it aims to explore the prospects of ethical consensus, where it can be found, and to identify methods for the peaceful accommodation of irreducible differences. The Institute's Intersocietal Relations Program studies the actual and potential effects of ethical agreement and disagreement on relations between states and between distinct communities within multinational states. As a facilitator of dialogue The Ethikon Institute takes no position on the issues that divide its participants. It serves not as an arbiter but as a forum for the amicable expression of diverse and sometimes contending views.

Introduction

— 1 —

A reader's guide

Brian Barry

The closing years of the twentieth century seem likely to be dominated by issues involving borders. There are strong forces making for the breaking up of states, as we have seen in the Balkans, the former Soviet Union and many other parts of the world. At the same time, there are also strong forces making for the transcending of state boundaries as finance and production become increasingly international. The moves towards integration within the European Economic Community are one institutional response to a phenomenon experienced by almost every country.

In this book, we focus on the crossing of state boundaries by people and by money. The issue that animates the project is the contrast between the way in which states treat the inflow of people and the way in which they treat the inflow of money. Every state claims the right to determine who shall be permitted to enter its territory and almost all exercise this right vigorously to set up restrictive (in many cases virtually prohibitive) restrictions on entry for the purpose of living and working in the country. Within the world as a whole tens of millions – quite possibly hundreds of millions – of people would emigrate if the country of their choice would accept them, but the vast majority are doomed to frustration. Yet at the same time most countries place few restrictions on the transfer of capital into them and many governments actively court foreign investment.

The object of the present book is to offer a systematic analysis of movements across international boundaries of both people and money. The hope is that, by juxtaposing the two, more light will be thrown on each than could be expected from separate analyses. At the same time, the exercise is intended as a contribution to political philosophy, which should be of value even to those with no special interest in the topics discussed here. For it is not often that one is able to see how a number of very

3

different approaches arrive at conclusions about a common set of problems. These are, moreover, problems that have not traditionally been
central to the concerns of any mainstream theory. As this book demonstrates, we can find out a lot about a theory by testing it out in unfamiliar
intellectual territory.

The exploration of our issues from a variety of perspectives is what gives
this book its special, and we believe unusually interesting, character. We
have attempted to include a number of the best established and most
elaborately worked out approaches here. We take up first the kind of
liberal egalitarian theorizing associated with names such as those of John —
Rawls and Ronald Dworkin. We then proceed to the kind of libertarian,
anti-statist, position represented by Robert Nozick or (a different strand
this) economic liberals such as F. A. Hayek. Next we consider the application of Marxist analysis to our topics. We then turn to the tradition of
natural law theorizing. Lastly, we look at a system of ideas which may
appear inimical to ethics: that of political realism within the study of
international relations. How far this style of realism is actually opposed to
ethical considerations is precisely one of the problems that will be posed
here.

The core of the book thus consists of five sections, each devoted to one
of these five perspectives. All of the five sections adhere to the same format.
There are three chapters within each. The first is an analysis of migration
from the point of view of the relevant perspective. The second chapter
performs the same office for transfers of money. The third and last chapter
takes the form of a commentary on the preceding two. After the five
sections, each devoted to a perspective, the book concludes with two
pieces that attempt to draw together some of the themes that have
emerged.

The advantage of this rigid system of organization is that it provides a
common reference point. It functions, one may say, as a grid. Within this
grid will be found a great variety of treatments of our topics. This is
inevitable. For each perspective has its own distinct way of conceiving the
issues, and a point that is central within one theory may be quite peripheral
within another. It would have been counterproductive for the editors to
have attempted to homogenize the essays collected here. For this would
have meant distorting the way in which the questions appear from different
viewpoints. We are content to have provided a framework that makes
comparison possible and, we hope, fruitful.

Bringing together a group of authors from five countries, five perspectives and a number of academic disciplines is not the easiest of tasks.
Getting them to collaborate is even less easy. Neither would have been
possible without the Ethikon Institute and, above all, the contribution of
its guiding spirit, Philip Valera. The initial impetus was provided by a

conference held at the spectacular and inspiring venue of Mont St Michel in September 1989. The subsequent chores of revision and responding to revisions made by others have no doubt been lightened by memories of that very congenial and productive meeting. Two of our authors, Paul Weithman and John Finnis, were not at the conference, and we owe a special debt to them for making their contributions subsequently.

2

If people were money . . .

Robert E. Goodin

In the penultimate year of the Reagan presidency, the United States expelled over a million illegal aliens and was decidedly bullish about it.[1] In the same year, the United States absorbed over two hundred billion dollars worth of direct foreign investment and was not even slightly sheepish about it.[2] Australia, Great Britain and, indeed much of the civilized and semi-civilized world had been doing much the same, albeit in a little less dramatic fashion, for the past decade or in some cases much more.[3]

The message is clear enough. Had immigrants been investments – had the people been money – their influx would have been welcomed with open arms. Instead, it was deeply resented and fiercely resisted.

Why is there such a disparity in policy responses? Surely foreign penetration is foreign penetration, whatever form it takes. What makes the inflow of people so very different from the inflow of finance capital? These chapters, collectively, are devoted to exploring those sorts of questions.

The nature of borders

The formal functions of international boundaries are purely juridical. They physically delimit the sphere of sovereignty.[4] They define jurisdictions. They specify, literally, how far the writ of any given sovereign runs. Formally, frontiers merely mark the point at which one body of law gives way to another.

In practice, international borders reflect various other realities and serve various other ends, as well. Power politics being what they are, sovereigns' writs tend to run just as far as they are willing and able to press them. So, unsurprisingly, international boundaries have historically tended also to

6

mark out a militarily defensible space, delimited by some substantially impenetrable physical barriers (the Alps, the Pyrenees or the English Channel).

Boundaries chosen purely for military purposes thus served – in the first instance, almost automatically – social functions as well. In so far as international borders corresponded to relatively impenetrable physical barriers, they substantially impeded movement of all sorts. It was hard to move anything – people or goods, just as surely as armies or cannons – across them. So the same thing that once kept out foreign princes also kept out foreigners quite generally, their persons as well as their commodities and their commercial influence. Devices designed to secure sovereign prerogatives also helped to secure a substantial measure of autarky in social and economic realms, as well.

Nowadays, however, physical barriers to the movement of people and more especially of money are not what they once were. Even for the economically destitute, hitching a ride across oceans or continents proves far from impossible. And money, of course, moves literally with the flick of the finger on the keyboard. What was once a given of nature has now become a matter of policy. It is now for us, collectively, to say how much movement we are prepared to allow across our borders.

How open should borders be?

The aim of this chapter is not to settle the question of whether borders should be open or closed. Those matters will be discussed at length, and from diverse perspectives, in later chapters. Here, I shall merely attempt to set the stage for those subsequent discussions by sketching the sorts of considerations that seem to figure most centrally in contemporary policy discussions in these areas.

The case for free movement

At least within the Anglo-American democracies, the standard way of arguing for freer movement seems to be liberal egalitarian in form.[5] The premises at work here are, essentially, two: one is egalitarianism; the other is universalism, which in the present context amounts principally to globalism. The first holds that distributions of life prospects ought to be roughly equal, or at least substantially more equal than they now are. The second holds that our focus, in making those comparisons, ought to be upon people in general rather than merely upon people living within some particular political jurisdiction.[6]

Within that logic, the concern for freer movement of people derives essentially from a perception of the limited scope of government-to-government capital transfers. Whether foreign aid or foreign loans, whether multilateral or bilateral, those programmes as we now know them all seem simply incapable of changing the lives of people in recipient countries in any big way.

They have limited success largely because they have limited funds. Rich countries simply put too little into international transfer programmes to make much difference. 'The majority of aid', it is said, 'is successful in terms of its own objectives.'[7] And that may well be true. But, alas, reducing global inequality is only one among many objectives of most such programmes – and a subsidiary one at that.

There is every reason to believe that a generously funded, well-targeted programme of foreign assistance could well work to reduce global economic inequalities. We now know enough about how to organize aid programmes to be pretty confident of accomplishing those goals, if only we were truly serious about them.[8] The point is precisely that the richer nations are not now, and seem unlikely soon to become, deeply committed to goals of global redistribution.

In such circumstances, we are driven to rely instead upon decidedly second-best mechanisms of global redistribution. If we cannot move enough money to where the needy people are, then we will have to count on moving as many of the needy people as possible to where the money is. In these circumstances, if we really want people in poorer countries to enjoy life chances even remotely similar to those of people in richer countries, then the best way of ensuring that seems to be for the poor people themselves to move to the richer country. (Even then, the guarantee is less than iron-clad: much depends on the skills of immigrants, the willingness of domestic employers to employ them and the willingness of governments to apply the same labour and social security laws to them.) Of course, there is likely to be even more political resistance to that policy than the other. Citizens of rich nations are likely to be even more reluctant to welcome lots of destitute foreigners into their country than they historically have been to shipping substantial sums of money abroad to relieve their suffering.

But that, in a way, is precisely the political point underlying exercises in moral philosophy on this topic. The goal of such exercises is precisely to put rich countries on the spot. The aim is to argue that, if arguments for international distributive justice are valid and if rich countries do not want to give generously of their money to meet the demands that those arguments impose, then they are morally obliged to pay instead in a currency that they hold even dearer.

Morally, rich countries faced with strong moral arguments for global redistribution have only two options. Ideally, they should provide the poor with substantial sums of foreign aid; failing that, as a moral minimum they must alternatively be willing to admit substantial numbers of immigrants from the poorest countries. If that second alternative is politically even more unacceptable than the first, and if morally those are the only two options, and if people are capable of being moved by reflections upon morality at all, then perhaps citizens of the richer countries might, on second thought, take a more generous attitude towards foreign aid.

This point can – and politically should – be put just that sharply. If the rich countries do not want to let foreigners in, then the very least they must do is send much more money to compensate them for their being kept out. Those capital transfers really must be understood as compensation rather than as charity. They are merely the fair recompense for their being blocked from doing something (that is, moving to a richer country) that could, and quite probably would, have resulted in their earning that much more for themselves.

The case against free movement

That, or something like it, probably approximates the political logic underlying most arguments for freer movement of people and of money between the rich and poor nations of the world. Against those considerations, however, are arrayed others which argue for preserving or perhaps even increasing barriers to movement of both sorts.

Some of those arguments are inspired by what has recently been termed 'communitarianism'. On this view, different people and peoples are morally entitled – and perhaps are morally enjoined – to lead their own different lives in their own different ways, without undue influence from other people in other communities organized on different premises.[9] That leads quite naturally to the view that people's moral concern may legitimately stop with those physically near and emotionally dear to them.[10] The moral permissibility of closed borders follows obviously and straightforwardly from that logic.[11]

How important you think that argument for closed borders to be depends, though, upon how you assess the larger claims of communitarianism. And that, in turn, depends upon how you understand those claims in the first place. Roughly speaking, is their argument for 'the rootedness of moral agents' a proposition about psychology or about ethics?

If it is the former, saying merely that everyone has to start somewhere – grow up in some particular community, and so on – then the claim is undoubtedly true but of doubtful relevance to moral assessment. Arguments of that sort might help explain people's natural prejudices; if the psychological forces at work are strong, perhaps such arguments might even serve to excuse people in acting on those prejudices. But it is in the nature of excuses that what is being excused remains morally wrong. There is nothing in the argument, thus understood, to lead us to suppose that it is morally worthy – positively desirable, as opposed to sadly excusable – for moral agents to confine their sympathies in such ways.

Sometimes communitarians seem to be claiming more, though. Sometimes they seem to say that it is not only psychologically understandable but also that it is morally desirable that people should root themselves in this way. Now, of course, if the psychological forces at work are so strong that that is the only way in which people can develop a moral sense at all – and, furthermore, having thus developed it they cannot widen it without losing it altogether – then it would indeed be desirable to develop a limited moral sense rather than none at all. All of that remains really very back-handed praise for narrow communitarian values, to be sure. But I simply cannot see how any stronger, positive moral claim for communitarianism might be grounded.

If communitarianism were true, it would provide a strong argument for closed borders. But the moral case for communitarianism itself seems to rest on relatively weak arguments, thus compromising in turn the communitarian case for closed borders. There is another way of justifying closed borders, though. Rather than appealing to narrow communitarian values, this argument works in essentially universalistic terms. Closed borders do not fall nearly so automatically out of this argument. Instead, it treats them as a second-best stopgap. On this argument, in the ideal world all borders would be open. It is only because we live in an imperfect world that we sometimes need closed borders to correct, control or contain those imperfections.

To elaborate, let me take as my text a passage from John Maynard Keynes. He begins his 1933 essay on 'National self-sufficiency' by saying:

> I was brought up, like most Englishmen, to respect free trade not only as an economic doctrine which a rational and instructed person could not doubt but almost as a part of the moral law. . . . I thought England's unshakeable free-trade convictions, maintained for nearly a hundred years, to be both the explanation before man and the justification before heaven of her economic supremacy.

But contrary to all those natural inclinations, Keynes reports that he had latterly been convinced of the need for barriers to free trade. He explains the logic of this new position as follows:

> There is no prospect for the next generation of a uniformity of economic systems throughout the world. . . . We all need [therefore] to be as free as possible of interference from economic changes elsewhere in order to make

our own favourite experiments towards the ideal social republic of the future; and . . . deliberate movement towards greater national self-sufficiency and economic isolation will make our task easier. . . .[12]

The logic of this second-best proposition seems impeccable. Every state, perhaps, ought to have a generous welfare state. Every state, perhaps, ought to pursue Keynes' proposed policies for driving the rate of interest to zero and, in that way, effectively to nationalize the control of finance capital. But no country can pursue those options all on its own. A particularly generous welfare state will always be at risk of being swamped with immigrants, so long as it allows people to move in freely from abroad.[13] A state deliberately pushing down interest rates will always risk finding its policies foiled by capital flight, in so far as it allows free movement of capital out of the country.[14] Only by closing its borders to those sorts of movements can a country confidently pursue for itself, and by itself, ideals for which other nations of the world are not yet ready.

Closed borders might be justified, then, either as a matter of principle or of pragmatism. My own inclination is to say that, if they are going to be justified at all, it can only be in the latter way.

In the balance of this chapter, however, I shall abstain from taking any position on the larger issue of which justification – if either – might truly warrant closing our borders, and to what extent. I shall instead be mounting a more limited plea for consistency across all our various policies touching on issues of transnational movement.

The demands of consistency

How open overall we want our borders to be is an important question, and one that admits of diverse answers from diverse moral perspectives. That question is complicated enough. But the real question facing policy-makers is yet more complicated still.

We are typically confronted with proposals for borders to be differentially open. There are suggestions for borders to be more open to the movement of some things than to others. Thus, people tend to urge one policy for governing the import of computers and quite another for the import of explosives, one policy for admitting foreigners as individuals and quite another for admitting the same number of aliens all at the same time as part of one large group (of refugees, for example).

Likewise, there are suggestions for borders to be more open to movement in one direction rather than another. Thus, for example, many are tempted to take a much more relaxed attitude towards exporting explosives than towards importing them, or to expelling a large group of political dissidents than to admitting a similarly large group of troublemakers from abroad.

That we typically do make such distinctions seems undeniable. Whether we are morally entitled to do so is, as always, a separate question. There may or may not be any good reasons for nations to have relatively closed borders. That is an open question. But on the face of things it would seem that if ethically valid reasons for closed borders can be found at all, then those reasons must presumably apply *systematically*; that is to say, they should presumably dictate that borders be closed to the same extent in all directions and for all purposes.

I shall say more about the nature, source and the strength of this presumption in favour of symmetrical treatment shortly. Before turning to that topic though, let us see what would follow from this argument from consistency if it were to be sustained.

First, the systematic application of principles governing trans-boundary movement would apparently preclude any distinction according to the direction of movement. Whatever reason there is to keep something from coming into the country, consistency would seem to require us to impose the same prohibition upon that thing going out. Consider, in particular, the contrast between states' emigration and immigration policies. Consistency would seem to require us to judge the movement of people in both directions by the same standards, however harsh or lenient those may be. This symmetry manifests itself in several ways. Historically, perhaps the most widely discussed has been the proposition – enshrined in the Magna Carta and in countless texts since – that citizens should have an equal right to leave and to return to their own country.[15] But by the same token, it seems ethically inconsistent on the face of things for countries (of NATO, for example) to mount a vigorous international campaign for the freedom (of, e.g. Soviet Jews) to emigrate, while at the same time rigorously restricting the number of immigrants they will themselves accept.[16]

The inconsistency at work there may be pragmatic rather than literally logical in form. Still, pragmatically, 'in a world where all the inhabitable space is divided between states, . . . everyone needs to have his right of domicile formally recognized by one of those states.'[17] And in light of that fact, it amounts to simple bad faith to insist that people be allowed to leave without any guarantee – a guarantee that could come only from our being prepared to act as the underwriter of last resort – that they will have somewhere to go. The bad faith might not matter, in any practical sense, so long as someone else is willing to take in those whom we will not. But even if others' generosity saves us from having to face the consequences of our paradoxical stance, a lingering sense of bad faith in this matter remains.[18]

Second, the systematic application of principles governing transboundary movement would apparently preclude any distinction according to the nature of the objects coming or going across the borders. Whatever reason we have for keeping out foreign objects of one sort, consistency would seem to require us to impose similar rules to keep out other objects of a similar sort, as well.

Consider, in particular, the contrast between the rules which states apply to the movement of people and to the movement of money across their borders. Consistency would seem to require states to judge the transnational migration of people and of money – movement of human capital and of financial capital – by similar standards, equally harshly or equally leniently. It is, on the face of things, ethically inconsistent for some countries (until recently, perhaps, Poland) to run a blocked currency alongside open doors to emigration. It is, on the face of things, equally inconsistent for other countries (of Africa, perhaps) to open their doors to skilled immigrants but refuse to permit direct overseas investment in certain sectors.

Contemporary practice

These inconsistencies – if inconsistencies they truly be – seem absolutely rife in the contemporary world. Different states have different worries and impose different rules in consequence. But whatever the particulars of those rules, whether or not a state is prepared to permit the movement of people depends crucially upon the direction in which they are proposing to move. States rarely decide issues governing emigration and immigration according to the same criteria.

It was not always so. For large parts of European history, it has been relatively easy for people to change their country of residence. The French Constitution of 1791 guarantees 'liberté d'aller, de rester, de partir': coming, staying and going were all on a par.[19] Throughout the nineteenth century, it remained the conventional wisdom that movement should be easy in both directions. There was, in context, nothing wildly unrealistic about the resolution of an 1889 International Emigration Conference saying, 'We affirm the right of the individual to come and go and dispose of his person and his destinies as he pleases.'[20]

With the end of World War I, though, came the regime of passports and visas.[21] So, by the time the Universal Declaration on Human Rights was signed in 1948, the right to emigrate and to immigrate were once again treated separately and quite differently. The text of Article 13(2) stipulates that 'everyone has the right to leave any country, including his own', but implicitly it is only a national who enjoys a right 'to return to his country'.[22] The right to leave the country is thus deemed universal, the right to enter restricted to nationals returning home. It is perfectly proper, we now seem to suppose, that immigration should be harder than emigration. But what principled grounds could be offered for supposing that that should be so?

By the same token, countries which are only too happy to borrow vast quantities of money from abroad are all too reluctant to allow very many people at all to immigrate from abroad. I have already quoted statistics on the United States, in that regard. Here is another way of looking at those same statistics: the extra 40 billion dollars' worth of direct foreign investment flowing into the United States in 1987 amounted to just under 1/100th of its Gross National Product; the 600,000 new legal immigrants which the country admitted in the same year amounted to less than 1/4000th of its entire population.[23]

Why were US policy-makers wildly excited about the one – proportionately, the smaller – and so little perturbed by the other? Whatever harm foreign control might do to the fabric of American society, it is on the face of things simply not credible to suppose that a single migrant can do forty times as much damage as putting control of the same proportion of the US economy in foreign hands.[24]

This apparent inconsistency is not confined to the United States, though. It is only the most notorious offender in recent years. The same inconsistency could easily enough be found in the way in which Australia is so very welcoming of Japanese money but not Japanese migrants, or in the way in which Britain is so very welcoming of the capital but not the persons of its Hong Kong subjects.[25]

The presumption of symmetry

These inconsistencies may prove to be more apparent than real, of course. Closer inspection of these issues from diverse ethical perspectives might yield good grounds for mixing and matching various policies, both as regards migration of people and of money and as regards inflows and outflows. The broad array of chapters that follow is such as to ensure that those argumentative possibilities are explored as systematically as possible.

In framing rules for transnational movements, what to treat differently and how differently to treat it depends upon what deeper theories we happen to embrace. In part, those are empirical theories concerning the causes and consequences of the movements in question. In important part, though, those are moral theories specifying which consequences to welcome and which to shun, which policy interventions to permit and which not.

Thus, in trying to defend against these charges of inconsistency, policy-makers will inevitably – if often only implicitly – be asserting the superiority of one moral theory over another. Differences between objects and between

directions of movement which matter from the perspective of one moral
theory – and which within it suffice to justify different treatment of two
cases – do not from the perspective of another. Analogies that seem apt
from one perspective seem false from another.

It must be admitted, though, that on almost any theory some sorts of
differential treatment in these matters is almost bound to be permissible.
That is only to be expected. It is absurd, on the face of things, to suppose
that the same rules should apply to the movement of people as to cattle,
gunpowder or microcomputers. Such diverse objects display obviously
different properties. It is only reasonable that they should be treated
differently, in rules governing cross-border movements as in many other
respects. But it is one thing to say that some such distinctions will presumably prove justified. It is quite another to presume that differential
treatment is permissible, prior to actually being offered any such justifications. Some distinctions will almost certainly prove justified, but not just
any old distinctions.

Presumably justifications for differential treatment can sometimes –
perhaps often – be found. Still, until adequate justification actually has been
provided for any particular distinction, the presumption must remain on the
side of treating all (presumptively like) cases alike. The burden of proving
the moral merits of differential treatment must rest with those proposing it.
Call this the principle of *no discrimination without justification*.[26]

This formulation might seem to make the case for consistent treatment
of movements across borders too weak to be of much interest. It casts the
case purely in terms of a presumption; and presumptions, by their nature,
can always be rebutted. But how strong or weak this argument turns out
to be depends upon how hard or easy it is to find good arguments for
rebutting the presumption in question. If in the case of trans-boundary
movements good arguments for differential treatment are thin on the
ground – as clearly they are in so many other cases of differential treatment
– then a mere presumption might in and of itself take us quite a long way
towards firm policy conclusions.

Human capital and finance capital

So many kinds of goods, so different in obviously important ways, flow
across state borders that it is plainly unreasonable to expect that presumption of identical treatment to prevail absolutely in all cases of transboundary
flows. Sometimes, though, that presumption does seem particularly robust.

Consider, for example, the problem of exporting hazardous products.
Since human physiology is pretty standard across the world, products that
are dangerous for Americans to use are probably dangerous for Indonesians

as well. So if something is too hazardous to be used in or imported into our own country, then surely it is right for there to be a strong presumption in favour of supposing that it is also too hazardous to be exported from our own to other countries.[27] That presumption, like all presumptions, is in principle rebuttable. In practice, though, it seems awfully hard to rebut.[28]

There is another analogy that seems at first sight similarly robust, one between the movement of people and the movement of money. Both, in economic terms, are forms of capital. The movement of people shifts human capital – the physical and intellectual capacities embodied in human bodies. The movement of money shifts financial capital, and with it the productive capacities that are procurable in exchange for money.

Economically, there is good reason for seeing labour and capital as analogous. Overall, they complement one another as factors of production; at the margins, they substitute for one another in that capacity. The standard Cobb-Douglas production function mathematically represents output simply as a function of labour and capital inputs, and of those alone. In that equation, it takes some of each to produce anything at all: with zero labour inputs you get zero output, and likewise with zero capital inputs. But at the margins, the two are capable of substituting for one another: the more you have of one, the less you will need of the other to produce any given quantity of outputs.

What is true of labour and capital contributions to production in general seems particularly true of their transnational flows in encouraging economic growth. The way in which the two substitute for one another in spurring growth in any particular industry is clear enough. So too is the way in which they can complement one another in developing basic infrastructure: to build a railroad, for example, poor and underpopulated countries have historically needed inflows of both capital and labour from abroad.[29]

For the purposes of economic modelling, it is clearly crucial to determine whether (or when) labour and capital complement or substitute for one another. For moral purposes, it is not so clear at all that we need to know whether the sign of the coefficient linking them is positive or negative. Consider an analogy from within a single national economy. We may well think that wages and profits ought, for the sake of consistency, to be taxed at the same rate, whatever the complicated economic interrelationships between those factors. No amount of evidence about whether higher wages lead to lower profits or to higher ones can alter the perceived requirements of fairness on that score.

Similarly, perhaps nothing morally follows from a determination of whether, in international flows, capital and labour substitute for one another or whether they complement one another. Be they economically substitutes or complements, morally it might none the less be argued that they are the same 'kind' of thing and ought be treated similarly in our rules governing their transnational movements.

Perhaps the best reason for regarding them so is the simple fact that the distinctions drawn by those resisting that analogy are so strained and self-serving. They seem little more than cynical attempts on the part of states to participate only in those aspects of a regime of free movement from which they themselves would benefit. The British, Americans, Australians and so on happily accept foreign money but only reluctantly accept unskilled (or even skilled) foreign peoples. The regimes of the old Eastern bloc let money and people in but not out. Developing states admit human capital, in the form of skilled settlers, but not finance capital.

There are good reasons, of an understandably self-interested kind, for all those policies. The states in question suppose, probably quite rightly, that the sorts of trans-boundary movement that they shun would work to their detriment. But while self-interest makes their position comprehensible, it hardly makes it moral. Quite the contrary, when the clearest argument for a distinction is so transparently self-interested, there must be something like a double presumption against that distinction, on moral grounds.

Even double presumptions can, of course, be overcome provided there are sufficiently strong countervailing arguments. The question at the core of this book, to be addressed in the chapters that follow, is whether any such arguments are available.

Spiking a subversive theorem

Although economic facts cannot by themselves answer moral questions, they can render those questions irrelevant. In discussing free movements of people and of money across international boundaries, there is one theorem which threatens to do just that. If true, it would seem to settle decisively the policy questions that give rise to all the moral argumentation, without settling the moral questions themselves one way or the other.

It has been proven – independently, by both Paul Samuelson and Abba Lerner – that under certain very special assumptions it really does not matter whether factors of production (labour, capital and such like) can move freely between countries. 'Factor prices', Samuelson writes, 'will be equalized' just so long as there is 'free international trade' in the commodities that are produced through the use of those factor inputs.[30]

Global egalitarians should, apparently, take heart from this theorem. If they want to equalize life prospects of everyone worldwide, they do not have to press for politically contentious policies of free immigration or free flow of capital or generous foreign aid. They need merely press a case that has been fought and won (intellectually, if not necessarily politically) long ago – a case for free trade. That in and of itself will, according to this theorem, ensure global equalization of wages. Wages will fall in countries, like Sweden and the United States, that are capital-rich and labour-poor; conversely, wages will rise in capital-poor countries where people are on average desperately impoverished.[31] And in that way the goals of global egalitarians can be realized without any movement of either people or of money across international boundaries.

However, that theorem – like most others of its ilk in mathematical economics – depends for its truth upon certain assumptions of a strong and often unrealistic sort. Whether it, or anything remotely resembling it, remains true under more realistic assumptions is an open question.[32]

There is one assumption in particular that is required for Samuelson's proof that seems especially troubling from the point of view of those who worry about international distributions. For his proof, Samuelson needs to presume that all the countries in question are not 'too unequal' in their endowments of all the various factors of production. But it is precisely the unequal initial endowments that has led to the inequalities that global egalitarians hope to rectify. As Samuelson himself admits, 'to . . . return to the real world . . . we must . . . study the uneven endowment of primary factors that does characterize the only globe we yet know.'[33]

There are other assumptions – equally if not more problematic – buried beneath the mathematics required to prove this theorem. Let us not belabour them here, however. Suffice it to say that the reason most people have for desiring freer movement of people or of capital across the world would simply not exist under the conditions the theorem in view presupposes. The problem of grossly unequal per capita income between countries, derived in part from grossly unequal factor endowments of those countries, is in effect just assumed away in that proof. Were that matters were only so simple, in the real world.

In closing

How open or closed should borders be? Should movement be completely free, or completely constrained, or something in between? In this initial sketch of the outlines of those issues as I see them, I have given some indication of my own perspective on such matters. But thereafter, I have tried to ensure that nothing that I have said turns upon my own position on those larger issues.

My fundamental argument has been cast, instead, in the form of a consistency claim. I have merely tried to motivate the presumption in favour of symmetry in our policies governing trans-boundary movements.

This presumption would hold that, however free or constrained such movement is to be, it ought to be equally free or constrained in both directions and for both money as well as for people. But how robust that presumption proves to be, and free movement of all sorts actually ought to be, from various different ethical perspectives, is a matter to which my fellow contributors now turn.

Notes

1. That is just under four times 1970 levels. See U.S. Department of Commerce, *Statistical Abstract of the United States 1989* (Washington, D.C.: Government Printing Office, 1989), table 296.
2. That is over seven times 1970 levels, even discounting for inflation, according to the *Statistical Abstract of the United States 1989*, tables 1359 and 748.
3. Britain and Australia are other conspicuous examples, but they are not unique. See Joseph Carens, "Nationalism and the Exclusion of Immigrants: Lessons from Australian Immigration Policy," *Open Borders? Closed Societies? The Ethical and Political Issues*, ed. Mark Gibney (Westport, Conn.: Greenwood Press, 1988), pp. 42–60; Ann Dummett and Andrew Nichol, *Subjects, Citizens, Aliens and Others: Nationality and Immigration Law* (London: Weidenfeld and Nicolson, 1990); and, more generally, Guy S. Goodwin-Gill, *International Law and the Movement of Persons* (Oxford: Clarendon Press, 1978) and Alan Dowty, *Closed Borders: The Contemporary Assault on Freedom of Movement* (New Haven, Conn.: Yale University Press, 1987).
4. For a delightful account of how medieval scholastics 'developed the Roman law texts concerning *jurisdictio* and *imperium* into a concept of sovereignty', see Harold J. Berman, *Law and Revolution: The Formation of the Western Legal Tradition* (Cambridge, Mass.: Harvard University Press, 1983), esp. pp. 288–92. For the later history of the concept, see: George Cornewall Lewis's *Remarks on the Use and Abuse of Some Political Terms* (London: B. Fellowes, 1832), pp. 33–58; J. R. Lucas, *The Principles of Politics* (Oxford: Clarendon Press, 1966), pp. 29–33; and S. I. Benn and R. S. Peters, *Social Principles and the Democratic State* (London: Allen & Unwin, 1959), chap. 12.
5. See, e.g., the discussions in: Michael Teitelbaum, "Right versus Right: Immigration and Refugee Policy in the United States," *Foreign Affairs*, 59 (1980), 221–59; Anon., "Developments in the Law: Immigration Policy and the Rights of Aliens," *Harvard Law Review*, 96 (1983), 1286–465; Dowty, *Closed Borders*; Peter G. Brown and Henry Shue, eds., *Boundaries: National Autonomy and Its Limits* and *The Border that Joins: Mexican Migrants and U.S. Responsibility* (Totowa, N.J.: Rowman & Littlefield, 1981 and 1983 respectively); and Joseph Carens, "Aliens and Citizens: The Case for Open Borders," *Review of Politics*, 49 (Spring 1987), 251–73.
6. This is very much a post-Rawlsian preoccupation. See Brian Barry, *The Liberal Theory of Justice* (Oxford: Clarendon Press, 1973), chap. 12; Charles Beitz, *Political Theory and International Relations* (Princeton, N.J.: Princeton

University Press, 1979), part 3; and Charles Beitz, "Cosmopolitan Ideals and National Sentiment," and Henry Shue, "The Burdens of Justice," *Journal of Philosophy*, 80 (1983), 591–600 and 600–8 respectively.

7. Robert Cassen, *Does Aid Work?* (Oxford: Clarendon Press, 1986), p. 294.

8. Ibid.

9. Michael J. Sandel, *Liberalism and the Limits of Justice* (Cambridge: Cambridge University Press, 1982) and Michael Walzer, *Spheres of Justice* (New York: Basic Books, 1983), chap. 2. Cf. Will Kymlicka, "Liberalism and Communitarianism," *Canadian Journal of Philosophy*, 18 (1988), 181–203 and, more generally, his *Liberalism, Community and Culture* (Oxford: Clarendon Press, 1989) and *Contemporary Political Philosophy* (Oxford: Clarendon Press, 1990), esp. chap. 6.

10. For an alternative interpretation, from within an impartial/universalistic ethic, of these special duties, see Philip Pettit and Robert Goodin, "The Possibility of Special Duties," *Canadian Journal of Philosophy*, 16 (1986), 651–76 and, for an application to international society, Goodin, "What Is So Special About Our Fellow Countrymen?" *Ethics*, 98 (1988), 663–86. Cf. Brian Barry, "Self-Government Revisited," *The Nature of Political Theory*, ed. David Miller and L. Siedentop (Oxford: Clarendon Press, 1983), 121–54 and David Miller, "The Ethical Significance of Nationality," *Ethics*, 98 (1988), 647–62.

11. This is, certainly in its practical consequences and to some extent in its underlying logic as well, an echo of older concerns with the legitimate authority of sovereigns to command the loyalty of their subjects. For a discussion see Frederick G. Whelan, "Citizenship and the Right to Leave," *American Political Science Review*, 75 (1981), 53–63.

12. John Maynard Keynes, "National Self-Sufficiency," *Collected Writings*, ed. Donald Moggridge (London: Macmillan, 1982), vol. 21, pp. 233–46 at 233–4 and 241. Superficially, Keynes' later policy positions suggest that his views changed during World War II, but he was arguably just pursuing the same ends by other means; see J. R. Crotty, "On Keynes and Capital Flight," *Journal of Economic Literature*, 21 (1983), 59–65. See similarly James E. Meade's 1934 paper for the New Fabian Research Bureau, "The Exchange Policy of a Socialist Government," *Collected Papers*, ed. Susan Howson (London: Unwin Hyman, 1988), vol, 3, pp. 11–26.

13. Walzer, *Spheres of Justice*, chap. 2. Teitelbaum, "Right versus Right". Cf. Joseph Carens, "Immigration and the Welfare State," *Democracy and the Welfare State*, ed. Amy Gutmann (Princeton, N.J.: Princeton University Press, 1988), pp. 207–30.

14. Keynes, "National Self-Sufficiency"; cf. Abba P. Lerner, *The Economics of Control* (London: Macmillan, 1946), chap. 29.

15. Magna Carta of 1215, chap. 42. See further Stig A. F. Jagerskiold, "Historical Aspects of the Right to Leave and to Return" and José D. Inglés, "The United Nations Study of Discrimination in Respect of the Right of Everyone to Leave Any Country, Including His Own, and to Return to His Country," both in Karel Vasak and Sidney Liskofsky, eds., *The Right to Leave and to Return* (New York: American Jewish Commission, 1976), pp. 3–20 and 475–85 respectively.

16. Israel itself got caught on one horn of this dilemma, admitting far more Soviet Jews than it could reasonably accommodate when the Soviets eventually lifted the barriers to their emigration.
17. Maurice Cranston, "The Political and Philosophical Aspects of the Right to Leave and to Return," in Vasak and Liskofsky, ibid., pp. 21–35 at p. 28.
18. Recall in this connection the history of the Jews immediately prior to and during World War II: many countries demanded that Hitler let Jews flee but none were particularly prepared to admit them. See Bernard Wasserstein, *Britain and the Jews of Europe, 1939–45* (London: Institute of Jewish Affairs, 1979).
19. Quoted in Cranston, p. 28.
20. Quoted in Brinley Thomas, *International Migration and Economic Development* (Paris: UNESCO, 1961), p. 9.
21. See Goodwin-Gill, *International Law and the Movement of Persons*, chap. 2.
22. Reproduced in Ian Brownlie, ed., *Basic Documents in International Law*, 3rd ed. (Oxford: Clarendon Press, 1983), pp. 251–6 at 253; the International Covenant on Civil and Political Rights, Article 12, reproduces these propositions almost verbatim. Of course, Article 14 goes on to say that 'everyone has the right to seek and enjoy in other countries asylum from persecutions' – at least in so far as they are for political crimes – but if the state denies them asylum then international law requires the refugees to leave.
23. *Statistical Abstract of the United States*, tables 1359, 685, 9, 2 and 46.
24. For those who prefer – rightly – to talk in terms of stocks rather than flows, here are the corresponding statistics: foreign direct investment in the United States in 1987 was 5.78 per cent of GNP, whereas the foreign-born were (in 1980, the last year for which statistics are available) 6.22 per cent of the entire US population. By that reckoning they are just about on a par – which still leaves us puzzling why there is such a disproportionate response to such proportionately similar phenomena.
25. Carens, "Nationalism and the Exclusion of Immigrants: Lessons from Australian Immigration Policy."
26. This principle is, of course, standard in the literature on justice, equality and discrimination. See, e.g.: William K. Frankena, "The Concept of Social Justice," *Social Justice*, ed. Richard B. Brandt (Englewood Cliffs, N.J.: Prentice-Hall, 1962), pp. 1–30; David Miller, *Social Justice* (Oxford: Clarendon Press, 1976); Bernard Williams, "The Idea of Equality," *Philosophy, Politics and Society*, 2nd series, ed. P. Laslett and W. G. Runciman (Oxford: Blackwell, 1962), pp. 110–31 and Douglas Rae, *Equalities* (Cambridge, Mass.: Harvard University Press, 1981).
27. This is a variation on the theme of "Exporting Hazards" so ably discussed by Henry Shue in an article of that title in *Ethics*, 91 (1981), 579–606, reprinted in *Boundaries*, ed. Brown and Shue, pp. 107–46.
28. See Robert E. Goodin, *Political Theory & Public Policy* (Chicago: University of Chicago Press, 1982), chap. 8 for further discussion.
29. Simon Kuznets, *Modern Economic Growth* (New Haven, Conn.: Yale University Press, 1966), pp. 40–56. 'Latin-American economists with whom I have spoken have not infrequently stressed the reduced flow of international private

investment as an important reason why even an underpopulated country such as Brazil cannot employ new European immigrants on the scale once possible'; Howard S. Ellis, "Are There Preferable Alternatives to International Migration as an Aid to Economic Development?" *Economics of International Migration*, ed. Brinley Thomas (London: Macmillan, 1958), pp. 347–64 at 354–5.

30. Paul A. Samuelson, "International Trade and the Equalization of Factor Prices," *Collected Works*, ed. Joseph E. Stiglitz (Cambridge, Mass.: MIT Press, 1966), vol. 2, pp. 847–55 at 853. The theorem was proven originally in using 'land' in place of capital, but Samuelson later extended the theorem using capital in its place; see his "Equalization by Trade of the Interest Rate Along with the Real Wage," *Collected Works*, vol. 2, pp. 909–24. Abba P. Lerner, "Factor Prices and International Trade," *Essays in Economic Analysis* (London: Macmillan, 1953), pp. 67–84.

31. Wolfgang F. Stopler and Paul A. Samuelson, "Protection and Real Wages," in Samuelson, *Collected Works*, vol. 2, pp. 831–46.

32. For a discussion of this theorem with particular reference to migration issues, see Thomas, *International Migration and Economic Development*, pp. 25–8.

33. Samuelson, "International Trade . . .," p. 853 and "Equalization by Trade . . .," p. 924.

Liberal Egalitarian
Perspectives

— 3 —

Migration and morality:
A liberal egalitarian perspective

Joseph H. Carens

What must we do to treat all human beings as free and equal moral persons? That is the question that liberal egalitarianism demands we ask of all institutions and social practices, including those affecting citizenship, borders and migration.

Like any tradition of moral discourse, liberal egalitarianism is filled with conflicting arguments. The issue of movement across borders has only recently received any sustained attention, but already one can find major splits among liberal egalitarians. Some claim there should be no restrictions on freedom of movement, or almost none; others say that states are morally entitled to admit or exclude whomever they want with only a few qualifications; still others adopt some position in between.[1] In this chapter, therefore, I will not claim to represent the consensus of the tradition. Instead I will offer my current view of what anyone committed to liberal egalitarianism ought to think about migration, noting along the way the major points of disagreement within the tradition and indicating the places where I feel least certain about my own argument.

Overall, my position is this. Liberal egalitarianism entails a deep commitment to freedom of movement as both an important liberty in itself and a prerequisite for other freedoms. Thus the presumption is for free migration and anyone who would defend restrictions faces a heavy burden of proof. Nevertheless, restrictions may sometimes be justified because they will promote liberty and equality in the long run or because they are necessary to preserve a distinct culture or way of life.

I

Like all those in the liberal tradition, liberal egalitarians care about human freedoms.[2] People should be free to pursue their own projects and to make their own choices about how they live their lives so long as this does not interfere with the legitimate claims of other individuals to do likewise. In addition, liberal egalitarians are committed to equal opportunity. Access to social positions should be determined by an individual's actual talents and capacities, not limited on the basis of arbitrary native characteristics (such as class, race, or sex). Finally, liberal egalitarians want to keep actual economic, social and political inequalities as small as possible, partly as a means of realizing equal freedom and equal opportunity and partly as a desirable end in itself.[3]

Freedom of movement is closely connected to each of these three concerns. First, the right to go where you want to go is itself an important freedom. It is precisely this freedom, and all that this freedom makes possible, that is taken away by imprisonment. Second, freedom of movement is essential for equality of opportunity. You have to be able to move to where the opportunities are in order to take advantage of them. Third, freedom of movement would contribute to a reduction of political, social and economic inequalities. There are millions of people in the Third World today who long for the freedom and economic opportunity they could find in affluent First World countries. Many of them take great risks to come: Haitians setting off in leaky boats, Salvadorians being smuggled across the border in hot, airless trucks, Tamils paying to be set adrift off the coast of Newfoundland. If the borders were open, millions more would move. The exclusion of so many poor and desperate people seems hard to justify from a perspective that takes seriously the claims of all individuals as free and equal moral persons.

Consider the case for freedom of movement in light of the liberal critique of feudal practices that determined a person's life chances on the basis of his or her birth. Citizenship in the modern world is a lot like feudal status in the medieval world. It is assigned at birth; for the most part it is not subject to change by the individual's will and efforts; and it has a major impact upon that person's life chances. To be born a citizen of an affluent country like Canada is like being born into the nobility (even though many belong to the lesser nobility). To be born a citizen of a poor country like Bangladesh is (for most) like being born into the peasantry in the Middle Ages. In this context, limiting entry to countries like Canada is a way of protecting a birthright privilege. Liberals objected to the way feudalism restricted freedom, including the freedom of individuals to move from one place to another in search of a better life. But modern practices of citizenship and state control over borders tie people to the land of their birth almost as effectively. If the feudal practices were wrong, what justifies the modern ones?

Some would respond to this challenge by drawing a distinction between freedom of exit and freedom of entry and arguing that the two are asymmetrical.[4] The former, the right to leave one's own state ought to be virtually absolute, precisely because restrictions resemble the objectionable feudal practices. But that does not imply a right to enter any particular place. From a liberal egalitarian perspective this answer is clearly unsatisfactory if entry is so restricted in most states that most people who want to leave have no place to go. That is certainly the case in the modern world. The liberal egalitarian branch of liberalism is sympathetic to the charge that liberal freedoms can be empty formalities under some circumstances. Liberal egalitarians want to pay attention to the conditions (material and other) that make formal freedoms meaningful and effective. So, a right of exit that does not carry with it some reasonable guarantee of entry will not seem adequate.

The initial allocation of citizenship on the basis of birthplace, parentage, or some combination thereof is not objectionable from a liberal egalitarian perspective. Indeed it is morally required because children are born into a community with ties to others that should be acknowledged. In principle, however, individuals should be free to change their membership at will.

Finally, compare freedom of movement *within* the state to freedom of movement across state borders. Like every freedom involving human action, freedom of movement is not unlimited, but because it is an important liberty limitations have to be justified in a way that gives equal weight to the claims of all. Some restrictions on movement are easy to justify, e.g. traffic regulations or a right to exclude others from one's home (assuming everyone has a home or a reasonable opportunity to obtain one). But imagine an attempt by officials in one city or county to keep out people from another. That sort of restriction is seen as fundamentally incompatible with a commitment to free and equal citizenship. Cities and provinces have borders but not ones that can be used to keep people in or out against their will. Indeed freedom of movement *within* the nation-state is widely acknowledged as a basic human right, and states are criticized for restricting internal movement even by those who accept the conventional view of state sovereignty. People *are* generally free to change their membership in sub-national political communities at will.

If it is so important for people to have the right to move freely within a state, is it not equally important for them to have the right to move across state borders? Every reason why one might want to move within a state may also be a reason for moving between states. One might want a job; one might fall in love with someone from another country; one might belong to a religion that has few adherents in one's native state and many in another; one might wish to pursue cultural opportunities that are only available in another land. The radical disjuncture that treats freedom of movement within the state as a moral imperative and freedom of movement across state borders as merely a matter of political discretion makes no sense from a perspective that takes seriously the freedom and equality of all individuals.

II

The arguments in the preceding section create at least a presumption for freedom of movement from a liberal egalitarian perspective. Can this presumption ever be overriden? One possible approach is to argue that restrictions on free movement are necessary in order to promote freedom and equality in the long run. On this view, free movement is an aspect of the liberal egalitarian ideal which we should ultimately try to achieve but to adopt the practice of open borders now would jeopardize those liberal egalitarian institutions and practices that currently exist and slow their development elsewhere.[5]

This argument takes several related forms, most of them focusing on the need to protect existing liberal egalitarian cultures and institutions (however imperfectly realized). First, there is the question of national security. Presumably an invading army is not entitled to unopposed entry on the grounds of free movement. But that does not entail any real modification because the principle of free movement does not entitle citizens to organize their own armies to challenge the authority of the state either. What about subversives? Again, if it is against the law for citizens to try to overthrow the state, that kind of activity would presumably justify refusal of entry to outsiders. So, people who pose a serious threat to national security can legitimately be excluded.

A related argument concerns the danger to a liberal egalitarian regime posed by a large influx of people who come from non-liberal societies, even if they do not come with any subversive intent. To put it another way, are people committed to treating all individuals as free and equal moral persons obliged to admit people who are not so committed? This is close to the familiar question of the toleration of the intolerant in liberal regimes. One conventional answer (which I accept) is that liberal regimes are obliged to tolerate the intolerant and respect their liberties so long as they do not pose an actual threat to the maintenance of liberal institutions. When they do pose a threat, however, their liberties may be curtailed in order to preserve the regime.[6] Here that answer would imply that restrictions on non-liberal entrants would be justified only if one had good reason to believe that they would threaten the liberal character of the regime if admitted. This entails the conclusion that it could be legitimate to exclude people for holding beliefs and values that are also held by people who are already members but only because of the presumed cumulative effect of their presence.

Would it be justifiable to expel non-liberal members because of their beliefs and values if their numbers grew large enough to constitute a threat? No. I argued above that the radical disjuncture between freedom of entry and freedom of exit in conventional morality is not justified. Nevertheless, there is something to the claim of asymmetry. Under many circumstances, the right to leave is much more important than the right to enter any particular place. It is only in the limiting case where there is nowhere to go that the two become equivalent, although as I noted above that limiting case is closely approximated in the real world for many people. Similarly, under many, perhaps most circumstances the right to remain in a country where one is already a member is much more fundamental than the right to get in. All of the ties that one creates in the course of living in a place mean that one normally (though not always) has a much more vital interest in being able to stay where one is than in being able to get in somewhere new. This is not a denigration of the importance of the freedom to move, but rather a claim that the freedom to remain is even more important. Thus, expulsions of members are almost never justified from a liberal egalitarian perspective.

Although it is a distraction from the threat to liberalism argument, it is worth pausing here to explore the implications of this point about expulsions for the issue of migrant workers and their families.[7] In the preceding paragraph, I deliberately used the term 'members' rather than 'citizens' because being a member of a society and having the moral claims of a member is not dependent upon having the formal status of a citizen. Indeed, one of the ways states may act unjustly is by denying citizenship to people who are members. When a state admits people to live and work in the territory it governs, it admits them to membership so long as they stay any significant period of time. It cannot do otherwise and still treat them as free and equal moral persons. Thus it is obliged to admit their immediate families as well and to open the doors to citizenship to them and their families. Even if they do not become citizens, they have a right to stay for all of the reasons discussed in the preceding paragraph. So, the state cannot rightly expel them even if circumstances have changed and it is no longer advantageous to have them. And again in parallel with the preceding paragraph, it is much worse to deport people who have already come and settled than to refuse entry to new workers.

These claims about membership and the right to remain are not altered even if the migrant workers were admitted under terms that explicitly provided for their return should circumstances change. Liberal egalitarianism places limits on freedom of contract, rendering void any agreements that are incompatible with equal respect for persons. And unlike most of the claims I make in this chapter about what liberal egalitarianism requires with respect to migration, these claims about migrant workers are generally reflected in the practices of contemporary liberal democratic societies.

To return to the threat to liberalism argument, another variant focuses not on beliefs and values but on sheer numbers. Given the size of the potential demand, if a rich country like Canada or the United States were to open its borders, the number of those coming might overwhelm the capacity of the society to cope, leading to chaos and a breakdown of public order.[8] The risk would be especially great if only one or two of the rich countries were to open their borders. One cannot assume that the potential immigrants would see the danger and refrain from coming because of the time lag between cause and effect, because of collective action problems, and so on. Call this the public order problem. Note that the 'public order' is not equivalent to the welfare state or whatever public policies are currently in place. It is a minimalist standard, referring only to the maintenance of law and order. A threat to public order could be used to justify restrictions on immigration on grounds that are compatible with respecting every individual as a free and equal moral person, because the breakdown of public order makes everyone worse off in terms of both liberty and welfare. In some ways, this is reminiscent of Garrett Hardin's famous lifeboat ethics argument.[9] It does no one any good to take so many people into the boat that it is swamped and everyone drowns.

Even if one accepts all of the arguments above as sources of possible constraint on entry, the basic commitment to free movement as the fundamental goal and underlying principle remains intact. Just as those in a lifeboat are positively obliged to take in as many as they can without jeopardizing the safety of the boat as a whole (a point that those fond of this analogy often neglect), the state is obliged to admit as many of those seeking entry as it can without jeopardizing national security, public order and the maintenance of liberal institutions.

One obvious danger, however, is that an expansive interpretation of the criteria in the preceding arguments will open the door to a flood of restrictions. For example, the United States has used the national security justification to deny entry (even for temporary visits) to people identified as homosexuals, as well as to all sorts of people whose views do not conform to the reigning American ideology. And if national security is linked to the state's economic performance (as it often is), any economic costs connected with immigration can be seen as threatening national security. Exclusionists in the nineteenth century in the United States cited the dangers of immigration from non-liberal societies as grounds for keeping out Catholics and Jews from Europe and all Asians and Africans. Canada and Australia had comparable restrictions on similar grounds. (Today Islamic fundamentalism seems to be the main target of those worried about non-liberal values.) And, of course, some people see a threat to public order in any new demand placed on a social system. They want a safety margin of fifty empty places in a lifeboat built for sixty.

Despite these sad examples, one should not exclude proper concerns, at least at the level of theory, because they are subject to exaggeration and abuse in practice. The task is to distinguish between reasonable and unreasonable uses of these sorts of arguments. As Rawls puts it in acknowledging that liberties may sometimes be restricted for the sake of public order and security, the hypothetical possibility of a threat is not enough. Rather there must be a 'reasonable expectation' that damage will occur in the absence of restrictions and the expectation has to be based on 'evidence and ways of reasoning acceptable to all'.[10] The same strictures apply to all attempts to justify restrictions on immigration along the lines sketched above, and none of the examples cited is really justified as a reasonable use of restrictive criteria.

A variation of the preceding arguments that is based on real concerns but is much more problematic from a liberal egalitarian perspective is what might be called the backlash argument.[11] On this view, the commitment to liberal egalitarian principles is not very secure even in liberal societies. Current citizens might object to the ethnic and cultural characteristics of new immigrants, fear them as competitors in the work-place, and perceive them as economic burdens placing excessive demands upon the social welfare system. At the least, this reaction might erode the sense of mutuality and community identification that makes egalitarian and redistributive programmes politically possible. At the worse, it might threaten the basic liberal democratic framework. A glance at current European politics makes it clear that this threat is all too real. In several countries, extreme right-wing parties, using veiled and not so veiled racist and neo-fascist appeals, have gained ground, primarily, it seems, by making opposition to current immigrants and future immigration a key element in their platforms. In this context, to open the borders more now might well provoke a political reaction that would quickly slam the doors shut and damage other liberal egalitarian institutions and policies as well.

Would this justify restrictions on immigration from a liberal egalitarian perspective? The answer must be 'no' at the level of principle and 'perhaps' at the level of practice. I am assuming here that the claims to exclude do not rest on some as yet unspecified valid argument. By hypothesis then we are dealing with a case in which restrictions on immigration would not be justified if one took a perspective in which all were regarded as free and equal moral persons. Those advocating exclusion are either putting forward claims that are intrinsically unjust (e.g. racist claims) or ones that are legitimate concerns (e.g. their economic interests) but outweighed by the claims of the potential immigrants (both in terms of their right to free movement and in terms of their own economic interests). The 'justification' for restrictions is simply that if no concessions are made to the exclusionists they may make things even worse. Put that way it is clearly no justification at all at the level of principle though one cannot say that such concessions are never prudent in practice.

Compare this issue to such questions as whether slaveowners should have been compensated for the loss of their property when slavery was abolished, whether holders of feudal privilege should have been compensated when those privileges were abolished and whether segregation should have been ended gradually (with 'all deliberate speed') rather than all at once. All of these questions were live issues once in political contexts where defenders of the old ways still had sufficient political power to resist change and perhaps even reverse it if pressed too hard. In none of these cases, it seems to me, were concessions required as a matter of principle, but in any of them they may have been defensible in practice as the best that could be achieved under the circumstances. The latter seems an appropriate moral guide to political action assuming a definition of the good that takes into account independent ethical constraints upon action. And so the backlash argument, too, may provide grounds of this limited sort for restrictions in some cases.

Finally, there are arguments for restriction that focus not on the protection of liberal egalitarian institutions and practices in states that currently have them but on their development elsewhere and on the reduction of global inequalities.[12] According to the 'brain drain' hypothesis, the movement of people from the Third World to the First World actually increases global inequalities because the best educated and most talented are among the most likely to move in order to take advantage of the greater professional and economic opportunities in affluent societies. Even among the poor, it is the most energetic and ambitious who move, and usually people from the lower middle classes rather than the worst off because the latter do not have the resources needed for migration. Thus migration actually involves a transfer of human resources from poor countries to rich ones. This often involves the loss of actual economic investments in the form of scarce and costly expenditures on education and training, but the greatest cost is the loss of people with the capacity to contribute to the transformation of their country's condition. Freer movement would only make the situation worse, making development in the Third World and a reduction of global inequalities even more unlikely than it is now.

A variant of this argument stresses politics rather than economics, drawing attention to the way in which easy exit may act as a safety valve for a repressive regime. It may be easier to silence domestic opposition by sending it abroad than by suppressing it internally. And if exit is an easy option, those living under a repressive regime may devote their energies to getting out rather than to transforming the system under which they live.

On the whole, I think these are the sorts of arguments that have given utilitarianism a bad name in some quarters, although, as is often the case, I do not think a clear thinking utilitarian would support them. What is particularly objectionable is the way they propose to extract benefits for some people by, in effect, imprisoning others. As is so often the case in discussing migration, it is helpful to compare internal migration with migration across state borders. Many states suffer from severe regional inequalities and it is often suggested that these inequalities are made worse by the movement of the brightest, best-trained people from poor regions to rich ones – an internal brain drain. But what would we think if Canada tried to cope with its regional disparities by prohibiting people from moving from Newfoundland to Ontario, or if Italy limited migration from Naples to Milan? The regional differences are a serious problem that states have a duty to address, but they would be wrong to try to solve this problem by limiting the basic freedoms of their citizens.

So, too, with the international brain drain. International inequality is a serious moral problem, but restricting movement is not a morally permissible tactic for dealing with it. And that assumes that it would be a useful tactic. In fact, the benefits themselves are extremely problematic. Emigrants contribute in various ways to their communities of origin (often through direct financial remittances), and it is far from clear that making them stay home would lead to the desired economic and political transformation. On the other hand, the cost to those denied permission to leave is clear and direct. Limitations of important freedoms should never be undertaken lightly. In the face of great uncertainty about their effects they should not be undertaken at all.

What about financial compensation for the costs of education and training? Here it is important to distinguish between basic education and advanced education or training. For the former no compensation is due. Everyone is entitled to basic education, and children cannot enter into binding contracts. Whatever investments a society makes in its young, it cannot rightly require direct repayment. Advanced training is somewhat different both because it is provided only to a few and because those receiving it are normally old enough to assume responsibility for their choices. If it is subsidized by the state, especially a state with comparatively few resources, it may be reasonable to expect the recipients to commit themselves to a few years of service in the country or to repay the costs of the training. But these sorts of expectations must be limited and reasonable. Liberal egalitarianism is incompatible with any form of indentured servitude.

In arguing that the state may not normally limit migration as a way of
enforcing a claim to the services of its citizens, I am not saying that people
have no obligations to their communities of origin. It is a familiar feature
of most liberal theories that the state should not enforce many sorts of
moral duties or obligations not just on the prudential grounds that enforcement will be costly or ineffective but on the principle that individuals
must have considerable scope to define their own lives and identities,
including the moral worlds that they inhabit. This does not mean that
all moral commitments are a matter of choice. From the individual's
perspective, the moral ties may be experienced as given, a product of
unchosen relationships with members of one's family, ethnic group, religious faith, or even political community. Take a black doctor in the United
States. He or she might or might not feel a special obligation to work in the
black community. If he or she does, he or she might or might not think that
other black doctors have a comparable obligation. Liberal egalitarianism
has nothing to say about these matters. It does not try to fill the whole
moral world. It does not deny the existence of such obligations or imply
that they are purely subjective and not subject to rational discussion. The
only limit that liberal egalitarianism places on such moral views and moral
commitments is that they must not conflict with the rights and duties that
liberal egaliteranism itself prescribes.

People from poor countries may feel a special obligation to use their
talents at home, and they may think that their compatriots have the
same obligation. Liberal egalitarianism does not deny or affirm this view.
It only denies the moral propriety of enforcing it through restrictions on
movement.

My arguments about the brain drain have focused on the countries of
origin. What about the countries of destination? It would be both pater-
nalistic and hypocritical for rich countries to say that they were closing
their borders to help the poor ones out. Moreover, given my arguments
above about the relationship between the right of exit and the right of
entry, it would be wrong to do so with the goal of denying potential
emigrants any place to go.

III

One objection to the line of argument I have been developing so far is that the
whole problem of freedom of movement is essentially epiphenomenal.
Other things being equal, one could expect that most people would not
want to leave the land where they were born and raised, a place whose
language, customs and ways of life are familiar. But other things are not
equal. There are vast economic inequalities among states, and some states

deny basic liberties to their own citizens. These are the circumstances that create such a vast potential for movement across borders and that make the issue of migration seem like an urgent moral problem. But from a liberal egalitarian perspective, these circumstances are at least as morally objectionable as restrictions on freedom of movement.[13] States have an obligation to respect their citizens' basic liberties, and rich states have an obligation to transfer resources and adopt other measures to reduce drastically the prevailing international economic inequalities. If they fulfilled these obligations, migration would no longer be a serious moral problem, because relatively few people would want to move and those who did could and would be accommodated somewhere.

If one replies that states will not meet these obligations, the response is that we gain nothing by focusing on another obligation which they are equally unlikely to fulfil. Most of the same practical and self-interested considerations that will prevent rich states from transferring significant resources to poor states, will keep them from opening their borders wide to poor immigrants. In struggling against injustice, it is a bad strategy to make the admission of new immigrants to rich countries a priority, because restrictions are a symptom, not a cause, of the real problems, because immigration can never be a solution for more than a relatively small number, no matter how open the borders, and because this focus on people who want to move from the Third World to the First World may perpetuate neo-colonial assumptions about the superiority of the First World.

I think there is something to be said for this objection. International inequalities and political oppression are certainly more important moral and political problems than restrictions on migration. The sense that the latter is an urgent problem derives in large part from the size of the potential demand and that in turn derives from international inequalities and other forms of injustice that free movement will do little to cure. Nevertheless, we cannot entirely ignore the question of immigration. In the long run, the transformation of the international politico-economic order might reduce the demand for international migration and the resistance to it, but, as Keynes said, in the long run we are all dead. We have to consider the moral claims of those whom we confront here and now (as well as the claims of future generations). For example, refugees who have no reasonable prospect of a return to their homes in the near term need a place to settle if they are to have any chance of a decent life. Moreover, we lack knowledge as well as will when it comes to radically reducing international inequalities, as is illustrated by the failures of most attempts to eliminate regional inequalities *within* states. In terms of politics, it is not clear that increasing aid and increasing immigration are really incompatible. In general, the same political actors support or oppose both.

But the objection that the demand for free movement is essentially epiphenomenal poses a theoretical challenge as well as a practical one. To what extent does my earlier claim about the liberal egalitarian commitment to free movement rest upon the current realities of international inequalities and political oppression? Would people have the right to move freely in a world without the deep injustices of the one we live in, or might there be legitimate grounds for restricting free movement, say, for the sake of a certain kind of community? In other words, is free movement epiphenomenal at the theoretical level, not derived directly from fundamental principles but rather from the application of those principles to the circumstances in which we find ourselves?

To explore this question, I propose to focus in the next two sections on the question of movement across borders when the states in question enjoy comparable levels of affluence and comparable liberal democratic political institutions.

IV

The epiphenomenon argument raises questions about the consequences of focusing on possible changes in migration policies in abstraction from other issues, but it does not directly challenge the principle that free movement is good from a liberal egalitarian perspective. Are there any elements in the liberal egalitarian tradition that would give pause to this general embrace of openness?

One possible source is the liberal egalitarian commitment to pluralism, and the consequent respect for difference and diversity. Consider first the case of Japan. Should Japan's immigration policy be the same as that of the United States or Canada? A commitment to free movement seems to require a positive response to this question, except that the public order constraint might kick in sooner because of the high population density in Japan. But to answer that question positively seems counter-intuitive, and not just because we assume that all states have the right to control their borders. Rather a positive response seems to imply that all states have a moral obligation to become like us – multicultural countries with large numbers of immigrants (or at least to open themselves to that possibility). (This sounds like a form of North American moral imperialism; our way is the only right way.)

Now that does not prove that the claim is wrong. Appeals to diversity and pluralism carry no weight when it comes to the violation of basic human rights. From a liberal egalitarian perspective all states are obliged to respect such rights regardless of their history, culture or traditions. As we have seen, it is possible to claim that freedom of movement is a basic human right from a liberal egalitarian perspective. But perhaps that claim does not pay sufficient attention to the costs that freedom of movement can impose.

To return to the Japanese case, Japan is a country with a highly homogeneous population. It is not completely homogeneous. There are religious differences and ethnic minorities in Japan as there are in every country. But most people in Japan share a common culture, tradition and history to a much greater extent than people do in countries like Canada and the United States. It seems reasonable to suppose that many Japanese cherish their distinctive way of life, that they want to preserve it and pass it on to their children because they find that it gives meaning and depth to their lives. They cannot pass it on unchanged, to be sure, because no way of life remains entirely unchanged, but they can hope to do so in a form that retains both its vitality and its continuity with the past. In these ways many Japanese may have a vital interest in the preservation of a distinctive Japanese culture; they may regard it as crucial to their life projects. From a liberal egalitarian perspective this concern for preserving Japanese culture counts as a legitimate interest, assuming (as I do) that this culture is compatible with respect for all human beings as free and equal moral persons.[14]

It also seems reasonable to suppose that this distinctive culture and way of life would be profoundly transformed if a significant number of immigrants came to live in Japan. A multicultural Japan would be a very different place. So, limits on new entrants would be necessary to preserve the culture if any significant number of people wanted to immigrate.

Would the limits be justified? That depends, I think, on why the people wanted to come. We have to weigh the claims of those trying to get in equally with the claims of those who are already inside, but to do that we have to know something about the nature of those claims. For example, suppose some non-Japanese person had married a Japanese citizen. It would clearly be wrong to exclude the non-Japanese spouse, even if mixed marriages were seen as subversive of Japanese culture. Here the fundamental right of individuals to marry whom they want and to live together, along with the fundamental right of the Japanese citizen not to be expelled from his or her home, should trump any communal concerns for the preservation of culture. (And, as far as I know, Japan does indeed admit spouses.)

Suppose, however, that people wanted to come to live and work in Japan as a way of pursuing economic opportunity. Should that trump the concern of the Japanese to preserve their culture? The answer might depend in part on the nature of the alternatives the potential immigrants face if Japan is closed. Recall that we have temporarily put to one side, by hypothesis, the problems of deep international inequalities and refugee-generating forms of oppression. Presumably, then, the potential immigrants have reasonable economic opportunities elsewhere, even if ones that are not quite as good. I do not see why an interest in marginally better economic opportunities should count more than an interest in preserving a culture.

One obvious rejoinder is that restricting immigration limits individual freedom, while cultural changes that develop as a by-product of un-coordinated individual actions do not violate any legitimate claims of individuals. The problem with this sort of response (which clearly does fit with some strains in the liberal tradition and even with some forms of liberal egalitarianism) is that it uses too narrow a definition of freedom. It excludes by fiat any concern for the cumulative, if unintended, conse-quences of individual actions. A richer concept of freedom will pay attention to the context of choice, to the extent to which background conditions make it possible for people to realize their most important goals and pursue their most important life projects. That is precisely the sort of approach that permits us to see the ways in which particular cultures can provide valuable resources for people and the costs associated with the loss of a culture, while still permitting a critical assessment of the consequences of the culture both for those who participate in it and for those who do not.

But if we say that exclusion may be justified to preserve Japanese culture, does that not open the door to any other state that wants to exclude others, or certain kinds of others, to preserve its culture and its way of life? Doesn't it legitimate racist immigration policies? What about the White Australia policy, for example? That was defended as an attempt to preserve a particular culture and way of life, as were similar racial and ethnic policies in Canada and the United States.[15]

From some viewpoints every form of exclusion that draws distinctions based on race, ethnicity, or cultural heritage is morally objectionable. I think, however, that one cannot make such a blanket judgement. Dif-ference does not always entail domination. One has to consider what a particular case of exclusion means, taking the historical, social and political context into account.[16] For example, the White Australia policy cannot be separated from British imperialism and European racism. That is why it was never a defensible form of exclusion.

Japan's exclusionary policy seems quite different. First it is universal, i.e. it applies to all non-Japanese. It is not aimed at some particular racial or ethnic group that is presumed to be inferior, and it is not tied to a history of domination of the excluded. Japan has a centuries-old tradition of ex-clusion based partly on fears of the consequences of European penetration. Of course, there is also the Japanese imperialism of the twentieth century, but that developed only after the West had forced Japan to end its isolation. Moreover, it was only during its period of imperialist expansion that Japan adopted a non-exclusionary policy, declaring all the subjects of the Japanese Empire to be Japanese citizens and bringing thousands of

Koreans into Japan as workers. Both before and after this period, Japan strictly limited new entrants. Unlike much of Western Europe, for example, Japan rejected proposals for guest worker programmes to solve labour shortages in the 1960s and 1970s. I trust that it is clear that I am in no way defending or excusing Japanese imperialism. On the contrary, my point is that the Japanese policy of exclusion was not a product of, and was in important ways antagonistic to, Japanese imperialism. In that respect, at least, exclusion was not linked to domination.

But does not a policy of exclusion always imply that the culture and the people being protected through exclusion are superior to the ones being excluded? Not necessarily. It may simply reflect an attachment to what is one's own. Presumably it does entail the view that this way of life is worth preserving, that it is better than whatever would replace it under conditions of openness. But that is not necessarily objectionable in itself. Besides, having relatively open borders may also generate a sense of cultural superiority, as the American case reveals.

I do not pretend to have established the legitimacy of Japanese exclusion. That would require a much more detailed and careful examination than I can provide here. What I do hope to have established is that such an examination would be worthwhile, that exclusion for the sake of preserving Japanese culture is not self-evidently wrong, at least in a context where we have temporarily assumed away the most urgent concerns (desperate poverty and fear of oppression) that motivate so many of those who actually want to move and that make their claims so powerful.

What if we let those concerns back in and at the same time assumed that the positive case for the preservation of a distinctive Japanese culture could be sustained? One possibility is that we would conclude that not all of the rich states should have precisely the same responsibilities regarding admission of new members and assistance to poor states. Perhaps it would be appropriate for Japan to meet most of its responsibilities through aid rather than through admissions. (I express these thoughts tentatively because I feel unsure about them.)

Even if one did follow this line of thought, however, Japan would face certain responsibilities regarding the admission and integration of 'outsiders'. For example, Japan should admit some reasonable number of refugees on a permanent basis. Their needs cannot be met by aid and Japan cannot rightly expect others to assume all the burdens of resettlement. Perhaps it would be acceptable to select among the refugees on the basis of their adaptability to or compatability with Japanese culture.

Even more important, Japan has a responsibility to treat its Korean minority differently. Most of the Koreans in Japan are people who were brought over to work in Japan during World War II or their descendants. They have lived in Japan for many years. Most of the children have never lived anywhere else, and many do not even speak any other language than Japanese. Japan has an obligation to treat these people as full members of society, to grant them citizenship easily if they wish it and to make their position as permanent residents more secure and more equitable if they prefer to retain their Korean citizenship.[17] In short, Japan's desire to protect its cultural cohesiveness is outweighed in some cases by the legitimate claims of others to entry and integration.

The discussion of Japan makes a preliminary case for exclusion for the sake of preserving a cultural tradition and a way of life. In Japan this cultural tradition and way of life are closely associated with the political boundaries of a sovereign state. But this does not establish anything about the moral status of the state as such nor does it rule out the possibility that there may be other communities with cultures and ways of life worth preserving that do not exist as states. Take, for example, the case of native communities in North America who are trying to preserve a traditional way of life within some defined land area. Most of what has been said about the Japanese case could also be said about them: they are trying to maintain a distinctive culture and way of life that gives meaning to those who inhabit it and which they regard as highly preferable to the way of life that would be entailed if they mixed with others, they cannot maintain this culture if any significant number of outsiders come to settle on their land and the reasons the outsiders have for coming (e.g. to use the land for recreational purposes) generally seem far less compelling than the reasons the natives have for keeping them out.[18]

I accept these general claims. Indeed the control that native peoples exercise over their land provides a striking exception to the general right of free mobility within the modern state, and one that is entirely justified from a liberal egalitarian perspective in my view. So, it is not the state as such that gives rise to a claim to exclude, but rather the existence of a community with a distinctive and valuable way of life that would be threatened by immigration.[19]

V

Can a parallel argument be developed on behalf of the state as such, perhaps on the grounds that each (legitimate) state has a distinct political culture worthy of preservation and protection? By 'political culture' I mean the collective self-understanding, the way citizens think of themselves and of their relationship with one another as this is reflected in their political institutions, policies and practices. One reason people have for wanting to restrict entry is their desire to protect the democratic autonomy of the community in which they live. This view presupposes that there is some significant space between what is morally required of all and morally prohibited to all so that different communities can legitimately make different choices about goals, institutions and policies, or, more broadly, about the ways they lead their collective lives. Call this the zone of the morally permissible. One need not think of this as a realm of mere preferences, however. The moral arguments that belong here (and are most apt to be used in real political debates) are ones about the history and character of the community rather than about universal rights and duties. Most forms of liberal egalitarianism do not pretend to settle all moral questions. So, different communities will make different decisions, adopt different policies and develop different characters. But these differences may be threatened by open borders.[20]

Let me offer a concrete example from a comparison between Canada and the United States.[21] (I write as someone born and raised in the United States who has lived in Canada for the past four years.) Canada has a national health insurance plan that pays for the medical care of all citizens and permanent residents. The United States does not. According to some estimates, 30 per cent of the American population has no health insurance, and many more are underinsured. Should Americans with serious health problems be able to move to Canada to take advantage of its health care system? Take those with AIDS as an example. This is an illness that requires a lot of expensive medical care over a long period, care that may simply be unavailable in the United States if one has no insurance. People with AIDS and without insurance might well choose to move to Canada if they could do so. But Canada's population as a whole is only 10 per cent of that of the United States. If even a small proportion of the Americans with AIDS moved, it would put a severe strain on the Canadian health care system. At present, Canadian immigration requirements keep out potential immigrants with medical problems that seem likely to put an unusually high financial burden on the health care system. Is that an unjust restriction on potential American immigrants?

Canada's health care system is only one example of a pervasive difference between Canada and the United States in social welfare policy. In one area after another Canada provides greater benefits to those in need, and, of course, Canadians pay much higher taxes than Americans to fund these programmes. If the borders were open and if many of the needy moved across, both the capacity and the willingness to support the programmes would be in jeopardy. The capacity would be threatened by the relative size of the Canadian and American populations, the willingness by the sense that Americans were taking advantage of Canadians (not so much the needy Americans, who would probably arouse both sympathy and resentment, as the greedy ones who refused to bear the costs of caring for their own and tried to shift these costs onto others). Restrictions on immigration from the United States therefore may help to make it possible for Canadians to take a different and more generous path from Americans when it comes to social policy. Does liberal egalitarianism require them to open the borders anyway?

If the questions in the last two paragraphs sound rhetorical, it is only because the presumption that states have the right to control entry is so deeply rooted in our thinking. One has only to shift the focus to intra-state movement to see why the questions are real and important. In the United States as in many federal systems, sub-units bear much of the responsibility for social policy and they differ greatly in the ways they carry out these responsibilities. For example, Wisconsin's welfare policies are much more generous (or much less stingy) than those of the neighbouring state of Illinois. Some Wisconsin officials claim that people are moving from Illinois to Wisconsin for the sake of these benefits. These officials propose to discourage the influx by reducing benefits for new residents during a temporary waiting period – a strategy that may or may not pass legislative and judicial scrutiny. But not even the most ardent advocates of exclusion think that they can prohibit people from moving to Wisconsin from Illinois or keep them from gaining access to all of the state's social programmes after a waiting period. This is not just a quirk of the US constitutional system. As we have seen, freedom of movement within the nation-state is widely regarded as a basic human right, and if this freedom is to be more than a mere formality, it necessarily entails that new arrivals have access to the rights and privileges that current residents enjoy, at least after the satisfaction of a modest residency requirement and, in some cases, immediately. But this freedom of movement has the same effect of eroding or at least limiting the democratic autonomy of Wisconsin as it would that of Canada.

Is that bad? Should Wisconsin have the right to keep out people from Illinois after all? Or should Canada be obliged to admit people from the United States? If the two cases are different, how and why are they different? I find these questions genuinely puzzling, but in the end I cannot see that sovereignty makes that much difference from a liberal egalitarian perspective. Despite my attachment to Canada's social welfare policies, I do not think they justify restrictions on movement. On the other hand, I do think that this commitment to free movement is compatible with short-term residency requirements so that one must live somewhere for a few months before becoming eligible for social programmes, and that such requirements would do a great deal to protect against the erosion of social programmes. Living in Canada, one cannot help but be aware of the importance some people (especially in Quebec) attach to maintaining the distinct culture and way of life of their province. It turns out to be possible to do so even within a context of free migration within the state and considerable immigration from outside. Despite its occasional effects on social policies, it is easy to exaggerate the impact of free movement within the state and also to ignore its importance to those who do take advantage of it. The same is true of movement across borders. Perhaps even the Japanese ought in principle to begin with a policy of open doors, closing them only if a substantial demand actually appears. Given the difficulties of fitting into Japanese society as an outsider, how many would actually want to settle there if they had reasonable opportunities elsewhere?

So, I return to the theme with which I began. Liberal egalitarianism entails a deep and powerful commitment to freedom of movement which can be overridden at the level of principle only with great difficulty.

VI

Let me turn briefly now to the question of how the responsibilities of one state with regard to migration are affected by what other states do. In principle, the failures of one state should increase the obligations of the others since there are people out there with legitimate needs and moral claims that are not being met. And it actually seems to work this way with regard to refugees at first. Thus the very existence of refugees reflects a failure of the state from which they have fled, and other states generally acknowledge that this imposes new obligations on them to care for people who were not previously their responsibility. But then by any reasonable specification of what a fair share of responsibility for refugees would require of each state, most states fail to live up to their responsibilities. (Except for the states that are next door to the refugees. They sometimes act admirably and in any event can rarely avoid bearing a disproportionate share of the burden.) Should we say that this second round of failures generates a new set of obligations for the few states that have acted responsibly? That seems an unpromising line, ratcheting up the level of responsibility until one is almost bound to fail. On the other hand, the needs of the refugees remain unmet. In practice, states, like people, tend to judge their own behaviour by what others do, so that states feel proud if they do more for refugees than most (and especially than the ones with whom they compare themselves.)

VII

I will conclude with a few remarks on criteria of inclusion and exclusion. Assuming that there will be some restrictions on entry, either for legitimate reasons like the public order constraint or for illegitimate ones like a desire to protect economic privilege, are there some criteria of inclusion and exclusion that are more (or less) objectionable than others from a liberal egalitarian perspective? Certainly need should be one important criterion for admission, and refugees seeking permanent resettlement rank very high on this score since they literally need a place to live. The claims of immediate family members (spouse, minor children) rank very highly as well. No one should be denied the right to live with his or her family. Other relatives also have some claim but not as strong a one.

To return to the criterion of need, if one accepts the brain drain hypothesis, it would seem appropriate to give priority to the least skilled and most needy among potential immigrants as this would have the least negative impact on the countries of origin. On the other hand, if one admits people with skills and education, it may reduce the backlash problem (which appears to be a real or potential problem in every country that accepts immigrants, especially refugees).

Are criteria that serve the interests of the receiving country always morally problematic in this way, defensible only on prudential grounds? Not necessarily. Taking linguistic and cultural compatibility into account does not seem objectionable if it is not a disguised form of racial or ethnic prejudice and if the cumulative effects of such policies by different countries do not leave out some groups altogether.

Criteria of selection that discriminate against potential immigrants on the basis of race, ethnicity, religion, sex, or sexual orientation are particularly objectionable from a liberal egalitarian perspective. Can these criteria ever be used legitimately to give priority to some? Again, one crucial question is whether they constitute *de facto* forms of discrimination. Consider four recent or current policies with these sorts of factors (I oversimplify a bit, but I think I describe the main lines accurately):

1. Britain removed citizenship from holders of overseas passports and citizens of commonwealth countries, except for those whose grandfather was born in Great Britain.
2. Ireland grants an automatic right to citizenship to anyone with a grandparent born in Ireland, provided that the person comes to Ireland to live.
3. Germany grants citizenship (upon application in Germany) to anyone of ethnic German descent, no matter how long since the person's ancestors lived in Germany.
4. Israel grants automatic citizenship to any Jew who comes to live in Israel.

Of these, the British law is the most objectionable from a liberal egalitarian perspective and the Irish law the least, despite their formal similarity. The British law is a thinly disguised form of racism. It was designed to preserve the citizenship rights of as many descendants of white settlers as possible while depriving as many Asians and Africans as possible of theirs. The Irish grandfather clause, by contrast, has no hidden exclusionary goal. It is merely an attempt to lure back the descendants of some of those who left. The German law is troubling for two related reasons. First, the explicit link between ethnicity and citizenship raises questions about whether those German citizens who are not ethnic Germans are really regarded as equal citizens. Second, the easy grant of citizenship to people who have never lived in Germany before and some of whom do not even speak the language contrasts sharply with the reluctance to grant citizenship automatically to the children of Turkish 'guest workers' even when the children were born and brought up in Germany (and sometimes speak no other language). Finally, the Israeli 'Law of Return' raises questions about whether the Arab citizens of Israel whose friends and relatives do not have comparably easy access to citizenship are really regarded as equal citizens. On the other hand, the Israeli law is tied both to national security concerns and to the historic purpose of Israel as a homeland for Jews.

VIII

Liberal egalitarians are committed to an idea of free movement, with only modest qualifications. That idea is not politically feasible today and so it mainly serves to provide a critical standard by which to assess existing restrictive practices and policies. While almost all forms of restriction on movement are wrong from a liberal egalitarian perspective, some practices and policies are worse than others. Expulsion is worse than a refusal to admit. Racism and other forms of discriminatory exclusion are worse than policies that exclude but do not distinguish in objectionable ways among those excluded. Ideals do not always translate directly into prescriptions for practice because of the second-best problems familiar from economic theory which have their analogue in moral theory. In theory this might seem to make it difficult to identify the policy implications of liberal egalitarianism with regard to free movement. One can doubtless imagine cases where the sudden opening of the borders of one country (with all the other circumstances of the modern world remaining unchanged) would do more harm than good from a liberal egalitarian perspective. In practice, however, we can usually ignore this concern because, in every polity, domestic political considerations will confine feasible policy options to a relatively narrow range, excluding alternatives that would entail major costs to current citizens. Given these political realities, liberal egalitarians should almost always press for more openness towards immigrants and refugees.

Notes

1. For a defence of few or no restrictions, see Joseph H. Carens, "Aliens and Citizens: The Case for Open Borders," *The Review of Politics*, 49 (Spring 1987), 251–73; Bruce Ackerman, *Social Justice in the Liberal State* (New Haven, Conn.: Yale University Press, 1980), pp. 89–95; Judith Lichtenberg, "National Boundaries and Moral Boundaries: A Cosmopolitan View," *Boundaries: National Autonomy and Its Limits*, ed. Peter Brown and Henry Shue (Totowa, N.J.: Rowman & Littlefield, 1981), pp. 79–100; and Roger Nett, "The Civil Right We Are Not Yet Ready For: The Right of Free Movement of People on the Face of the Earth," *Ethics*, 81 (1971) 212–27. For the state's right to control entry, see Michael Walzer, *Spheres of Justice* (New York: Basic Books, 1983), pp. 31–63. For the middle position, see Frederick Whelan, "Citizenship and Freedom of Movement: An Open Admission Policy:" *Open Borders? Closed Societies?: The Ethical and Political Issues*, ed. Mark Gibney (Westport, Conn.: Greenwood Press, 1988), pp. 3–39.
2. The arguments in this section draw upon Carens, "Aliens and Citizens" and Whelan, "Citizenship and Freedom of Movement."
3. This brief sketch necessarily covers over deep disagreements among liberal egalitarians with regard to many issues such as how much inequality is compatible with or required by the commitment to freedom, whether affirmative action for groups historically subject to discrimination is a violation of, or a means of realizing, liberal egalitarian principles, what are the foundations (if any) of liberal egalitarian commitments, and so on.
4. See Walzer, *Spheres of Justice*. For a detailed discussion of the right of exit see Frederick Whelan, "Citizenship and the Right to Leave," *American Political Science Review*, 75 (1981), 636–53.
5. I have discussed these sorts of arguments previously in "Aliens and Citizens." For other treatments see Ackerman, *Social Justice*; Whelan, "Citizenship and Freedom of Movement," and an unpublished paper by Whelan entitled "Freedom of International Movement: Some Reservations."
6. Here I follow John Rawls, *A Theory of Justice* (Cambridge, Mass.: Harvard University Press, 1971), pp. 216–21.
7. I develop the claims in the next two paragraphs at greater length in "Membership and Morality: Admission to Citizenship in Liberal Democratic States", *Immigration and the Politics of Citizenship in Europe and North America*, ed. William Rogers Brubaker (Lanham, Md.: German Marshall Fund Of America and University Press of America, 1989), pp. 31–49.
8. For one discussion of the potential demand, see Michael Teitelbaum, "Right versus Right: Immigration and Refugee Policy in the United States," *Foreign Affairs*, 59 (1980), 21–59.
9. Garrett Hardin, "Living on a Lifeboat," *Bioscience* (October 1974).
10. Rawls, *A Theory of Justice*, p. 213.
11. For an explicit use of this argument, see Teitelbaum, "Right versus Right."
12. Whelan offers a clear presentation of these arguments in "Freedom of International Movement."

13. See, e.g., Charles Beitz, *Political Theory and International Relations* (Princeton, N.J.: Princeton University Press, 1979); Brian Barry, "Humanity and Justice in Global Perspective," *Ethics, Economics, and the Law: Nomos XXIV*, ed. J. Roland Pennock and John W. Chapman (New York: New York University Press, 1982), pp. 219–52; and David A. J. Richards, "International Distributive Justice," in Pennock and Chapman, pp. 275–99.

14. For discussions of the ways in which liberal individualism is compatible with the view that people may have an interest in maintaining and passing on a culture, see Brian Barry, "Self-Government Revisited", *The Nature of Political Theory*, ed. David Miller and Larry Siedentop (Oxford: Clarendon Press, 1983) and Will Kymlicka, *Liberalism, Community and Culture* (Oxford: Oxford University Press, 1989).

15. For a fuller discussion of the White Australia policy, see Joseph H. Carens, "Nationalism and the Exclusion of Immigrants: Lessons from Australian Immigration Policy", *Open Borders? Closed Societies: The Ethical and Political Issues*, ed. Mark Gibney (Westport, Ct: Greenwood Press, 1988), pp. 41–60.

16. For a fuller defence of this approach see Joseph H. Carens, "Difference and Domination: Reflections on the Relation between Pluralism and Equality," *Majorities and Minorities: NOMOS XXXII*, ed. John Chapman and Alan Wertheimer (New York: New York University Press, 1990), pp. 226–50.

17. The claims made here for Koreans in Japan parallel those made above for migrant workers.

18. I have explored these issues more fully in an unpublished paper entitled "Migration, Morality, and the Nation-State."

19. For a valuable discussion of minority rights, especially the rights of native people in liberal societies, see Kymlicka, *Liberalism, Community and Culture.*

20. This concern for the capacity of communities to define their own character lies at the heart of Walzer's defence of their right to closure. See note 1.

21. I explore the relevance of differences in social welfare policy between Canada and the United States in a similar way in "Immigration and the Welfare State," *Democracy and the Welfare State*, ed. Amy Gutmann (Princeton, N.J.: Princeton University Press, 1988), pp. 207–30.

— 4 —

Ethics and international economic relations

I. M. D. Little

It may be useful to start by underlining an important difference between the viewpoint I am going to take and that of many moral philosophers. I do not believe in natural rights, laws, or liberties; by which I mean rights, laws, or liberties that are independent of any community or society. I accept that people may have rights, but these rights are created by, and are nugatory without, a moral community.

My brief is to take a liberal egalitarian point of view. What does this mean? There are two extreme doctrines. One is that there should be no restriction of liberty for the purpose of pursuing end-state equality. The other is that every restriction of liberty is justified that leads to greater equality. By 'equality' I mean economic equality somehow defined, not equality of 'respect or concern'. I take it, as most do, that there may be tension between the two.

I do not know of anyone who subscribes to the latter doctrine. The former has been argued by Nozick.[1] Oddly enough it is also the view of Rawls, who claimed to make liberty lexically prior to equality.[2] Despite this, of course, he ends up with his famous difference principle, to the effect that inequality is justified only to the extent that it benefits a representative member of the poorest class. I have found his reconciliation of these apparently conflicting doctrines unconvincing.[3] But that need not worry those who take the view that some but not all liberties may be restricted for the sake of equality. I am happy to include myself in this class of persons. This is hardly going out on a limb. I am only ruling out what I regard as extreme views.

There are many possible measures of equality.[4] In taking an egalitarian viewpoint in any degree one has to assume that there are some measurable changes in wealth distribution that would both indicate greater equality

48

and be regarded by egalitarians as desirable. An acceptable measure of equality might reflect only the relative position of the poorest.

The view is advanced elsewhere in this volume by Lal that a state has no right to restrict liberty (e.g. the liberty of a person to dispose of his property in any way he wishes) for the sake of achieving more end-state equality; but that it can justly do this to relieve poverty. Poverty relief is distinguished from redistribution on the grounds that the former is a public good, and the very purpose of a state is to provide public goods. I find this argument difficult to accept. To include poverty relief, or a safety net, as a public good, like defence or law and order, seems to be straining the definition of 'public goods'. More important, if the reduction of poverty is a public good it can be argued on very similar, even identical, grounds that greater equality of wealth is also a public good. I propose to include poverty reduction under the banner of equality.

The questions to be discussed here mostly concern what restrictions on international movements of capital and commodities a state is justified in enforcing. The division of the discussion between migration of people, and of goods, services and capital is rather artificial. Nothing can be said from an ethical viewpoint about either without deciding what obligations a state has to foreigners. If, for instance, it was agreed that the state existed solely for the benefit of its own citizens, or some class of its own citizens, then the value of restrictions to be imposed on international movements (if any) would be a function only of the economic consequences for its own citizens. However, even if some restriction were deemed valuable, it might be unacceptable on grounds of undue denial of liberty.

It may be useful to start with what is, I think, an extreme view. Imagine a Nozickian minimal state established by notional contract for defence, law and order. It has duties and rights only towards its own citizens. Who are they? The original contractors, and, it must obviously be supposed, their descendants. I can already imagine problems. For instance what about adopted children? Could I adopt a thousand boat people? Let us side-step such problems by assuming that the original contract somehow defines citizen-worthy descent. Such a state would surely have no right to prevent its citizens dealing with foreigners. But foreigners themselves can have no rights. The state should not stop them, but they would be unlikely to buy land and reside, or make investments, with no protection at all. There would no doubt be some international trade, but perhaps not much for there could be no international enforcement contracts.

To my very limited knowledge, contract theorists – indeed moral and political philosophers in general – are very weak on international matters. This is true for instance of Rawls. He does imagine representatives of states meeting behind a veil of ignorance. According to him they come up with more or less conventional principles to regulate inter-state behaviour, but not with any principles of distributive justice. It is not altogether clear why this should be so. But one can suggest a reason. The existence of states is taken as given, and their representatives are not supposed to be suggesting rules for world government. Unlike the constitution of a state, there is no mechanism for realizing principles of distributive justice. Moreover, if the veiled participants are invited to take states as they are in reality (as the veiled participants in the conference establishing justice within a state are supposed to take human beings as they are), then we have the familiar difficulty that states are unjust, which makes it difficult to justify an international difference principle.

It does not help to suppose that the veiled participants are simply human beings, not representatives of any state. They would then be forming principles for world justice. But how futile if they cannot usefully propose a constitution for the world! It is no use agreeing to a maximin principle if there is to be no constitution under which a set of rules embodying that principle can be enforced. It is also worth remarking that such veiled participants would probably not subscribe to the conventional inter-state principles. For instance, why should it not be just to invade an unjust state, or at least interfere with its internal affairs?

Let us forget about contract theories, and be realistic. States have been constituted by force, and many of them deny their subjects liberties that most people would regard as important (and some as natural or basic). Few show much concern for equality. How do we want a relatively wealthy, democratic and egalitarian state to behave in these circumstances? Do we want it to treat foreigners purely as instruments for the economic welfare of its own people? If so, it would be entitled to regulate migration, trade and capital movements with this end in view, and would be limited only by the requirement that in so doing it must not trespass too much on the liberty of its own citizens.

The last proviso is surely necessary. Without it the state might say that I could invest my money abroad since there is an anticipated return (which it taxes). But I would not be allowed to subscribe to Oxfam.[5] However, even with this proviso, most people who consider themselves as liberal and to some degree egalitarian would surely think that it is going too far for the state to treat foreigners solely as instruments.

However, it must be noticed that at least in the matter of migration states treating foreigners solely as instruments comes close to reality. Migrants come in rather freely if they are wealthy and will pay taxes, or are talented and can be expected eventually to contribute more than they cost. All states now prevent, if they can, large numbers of poor migrants. If poor they would probably make the state's own poor worse off, and if too numerous they would not assimilate, and if allowed to settle would create ethnic or communal problems that can seriously undermine the well-being of existing citizens. (Emigration presents different problems. I deal with this below.) One hardly needs to add that trade and capital movements are regulated in like manner. Governments protect their own industries, especially labour-intensive industries, without thought for their employment potential in developing countries, and so on. And where a country does not regulate, that is either because *laissez-faire* is regarded as anyway the best policy from the point of view of its own citizens or because it does not want to restrict liberty too much.

But what of international aid? Is that not an exception? Governments do not generally argue as if it were. Aid is generally justified on grounds of self-interest (usually unconvincingly to my mind). Despite the existence of a small constituency for aid on the utilitarian principle that it is good for the rich to give to the poor (and that some part of the aid will percolate to the relatively poor in most poor countries), governments are probably correct in thinking that such arguments have little general appeal (they seem to have more appeal in Holland, Denmark, Norway and Sweden, than elsewhere). Disasters are an exception. The reasons are clear. People are shocked into sympathizing with the victims. To some extent the same seems to apply to migration. The distinction made between political and economic refugees hangs on this.

In general, the governmental behaviour I have described seems to reflect popular thinking. Protests even from intellectuals are usually quite muted. Can we define a core of widely accepted ethical thinking that underlies the manner in which states actually regulate or do not regulate dealings with foreigners?[6]

Clearly it is not universal utilitarianism. Even if poor states had benevolent and efficient governments with a proper concern for the mass of their peoples, there would be almost no support for the massive transfers which such utilitarianism would seem to imply. Nevertheless, I suggest that a weighted and constrained utilitarianism best fits the case. First, utilitarianism has to be constrained by rights, for people do believe in rights and corresponding duties. To use a familiar philosophical example, it is my duty to save my tiresome mother from fire, rather than the rich visiting philanthropist. Equally, rights (positive rights) have to be constrained by utilitarianism. In accepting a liberal egalitarian stance whereby some rights may be traded against equality, we have already accepted that.

Second, utility has to be weighted by social distance; charity begins at home. There is little doubt that the marginal utility of someone with whom one is acquainted weighs more than that of an unknown Bangladeshi (except sometimes if a flood is vividly reported on television). I do not think this is wholly a matter of special duties, such as the special duty most people think they owe to their families or their dogs. Furthermore, if duties extend far beyond rather narrow boundaries of kith, kin and friendship they seem to require a utilitarian base. Admittedly, duties may sometimes trump utility. Who thinks it wrong for a testator to leave at least some of his estate to his rich son? But what grounds are there for believing that a rich person has a duty to give to poor people who are remote from him? Only that they are poor. Even if we substitute 'lack of basic needs' for poverty, I think that is still utilitarianism.[7] This is not to say that some people may think more in terms of rights than utilities. Thus in the case of a famine a person might be more moved by the argument from a right to live than by the high marginal utility of a starving person. But rights also suffer from social distance in the sense that the further removed a person is the more one is inclined to think that there is someone else, or some other organization or state, whose duty it is to help. For myself, I might add, nationality is not a hurdle in assessing effective social distance. I am more likely to give to Oxfam than to a charity whose recipients are equally unknown deprived Britons. But I guess I may be in a minority.

I have thus far concentrated on foreigners. But international movements or transactions may also be regulated for egalitarian reasons, with due regard to liberty, within one's own country. This has been treated only in passing. Protectionism is an obvious example. Another example of great interest to developing countries is emigration and the related control of capital movements. Most liberals probably think it an intolerable affront to personal freedom to prevent a person emigrating. But if he is paid less than his contribution to society in that country, possibly for egalitarian reasons, then the country and perhaps its poorer members may suffer, though they may not. (Remittances have been, since 1974, an important part of the national income of South Asian countries, as well as Turkey and North Africa.) Even so, most liberal egalitarians (certainly myself) think he must be allowed to go. Jagdish Bhagwati has tried to resolve this conflict by suggesting that the host country should put a special tax on these migrants and return it to the country of origin. Ingenious, but a non-starter!

On top of this, should the migrant be allowed to take his fortune with him? There would be more disagreement on this score. Prima facie, if a government has a right to tax his property for redistributive reasons it should equally have a right to exact an equivalent once and for all tax on exit. In brief, he should be allowed to take a part of his fortune (the rest should be returned to him if he came back).

What should I deduce from the actual behaviour of Second and Third World countries? Many regulate and some virtually prohibit emigration. Very few permit more than a token amount of money to be taken. They do not behave in a liberal manner, but this is seldom for egalitarian reasons. Different cultures weigh liberalism and egalitarianism differently. The weight of one or the other may indeed approach zero.

Let me now address myself more specifically to some of the questions that form the subject matter of this book concentrating on movements of merchandise and money. But it is unlikely that any unambiguous answers can be given. The taking of a liberal egalitarian stance rules out only some extreme views. Moreover, the undercurrent of utilitarianism that I have admitted implies that policies must be judged by their consequences. The consequences are for economics. Needless to say they are usually debatable. But they cannot be usefully debated in a forum composed predominantly of philosophers and political theorists. Where economic consequences are involved I can give only my own views.

The essential standpoint I am taking is that a government is there to maximize some function of the utility of its citizens, subject to certain rights not being trampled on. But foreigners are not to be treated solely as instruments. There are degrees of foreignness ranging from long-resident aliens to totally unknown inhabitants of distant lands. Some human sympathy is felt by most or all people. So one does not want one's government to put all foreigners beyond the pale; some consideration should be shown to all human beings. Thus negative rights should always be respected. But positive rights to some standard of living are not recognised at least in the case of non-residents. However, some very limited aid should be given on utilitarian grounds. (Aid is less than 0.5 per cent of national income for most rich countries, and some even of this can be credited to self-interest.)

Speaking more personally I would myself like my government to give more aid, despite my knowing that it is very difficult to give aid effectively for the poor and that much is wasted. Of course there is a minority of liberal egalitarians who would go much further. But if my constituency is to include most people who would think of themselves as liberals, and who agree with some element of redistribution within their own country, then I cannot go much further.

It obviously follows from what has been said that it may be ethically appropriate for any country to restrict capital movements in or out. The circumstances are that such restriction increases the welfare of its citizens.

But should there be no international limitations on the sovereign rights of a state in this or other respects in the name of 'global distributive justice'? To speak of global justice at all requires, I believe, a global moral community (this follows from my rejection of natural law). I cannot conceive of justice as between, say, those on Earth and those on some planet in another galaxy (supposing that we on Earth could know of their existence and whether they were rich or poor relative to ourselves, but could never communicate). I admire people who try to develop such a community for this globe, but it hardly exists. Therefore, it hardly makes sense to speak of global justice. But one can, of course, favour a more equal distribution, regardless of nationality, without any belief in global justice.

Some fifteen years ago, the idea of a 'New International Economic Order' (NIEO) was mooted and actively demanded by the 'Group of 77' (which includes nearly all developing countries numbering many more than 77). But the developing country proponents of the NIEO had greater equality of states in mind, not people. There was a strong emphasis on sovereignty; and they resented the idea that their poor were anyone's concern but their own.

The actual suggested constituents of a NIEO almost all implied more aid, and more international controls. In my opinion the controls would have done the poor of the world no good. The aid component of the proposed measures would probably not have increased total aid (donors are not that easily fooled). Most of the measures proposed paid no attention to the relative poverty of developing countries, and on balance the wealthier would have benefited most (if any benefited). The aid component would have been without strings. But in my opinion aid (grants and concessionary loans) can be justified only if they go predominantly to the poorest countries, and sustained only if the public in the donor countries can be assured that they go to countries with reasonably viable general economic policies that show some concern for the welfare of the mass of the people. Strings are needed. The NIEO concept seems to have faded away.[8]

I have briefly considered aid. Let me finally address some other specific international concerns. I shall do this from the viewpoint already described, but I shall make that viewpoint a little more focused by supposing that as a rich-country citizen I believe that helping the poorest people on Earth has a higher priority than it appears to be accorded by the governments of industrialized countries. What can and should be done in suggesting any institutional reforms still depends both on their practicality, including what can be made acceptable to poor countries, and on the economic consequences. I will illustrate the problems taking only a few examples.

Debt is the hottest current topic. Essentially, the burning question is how much debt, if any, should be forgiven — and whose debt, and who should bear the cost. A longer-run institutional question might be whether international borrowing and lending should be controlled in some way — with such control becoming part of an international economic order. Note that this would be the institution of an order rather than its reform, for the debt arose from disorder.

The background is probably relevant to both questions. In 1974 OPEC created an enormous payments surplus. If a major recession was to be avoided this had to be offset by other countries creating corresponding deficits through expansionary policies. Inflation was also magnified by the oil price rises, which made the industrialized countries reluctant to expand. Developing countries were less reluctant. So the commercial banks recycled the 'petro-dollars' to some of them (for several years at extremely low real interest rates). All would have been well if enough of this borrowing had been devoted to investments with a return which would at least cover the payment of interest on the debt. In fact most of it was used for investment, but much of this investment produced little or nothing. Debt was already high, but not impossibly so, when the second oil-price shock hit. Many countries found retrenchment too difficult and continued to borrow at an alarming rate at the now high rates of interest that had come about largely as a result of President Reagan's economic policies, until the crunch came when they ceased to be able to borrow.

The above scenario applies to a good number of countries, but not all. Some countries, e.g. Nigeria, Mexico and Venezuela, experienced highly favourable external shocks, still borrowed excessively and are now in deep trouble. In Asia, the scenario applies only to the Philippines, which in many ways resembles Latin American rather than other Asian countries.

Now should the debt, or some of it, be forgiven? The assumed emphasis on poverty suggests not, except in the case of some African countries (where indeed some debt has been forgiven). A famous Indian economist, T. N. Srinivasan, has protested against debt-forgiveness.[9] India has little debt and a high proportion of the world's poorest people. Rather than forgive debt to relatively wealthy Latin American countries aid to India should be increased. If taxpayers are to bear the cost of debt-forgiveness it is likely that it would be competitive with other forms of aid which might therefore be reduced.

Other ethical problems arise. The conceptions of justice I have discussed say nothing about deserts (what is deserved, not barren areas). Yet some commentators on the debt problem seem to put this up front. The highly indebted countries were incapable of managing their affairs properly. So it is their fault. Alternatively, the bankers were very foolish and moreover pushed the developing countries into borrowing (but what about *caveat emptor*?). Bank equity holders and senior staff should suffer (but that would not be enough for not many banks could be allowed to go bankrupt). Yet again, one can argue that the citizens and taxpayers of the rich countries benefited, for if the bankers and their borrowers had not been foolish there would have been a deeper recession in the 1970s. Finally, arguments from moral hazard are raised.

Personally, I am not much moved by arguments about deserts or moral hazard. Countries and banks are not people and do not learn in the same way. Those countries that repudiated their debts in the 1930s were in the van of the credit worthy in the 1970s: and there will not be another debt crisis for forty years. Personally, and *pace* T. N. Srinivasan, I would favour quite a lot of debt-forgiveness, but I am not prompted to this view by any conception of global justice.

Does the debt situation suggest that there should in future be more international control of borrowing and lending to be part of the international order? Bank surveillance and control of foreign borrowing and lending by a country's own banks and other institutions is prima facie a country's own concern. Certainly, developing countries would be, and have been, up-tight about any limit on their freedom to borrow on the Euro-dollar market (which might be required in the interests of a stable international currency). Of course, that does not settle the question. I fear the matter is too complex, and I am not expert enough, to go further into it. But I suspect that a very cumbersome and overrestrictive apparatus might be created to fight the last war.

Let me turn to something easier – multinational corporations. Tremendous heat was generated in the 1970s on this subject by some developing country governments and spokesmen and by the 'development establishment'. That multinationals might do economic harm in innumerable ways was hypothesized: but, above all, the fear was that they might undermine a country's independence. Of course a country has a right to control incoming foreign investment; every country I know of does. They also have a right to make foreign companies fulfil certain conditions of operation; many do. When a country has a highly distorted price mechanism it is true that some investments by foreigners may do harm (just as it is true that some investments by natives may do harm). This is because the distortions (by definition) thrust a wedge between private and social profitability. Some control could be a second- or third-best solution to this problem. But domestic economic reforms would be better.

The sheer volume of foreign interests – in industrial investment or real estate – either overall or in particular industries or areas could threaten independence. Suppose Germans bought one of the northern Swiss cantons lock, stock, and barrel! But countries are in control, and quite sufficiently xenophobic. So what has this to do with the international order? Or international justice? The furore of the 1970s did result in a small UN institute. I have never heard of it since; the heat has died. Multinationals are now more welcome, and controls have been somewhat reduced (rightly, in my opinion). This is not because of any change in the behaviour of multinationals, or any institutional change. It seems simply to have been because radical opponents of capitalism and nationalist opponents of foreign capitalists shouted too loud and lost their voices.

Lastly, take trade. This is an easy one to end with. There is no doubt that industrial protection on the part of the rich countries harms the poor in the poorest countries.[10] To my mind, the high protection which the governments of poor countries insist on (very gradually this insistence is waning) also harms the poor in almost all countries.[11] I believe it also harms their development in a more general sense.

There has been a tendency to globalize problems that are not global at all, not even international. But protection is not one of these. There is a strong argument for an international institute. This is because almost every country has a tendency, indeed seems to feel a compulsion, to use trade restrictions to solve some internal problem. There is, even from the individual country's point of view, almost always a better way of dealing with the problem – but in the short run trade restrictions seem easiest, politically or administratively. In the long run I believe all lose. An international institution that ties countries' hands can do much good. Of course, there is such an institution; in its heyday the GATT did much good. For reasons I need not go into it is in sad decline. This has been the fault of both rich and poor countries.

If it is desirable to tie countries' hands in the area of trade, why not in other areas? For instance, could not controls over international investment be subject to limitations imposed by an international agreement embodied in a monitoring quasi-judicial institute similar to the GATT? Am I not being inconsistent in seeing trade and not international investment as a global problem? In principle I am; but perhaps not in practice. I think a beneficial agreement with teeth would be too difficult to reach.

I believe something rather close to free trade and freedom of international investment is in the interest of all countries. But on top of this I would regard it as a bonus that the poor of the world would stand to gain most provided that the economic policies of countries were themselves reasonably neutral and did not bias production in ways that limited the extent to which the masses could benefit. Liberalism and egalitarianism should not here be in any global conflict.

Notes

1. Robert Nozick, *Anarchy, State, and Utopia* (New York: Basic Books, 1974; Oxford: Basil Blackwell, 1974).
2. John Rawls, *A Theory of Justice* (Cambridge, Mass: Harvard University Press, 1971).
3. See I. M. D. Little, "Distributive Justice and the New International Order," *Issues in International Economics*, ed. Oppenheimer, (Northumberland, England Oriel Press, 1980), pp. 37–53.
4. See, e.g., A. K. Sen, *On Economic Inequality* (Oxford: Clarendon Press, 1972).

5. This could be regarded as a rather extreme case of equality within a state constituting an argument for regulating international transactions, and circumscribing liberty. There are more realistic cases, not involving a diminution of world equality, which I shall discuss below.

6. Brian Barry has suggested that this question implies acceptance of the moral possibility of forming a social welfare function from individual values, an idea that I rejected thirty-seven years ago (see I. M. D. Little, "Social Choice and Individual Values," *Journal of Political Economy*, vol. LX, no. 5 (October 1952), reprinted in *Rational Man and Irrational Society? An Introduction and Source Book*, eds Brian Barry and Russell Hardin (Beverly Hills, Calif.: Sage, 1982). In asking whether there is some widely accepted ethical thinking (on the part of those who would consider themselves both liberal and mildly egalitarian) to which governments are sensitive, I insist that I am not concurring in anything so diabolical as the construction of a social welfare function. To argue that some degree of consensus may exist, surely does not commit one to any belief in an objective moral code, or the dictatorship of some metaphysical general will. I have reread and am fully convinced by what I wrote in 1952.

7. A weighted utilitarianism can envelop almost any theory. Rawls' theory may even gain by thinking of it as utilitarianism with a weight of 1 for the disadvantaged, and zero for the others. It can also deal with Sen's objections to utilitarianism – that cripples and Indian peasant women should get more than they would if society's objective was to maximize utility. Furthermore, it is hardly less subjective. There is already room for a good deal of disagreement about relative marginal utilities.

8. I considered the components of the NIEO in *Economic Development – Theory, Policy and International Relations* (New York: Basic Books, 1982), chap. 17.

9. W. H. Buiter and T. N. Srinivasan, "Rewarding the Profligate and Punishing the Prudent and Poor," *World Development*, vol. 15(3), 411–17.

10. I have written 'industrial protection', because it is possible to argue that rich country agricultural protectionism benefits the poor in some food-deficit developing countries. On balance, I think I would argue that it is harmful, but prefer to side-step the issue.

11. High protectionism in poor countries has favoured industry and urban areas against agriculture and rural areas where most of the poorest people are. Within industry it favours capital intensive industry, thus limiting the demand for labour. Creating a high demand for labour is the best way of helping the poor. Freer trade is likely to be inegalitarian only in those few countries where the landed interest is rich. Taxation could eliminate this problem. But if for political reasons taxing the pastoralists or latifundians at the front door is ruled out, then industrial protection may be a way of imposing taxation at the back door. This has been given as a reason for protection in Australia.

——— 5 ———

Commentary: Liberalism and migration

James Woodward

As a commentator on the chapters by Joseph Carens and Ian Little, I find myself in the position of disagreeing far more with Carens than with Little about the implications of liberal egalitarianism. I shall therefore focus primarily on the contribution by Carens. The course of my discussion will take the following form.

In Section I, I shall argue against the claim, defended both in Carens' chapter and in several other chapters, that there is a basic human right to move freely across national borders. I shall also criticize the contention that a commitment to liberal egalitarian ideals requires acceptance of such a right. I shall then consider a second rationale for permitting extensive immigration: the claim that justice requires that we take steps to improve the condition of worse-off groups in the world generally, and that permitting extensive immigration from poor to affluent countries would be a way of accomplishing this end. I shall argue that while there are indeed humanitarian considerations favouring limited admission of some poor immigrants to affluent countries, extensive immigration will be of rather limited effectiveness as an anti-poverty strategy and that, moreover, it is likely that there will be important moral costs to permitting such immigration.

Section II draws attention to the most important of these costs, which has to do with the potential consequences of extensive immigration for the kinds of public institutions and social welfare policies that liberal egalitarians value. Section III argues in a preliminary way that these costs may be of sufficient weight to justify significant restrictions on immigration. In Section IV, I try to provide, again in a sketchy way, more theoretical backing for these claims, by exploring some rationales for restricting immigration within a broadly Rawlsian or contractual framework. In this

59

section, I also take up some issues regarding international distributive justice and the obligation to provide foreign aid raised in Little's chapter and suggest that there is more to be said for his sceptical treatment of these matters than many philosophers suppose. Finally, Section V draws attention to some current trends regarding immigration, not mentioned by either Carens or Little, which probably will decisively shape future moral discussion.

Immigrate to
emmigrate from

I

Let me begin by distinguishing two quite different rationales for extensive freedom of movement, both of which can be found in Carens' chapter. The first rationale appeals to the idea that there is a basic human right to immigrate; the second to the idea that immigration is an effective way of dealing with poverty and inequality. I shall suggest that once these rationales are distinguished, each is subject to different objections, which together seem to undercut any very general case for freedom of movement across borders of the sort which Carens wishes to make.

In its purest and most unqualified form, the first rationale involves the idea that there is a fundamental right or liberty, possessed by all persons, to immigrate to whatever country they want. This right is on a par with other, more familiar fundamental rights and liberties (like freedom from involuntary servitude, to use Carens' analogy) and follows directly from our status as free and equal moral agents. Carens explicitly commits himself to such a right at a number of points in his chapter. After asking in his opening sentence, 'What must we do to treat all human beings as free and equal moral persons?', he tells us that, 'Liberal equilitarianism entails a deep commitment to freedom of movement as both an important liberty in itself and a prerequisite for other freedoms' (see page 25). Elsewhere he claims that, 'citizenship in the modern world is a lot like feudal status in the medieval world' and that 'modern practices of citizenship and state control over borders tie people to the land of their birth almost as effectively [as feudal practices]' (see page 26–7). A similar idea is suggested by Carens' argument that 'freedom of movement within the nation-state is widely acknowledged as a basic human right' and that the same considerations which support this right will also support a 'right to move across state borders'. If restrictions on immigration and citizenship are really like assignments of feudal status, they will violate fundamental human rights, and will presumably be justifiable (if at all) only in very unusual circumstances. For example, such restrictions might be justified if continued immigration would result in a breakdown of public order (to mention one kind of restriction accepted as legitimate by Carens) but presumably would not be justified by less weighty reasons.

A second rationale involves thinking of freedom of movement as a strategy for dealing with poverty and inequality in the Third World. Carens appeals to this rationale when he writes:

> freedom of movement would contribute to a reduction of political, social and economic inequalities. There are millions of people in the Third World today who long for the freedom and economic opportunity they could find in affluent First World countries. Many of them take great risks to come: Haitians setting off in leaky boats, Salvadorians being smuggled across the border in hot, airless trucks, Tamils paying to be set adrift off the coast of Newfoundland. If the borders were open, millions more would move. The exclusion of so many poor and desperate people seems hard to justify from a perspective that takes seriously the claims of all individuals as free and equal moral persons. (see page 26)

Carens seems to think of these two rationales as complementary, but in fact they appear to me to be in considerable tension with one another and to have very different implications for immigration policy, given plausible empirical assumptions. One way to bring out the difference is to note their different implications for the issue of whether affluent countries should give (or are obligated to give) priority in accepting immigrants to those who are the poorest and most in need, if all who wish to enter cannot be admitted. Carens endorses such a policy and, given certain obvious empirical assumptions, the second rationale supports it. By contrast, the first rationale not only fails to justify such a policy but seems prima facie inconsistent with it. Suppose that all have a fundamental human right to enter, but the consequences of allowing everyone to act on this right are judged to be morally unacceptable. Then the natural way of respecting the force of this right, within an egalitarian framework, would be some policy that can be justified in terms of equal treatment of all who wish to exercise their right (e.g. a lottery system that gives every prospective immigrant, rich or poor, an equal chance to enter, or some other system that embodies some other relevant notion of equality of opportunity or access).

A system of giving priority to the needy in immigration, although supported by the second rationale, is simply not the system to which we would be led if we take the first rationale seriously. Within the liberal egalitarian tradition, those who make use of notions like 'basic human rights' do not think it is justifiable to adopt policies which differentially respect (or give priority to the satisfaction of) rights held by needy people over the rights of non-needy people. Consider, for example, Rawls' theory. If freedom of movement is a fundamental human right or liberty, then it falls within the scope of Rawls' first principle, which assigns equal liberty to all and which takes priority over the distributive considerations aimed at improving the condition of the worse off which figure in the difference principle. Conversely, if we think that immigration policies giving priority to the most needy are justifiable, this is an indication that we do not really think that there is a basic human right to immigrate or that restrictions on immigration are the moral equivalent of feudalism. Instead, we are thinking of freedom of movement as a socio-economic good of a sort that falls within the scope of the difference principle. *Rawls's*

We can further bring out the significance of this point, and the differences between the two rationales, by asking, as Carens himself does, what sorts of immigration rights people would have in a counterfactual world in which socio-economic inequalities between states are much less severe than they are at present, or alternatively, by confining our attention to immigration between affluent states in the actual world. My own judgement (and I think the judgement of many others) is that the case for any general right of free movement between countries is considerably diminished in such circumstances. If Bangladesh were as affluent as Sweden, but large numbers of Bangladeshis none the less wished to live in Sweden (preferring, let us suppose, a cooler climate) then, even if the Swedes could accommodate them without great hardship, it is hard to believe that the Swedes violate the Bangladeshis' fundamental human rights by denying them entry. Similarly, if a million Frenchmen wish to immigrate to Japan, because of marginally better economic opportunities there, I think that few people (including the French and Japanese) would hold that the Japanese have a stringent obligation to admit them.

All of this suggests that much of the force of Carens' advocacy of relatively unrestricted freedom of movement really derives from the second rationale – it is his images of poor and desperate people from poor countries ('Salvadorians being smuggled across the border in hot, airless trucks') trying to enter affluent countries like the United States and Canada and the idea that their lives would be greatly improved if they were able to do this, which is responsible for much of the appeal of his claims on behalf of freedom of movement. Replace the Salvadorians with a wealthy German businessman, and the idea that his 'basic human rights' are violated if he is denied entry looks a lot less appealing. But if this is so, the comparisons of immigration restrictions to extensive restrictions on internal movement or to assigned feudal status are just so much idle rhetoric.

One possible response to this, suggested by at least some of Carens' language both in the present chapter and elsewhere, is that regardless of the immediate responses of many of us to the cases described in the preceding paragraph, it none the less remains true that liberal egalitarianism or, more generally, a moral framework which treats all human beings as free and moral persons implies a fundamental right to immigrate to whatever country one wishes. Unless we wish to abandon this moral framework, we are, willy nilly, committed to recognizing this right. One way of trying to assess this contention is to ask whether various moral theories thought to express the fundamental commitments of liberal equalitarianism entail such a right. I shall try to do this, albeit in a very sketchy way, for one such theory – Rawls' theory of justice – in Section IV below. Another way of trying to evaluate this contention is to ask whether groups or communities of people who seem to come closest to embodying a commitment to liberal egalitarian ideals and who are in a position to make a decision about the matter under conditions of relatively full information and in the relative absence of distorting and coercive pressures, seem to acknowledge such rights of unrestrictive immigration. (This approach may seem particularly attractive if one is sceptical that any of the extant candidates, including Rawls' theory, very adequately captures the underlying ideals of liberal egalitarianism.)

Applying this idea, one is immediately struck by the fact that many of the societies which seem most fully committed to liberal egalitarian ideals (the welfare states of Western and Northern Europe, including particularly the Scandinavian countries) have quite restrictive immigration and citizenship policies. Among countries in this group which permit relatively extensive immigration, it is the United States which has adopted policies that are the most favourable to the admission of poor and desperate people. But among countries in this group it is also the United States that has the least fully developed welfare state, public institutions which are furthest from those which liberal egalitarians would regard as ideal and perhaps the largest proportion of citizens who hold social and political attitudes which are relatively unsympathetic to many elements of liberal egalitarianism. Moreover, no country in the general group of democratic welfare states permits either unrestricted immigration or anything like the level of immigration which might emerge as a compromise between a basic right of free movement and the need to maintain public order. To the best of my knowledge there are no significant political groups, parties or constituencies within any of the societies of this group – and in particular, no groups on the left/liberal side of the political spectrum – which advocate immigration of this magnitude. There are indeed individuals and organizations who advocate very extensive immigration, but they lack serious political followings, and at least in the United States, many of the most visible of these come from the political right.[1] Finally, unlike other widely acknowledged basic human rights (such as rights protecting free speech, or freedom of religion or rights protecting against arbitrary arrest and imprisonment), claims of an unrestricted right of free movement across borders are rarely, if ever, found, in standard enumerations of rights in the constitutions or legal systems of liberal egalitarian countries (or for that matter, in those of non-liberal egalitarian countries), or in the proclamations of international forums and organizations like the United Nations. In short, the observed pattern of attitudes and behaviours is very different from what we would naively expect if it were true, as Carens claims, that 'liberal egalitarianism entails a deep commitment to freedom of movement' (see page 25). I shall return to this point below.

Of course, these considerations are hardly conclusive. Perhaps liberal egalitarians have failed, for self-interested reasons, or out of logical ineptitude to recognize the implications of their own ideals. Still, these considerations seem to cast additional doubt on the claim that there is a basic human right to immigrate and on the claim that liberal egalitarians must be committed to such a right.

In fact Carens himself seems to me to implicitly concede this when he discusses, in later portions of his chapter, possible grounds for restricting immigration. There, in addition to the public order constraint, he is willing to take seriously (and indeed, seems to endorse) the claim that Japan is justified in denying entry to prospective immigrants in order to preserve Japan's cultural identity, at least if such immigrants merely desire better economic opportunities. (see pages 36–40)[2] Whether or not this is a good reason for barring entry, it is not a reason that fits very comfortably with the contention that there is a fundamental right to immigrate. If denying someone (or at least someone who is impoverished) entry is morally tantamount to treating him as a serf, it seems plain (to me at least) that the desire of a community to preserve its cultural identity or homogeneity is not remotely weighty enough to justify such treatment.

Let us then turn to the second of the two rationales distinguished above – to the plight of the Third World poor and with immigration to affluent countries as a strategy for dealing with their poverty. There are, it seems to me, at least two dimensions along which we can assess the suggestion that affluent countries ought to permit extensive immigration as a strategy for dealing with Third World poverty. First, (a) we may ask how effective the strategy is likely to be in accomplishing its intended object. Second, (b) supposing the strategy is likely to be effective, we may ask whether there are compelling reasons, moral or otherwise, for citizens of affluent countries to adopt this strategy. I shall comment very briefly on (a) here, and on (b) in Sections III and IV.

The effectiveness of extensive immigration as an anti-poverty strategy plainly depends upon a number of complex empirical considerations, which I have neither the space nor the competence to assess. None the less, there are obvious grounds for scepticism, some of which Carens himself concedes (see pages 35ff). First, even on the most optimistic assumptions about the willingness of affluent countries to accept immigrants, the proportion of the world's poor who might be helped in this way will be very small. Second, any feasible version of the strategy will be very imperfectly targeted on those groups that are most desperate and in need of help. For example, if we confine our attention to those who are less well off among actual and prospective immigrants to the United States, it seems clear that this group by no means includes those who are the poorest and most needy. The majority of less well-off immigrants to the United States come from Latin America. Although many are poor by North American standards, they are not remotely as poor as many people in Africa and South Asia. Actual immigrants are typically also far from being among the worst off in the population from which they come. Those who are able to make the trip to the United States must possess some economic resources, reasonably good physical health and typically will have skills and abilities that make them employable in US labour markets. They also tend to be young and male. A consistent strategy of targeting the very poorest and most needy groups in the Third World, as some of Carens' language seems to suggest (and which would perhaps also be suggested by a global version of Rawls' Difference Principle – see below), would require that the United States discourage the admission of most recent immigrants, and instead pursue an active policy of recruiting immigrants (providing them with the resources to come to the United States) from much poorer groups.

A third point (recognized by both Carens and Little) is that the widespread desire to immigrate derives, to a larger degree, from the existence of unjust, oppressive, corrupt and incompetent Third World governments who fail to fulfil basic obligations to their citizens or to provide material conditions in which they can live decent lives. Any strategy that makes progress in ameliorating Third World poverty and deprivation will need to involve more fundamental changes in the behaviour of such governments (and in the behaviour of affluent countries like the United States and the Soviet Union which support many of them). Such changes and the kinds of social and economic developments they would make possible would reduce the desire of many people in poor countries to move to affluent countries (immigration, especially for poor people, is a costly and risky undertaking); in the absence of such changes, the demand for entry into affluent countries will continue to far exceed any possibility of actually satisfying it. In short, the strategy of permitting extensive immigration does not attack the root causes of poverty and inequality and is not a strategy that will lend to improvements in the lives of most of the world's poor.

A final point concerns the likely experiences of very poor and unskilled immigrants once they arrive in affluent countries. Carens is curiously silent (at least in the chapter under discussion) about this subject; it is as though he supposes that once immigrants are allowed to take up physical residence in affluent countries (and I assume, to become citizens) their most serious problems will be behind them. But whether this is so (and whether extensive immigration turns out to be an effective strategy for fighting poverty) depends very much on what conditions for the immigrants are like after entry. This in turn depends on what the labour market experience and employment prospects of immigrants will be, and on how they are treated by the social welfare system of the host country. Although, at least in the United States, unemployment rates and rates of participation in the welfare system among present immigrants as a whole compare favourably with corresponding rates for native Americans, this masks considerable heterogeneity in the performance of different immigrant groups. Among some groups – not surprisingly those who tend to be relatively unskilled and to come from predominantly rural, agricultural societies – unemployment rates, and poverty and welfare participation rates are extremely high.[3] Although it is of course an empirical question how very large numbers of unskilled immigrants from such backgrounds would fare in the labour markets of affluent countries, I see no particular reason for optimism.

This in turn raises the question of the response of the social welfare systems of affluent countries to the large-scale immigration Carens advocates. Average welfare benefits (even in the United States, which as Carens says, are low in comparison with many other affluent countries) are typically many times the per capita income in poor countries. Unquestionably in many cases, participation in the social welfare system provided by affluent countries will raise the level of well-being of immigrants.[4] The availability of such benefits thus will be an inducement to immigration, even for those who are not confident of their ability to find employment. While it is true that, within a liberal egalitarian framework, it is desirable that such benefits be available to residents who need them, we also need to ask what the likely effect of extensive participation by newly arrived immigrants will be on the level and kind of state benefits and services. Will voters and political parties wish to support the very much higher levels of social spending required to fund full immigrant participation? Will attempts be made to restrict the access of immigrants to such benefits? What will the effects of immigrant participation be on the level of benefits and services available to present citizens? I think it is hard to be confident that anything like the present level of services and benefits will be available to immigrants.

I shall return to some of these issues below. I raise them, not because I am confident of the answers, but to underscore how important it is, in evaluating arguments for extensive immigration as a way of relieving poverty, to think in a concrete, realistic way about the mechanisms for the amelioration of poverty that we can expect to be available in affluent countries, once borders have been opened. In particular, before following Carens' advice to admit poor immigrants up to that point at which a breakdown of public order threatens, liberal egalitarians will wish to think about such obvious practical issues as how they will be fed, sheltered, clothed, educated, provided with medical services, and so forth. (Alternatively, we may decide that it is not the responsibility of government to see to it that immigrants are provided with these things, or that immigration should be allowed to continue even if immigrants cannot be provided with these things. But then – to anticipate a point for which I shall argue in more detail below – we are abandoning fundamental liberal egalitarian ideals.)

In questioning the effectiveness of extensive immigration as an anti-poverty strategy, I do not of course mean to deny that immigration (at some appropriate level) can provide important benefits to poor people who wish to immigrate. I fully agree, furthermore, that within a liberal egalitarian framework, this fact constitutes a reason in favour of permitting such immigration. My point is rather that the considerations supporting immigration, although quite real, are different from, and (I would claim) less compelling, than those to which Carens appeals. The case for extensive immigration cannot rest on a fundamental human right to move freely across borders (in the absence of catastrophic consequences) for there is no such right. And as a device for reducing Third World poverty, immigration is at best one strategy among several that may be pursued. Even under the most optimistic empirical assumptions, it offers only a very partial and limited solution to such problems of poverty and economic inequality. Moreover, if the strategy is to be effective in substantially improving the prospects of those who do immigrate, it seems unlikely that it will support immigration of the magnitude Carens favours. Those who will be most helped by immigration will be (unsurprisingly) those with skills needed in the economies of affluent countries and these will be far from the poorest among prospective immigrants. Finally, once the case for limited immigration is understood in this more modest light (not as a matter of fundamental right, or as a central component in a crash programme for the elimination of Third World poverty), issues about the relative moral importance of the considerations favouring admission of immigrants *vis-à-vis* other competing considerations that may favour restricting immigration within a liberal egalitarian framework naturally arise. Decisions about the appropriate kind and level of immigration begin to look like a matter of balancing a number of different considerations, rather than as straightforward entailments of some single, overriding moral requirement. I shall develop this claim in more detail in the following sections.

II

I turn now to what seems to me to be the most persuasive rationale – within a liberal egalitarian framework – for limiting free movement across borders. This has to do with the possible problems such movement may pose for sustaining the institutions, policies and values characteristic of states presently committed to liberal egalitarianism. There are several, related concerns here. One has to do with the possibility that competition within the labour market between immigrants and present citizens who are poor or disadvantaged may work to the disadvantage of the latter group and may increase income inequality. Another has to do with the direct impact of extensive immigration on social services like public education, health care, and unemployment, disability and welfare pro-grammes of various kinds. A third, very closely related concern, has to do with the more diffuse consequences of immigration for the character, ideals and politics of liberal egalitarian states. My argument in this section will be that there is a serious tension between the demand for anything like open borders and the desire of states to maintain institutions and policies supported by liberal egalitarian values within their borders. I will then try to show, in Section III, that obligations to maintain these institutions and policies owed to present citizens will sometimes defeat the claims of immigrants to enter. I shall focus mainly on the United States, both because it has probably moved furthest in the direction of the kind of immigration policy Carens favours and because it is the country I know best.

However, before proceeding, some qualifications and disclaimers are in order. First, it is important to bear in mind throughout my subsequent remarks that immigrants can create new resources, wealth, jobs and opportunities and can greatly enrich a nation's cultural life. They do not merely withdraw resources from a stock of fixed size. Immigrants thus can provide substantial benefits not only to themselves, but also to (many) citizens in the countries to which they immigrate, benefits which may outweigh whatever costs may be associated with immigration. But whether immigration will in fact have such a beneficial net effect depends very much, in my view, on its character and magnitude, and on economic, political and demographic conditions in the host country. Thus, while the remarks that follow attempt to draw attention to some possible serious costs of the sort of immigration policy Carens favours, I do not mean to deny (and in fact think that it is true – see Section V below) that there are at present good reasons of both a moral and self-interested sort, favouring substantial immigration into many affluent countries. My target is not substantial immigration *per se*, but rather Carens' idea that (subject to the qualifications he mentions) something like a policy of open borders is morally required of affluent countries and that the adverse import of extensive immigration on liberal egalitarian institutions is not a compelling reason for restricting entry.

Second, my impression is that there is relatively little systematic knowledge about the social and economic consequences of current levels of immigration to affluent countries.[5] And of course much less is known about the likely consequences of various hypothetical immigration policies which might be adopted by affluent countries. Because of this, and because the consequences of social policies often turn out to be very different from what even well-informed experts anticipate, my discussion of these consequences will be speculative at best. Should the kind of immigration Carens favours occur, its actual results may thus very well turn out to undercut and render irrelevant the kinds of worries I shall be raising. None the less, in my view, it would be irresponsible not to try to think about the possible consequences to affluent countries of extensive movements across their borders. Our inability to forecast accurately these consequences does not mean that we are entitled to treat them as irrelevant or inevitably benign. And, of course, even if we do not know now what the upshot of some hypothetical immigration policy would be, we can still ask what moral weight we should attach to various possible consequences of that policy, were they to occur.

I begin with concerns about wage competition. These concerns have often figured heavily in the opposition of organized labour and other groups in affluent countries to extensive immigration, or at least policies which favour admission of large numbers of unskilled immigrants. They are also expressed in Ian Little's paper. None the less, at least at present levels of immigration in the United States, econometric studies seem to show that immigrants have a negligible effect on non-immigrant (native) wage levels. (There is, however, evidence that more recent immigrants do depress the wage levels of earlier immigrants.)[6] However, these studies, which are based on cross-sectional data, tell us little about the effects of the much more extensive immigration that would presumably result if we were to adopt anything like an 'open borders' policy. While the impact will obviously depend upon the level and composition of immigration, I assume that there is at least a serious possibility that the effect of such a policy would be to depress incomes among some groups of natives and immigrants from what those levels would be in the absence of extensive immigration. If such an effect were to occur, it seems plausible that those groups most seriously affected would be the least well off among present immigrants and non-immigrants. Particularly in an economic environment which is already marked by increasing inequality and falling or stagnant wages in less well-paying jobs,[7] extensive immigration may

exacerbate inequality and further diminish the prospects of the worse off.
I also take it that some concern to protect the interest of the least well off
among its citizens and to improve their prospects is one of the characteristic features of contemporary liberal egalitarian states.

What about the impact of immigration on various kinds of social
welfare services? Some observers suggest that because immigrants to the
United States at present tend to be young, healthy and employed, they
contribute more in taxes to social programmes than they receive in
benefits.[8] Other investigations suggest a different or at least more complex
picture, in which different immigrant groups vary enormously in their
participation in and fiscal impact on such programmes.[9] Although I know
of no systematic study, it seems fairly clear that at least in some local areas
(e.g. Los Angeles) present levels of immigration have created very serious
problems for some public schools and public health institutions. Here
again, I think it would be very hard to deny that it is at least a serious
possibility that a policy permitting very much higher levels of immigration
(and particularly, a policy of giving preference to poor and unskilled
immigrants) would have the effect of very seriously overloading many
public institutions and social welfare programmes. These, if they were to
continue to exist at all, would require much higher levels of funding, which
might not turn out to be politically sustainable.

A closely related but more diffuse concern has to do with the impact of
extensive immigration on the values, attitudes and behaviour of present
citizens. Many multicultural and multiethnic societies are characterized by
high levels of ethnic tension, suspicion and violence. Such racial and
cultural enmity makes enormously more difficult the task of maintaining
democratic communities devoted to the sorts of political goals that liberal
egalitarians (or for that matter, liberals and democrats of all varieties)
regard as worthwhile. Indeed, one standard explanation for the relatively
underdeveloped character of welfare state institutions in the United States
points to the existence of cultural and ethnic differences that have impeded
the creation of a consensus regarding the desirability of such institutions.
However much we may deplore the existence of racial and cultural conflict,
it remains the case that it is much easier for many people to live peacefully
with, care about and identify with people who are ethnically and culturally
like themselves. The difficulties of successful cooperation are only increased when there are sharp economic differences as well.

These facts generate further concerns about the consequences of
extensive immigration for states with a substantial commitment to liberal
egalitarian ideals. One consequence of such immigration may be the rise of
political parties which attempt to exploit racial tensions, a consequence
which is very much in evidence in France and Germany as I write these
comments. Another consequence may be the disruption of the operation of

many public institutions or services, such as schools and transportation and recreational facilities, not just because of limitations on fiscal resources, but also because of increasingly sharp cultural and economic differences, and (especially in the case of public schools) because of the breakdown of any cultural consensus regarding the character and goals of such institutions. This in turn may lead these citizens who are able to withdraw from these institutions and to look for more private ways of meeting the needs previously addressed by these institutions. (They thus turn to private, rather than public schools, to automobiles rather than public transportation, to private rather than public recreational facilities, and so forth.) It is all too easy to imagine the kind of society that may result: it would be a society that is in many respects more like that advocated by libertarians or enthusiasts for free-market capitalism than the kind of society liberal egalitarians hope for. It would be a society in which there are very sharp inequalities in wealth and opportunity, in which important public services are non-existent or greatly underfunded, and in which people make whatever private contractual arrangements they can regarding education, health care and related matters. The development of communities having this sort of character is already well advanced in American cities like New York and Los Angeles and while no doubt many factors are responsible, it seems very plausible that the presence of large numbers of people of very diverse cultural backgrounds, many of them quite poor, contributes to these changes. And it is likely that immigration of the character and magnitude favoured by Carens would sharply accelerate them.[10]

I take it that to a large extent it is fear of the consequences I have described that explains the lack of enthusiasm, noted above, for extensive immigration on the part of many states with liberal egalitarian policies and institutions and on the part of political groups committed to liberal egalitarian ideals. And conversely, indifference to (or even a desire for) such outcomes plays a not insignificant role in the support for extensive immigration on the part of at least some groups on the right.

My claim, then, is that given plausible empirical assumptions, there is a serious tension, if not an outright contradiction, between the desire of a state to promote liberal egalitarian policies within its borders, and anything like a policy of open borders. If I have understood him correctly, Carens acknowledges this point, but he does not, in my view, accord it the prominence within his discussion that it deserves. He considers the example of the Canadian national health care system and concedes that if needy Americans without medical coverage were free to move across the border and receive health care under this system, 'both the capacity and the willingness to support the programmes would be in jeopardy' (see page 41). Although he does not explicitly say so, presumably he would also agree that opening Canada's borders and access to its health care system to the entire world would make the collapse of the system very much more likely, and that similar consequences would follow for many other social welfare programmes.

Carens resolves the conflict between freedom of movement and social welfare policies by opting, at best at the level of 'principle', for the former. He writes, 'Despite my attachment to Canada's social welfare policies, I do not think that they justify restrictions on movement' (see page 42). I take it that this conclusion is implied by Carens' claims about freedom of movement as a basic human right, but he also gives a more specific argument immediately after the sentence quoted above, which goes something like this: It would not be justifiable to restrict freedom of movement within a state in order to maintain existing social welfare policies. This shows the moral importance of freedom of movement in comparison with these policies. Moreover, the same considerations which support internal freedom of movement also support freedom of movement between states. (The mere fact of sovereignty cannot make a fundamental moral difference within a liberal egalitarian framework.) Thus a similar conclusion follows about restriction on movement across borders to support social welfare policies.

I shall try to provide some reasons for rejecting this argument in Sections III and IV below. Here I confine myself to two preliminary observations. The first is that there is no realistic possibility of any community with a serious attachment to liberal egalitarian social welfare policies voluntarily permitting immigration of a kind that would destroy those policies. There is thus, on Carens' account, an extremely sharp split between what we are supposedly morally obligated to do, and what in fact most liberal egalitarians actually will be motivated to do (or even what most liberal egalitarians will believe that they ought to do).

The second is that a commitment to the characteristic policies and institutions of the modern welfare state is, one would have thought, a key feature which distinguishes liberal egalitarianism from such competing political traditions as libertarianism which require the dismantling of such policies and institutions. Can it really be true that a commitment to liberal egalitarian values implies that one must embrace policies that would lead to just this dismantling? Perhaps this implication does indeed hold, but if so, I think it would be difficult to regard this fact as in any way a vindication of liberal egalitarian values; instead it seems to me more nearly to demonstrate their political irrelevance or incoherence. If some (supposed) formulation of liberal egalitarianism does indeed have this implication, I think that the first possibility for liberal egalitarians to consider is that the formulation in question does not really capture liberal egalitarian values.

III

In this section I want to argue in support of the claim that if extensive immigration would indeed have the deleterious consequences for the liberal egalitarian policies and institutions outlined above this would constitute a good reason for restricting such immigration. There is a tendency, which I think is very visible in Carens' chapter, to think of the moral problem concerning immigration as one of altruism versus self-interest. Should we be selfish and establish stringent barriers to entry or should we do the morally right thing and remove those barriers? It seems to me that this way of posing the problem misses much of its structure. As I see it, the issue is largely one of conflicting obligations or moral claims – the claims of immigrants to enter (and of present citizens who may benefit from their immigration) versus the claims of other citizens to various kinds of social services, benefits and opportunities which may be undermined by extensive immigration.

My contention is that the claims of present citizens who may be harmed by immigration can sometimes defeat the claims of those who wish to immigrate. As a point of departure, we may note that this is the way in which all governments and most people in both poor and rich countries think, at least when they are contemplating extensive immigration into their own countries. The citizens and government of Mexico, for example, may wish that the United States would permit more immigration from Mexico, but my guess is that they do not regard Mexico as under a parallel obligation to admit and care for large numbers of people from other countries. Moreover, this way of thinking has parallels in many other areas of life, in which we also suppose that obligations which are already in place to present members of institutions and organizations, can sometimes defeat the claims of needy newcomers to participate in those organizations. Suppose that you have two children, for whom you can care very adequately. An opportunity arises to adopt twelve more very needy children. If you do this, the resources and attention you will be able to devote to your present children will be very much diminished; perhaps they will fall below some baseline you regard as minimally acceptable. Still, we may suppose, all fourteen of your children will be better off than the additional twelve prior to adoption. Many people will think that considerations of self-interest aside, you ought not to adopt in this situation. The fact that by adopting you would fail to meet obligations which are already in place to your present children is a good (moral) reason for not adopting. Perhaps it is true that if you had no children and wished to adopt, you ought to give special consideration to those who are most needy. But this is not the situation you face – you already have

children and already have obligations to them. A similar conclusion seems
to hold in connection with many other organizations and institutions (for
example, private schools, hospitals, shelters for homeless people) when
there is no prior, agreed upon understanding that they will take all comers.
Why should not a parallel argument apply in connection with the obligations of states to their present residents or citizens?

In fact, Carens himself seems, at least at one point in his chapter, to
accept such an argument. He claims, in connection with migrant workers,
that 'it is much worse to deport people who have already come and settled
than to refuse entry to new workers' (see page 29). I fully agree with this
sentiment, as I think do the governments and citizens of most affluent
countries. These governments have been very reluctant to expel guest
workers who have lived for some time in their countries, even when their
services are no longer required. These governments have not shown a
corresponding reluctance to bar the entry of other prospective immigrants,
many of whom are far worse off than the guest workers. This asymmetry
is naturally explained if we assume that states and citizens acquire obligations to long-time residents of their countries which are different from
their obligations to needy non-residents who wish to enter.

One possible response to this argument is that it simply assumes the
moral legitimacy of present arrangements concerning national sovereignty,
arrangements that are deeply morally problematic. It may be said that
in matters like immigration policy, one should not just appeal to the obligations and requirements which derive from organizations and institutions as presently constituted or presently understood by their members.
Instead one needs to evaluate those institutional arrangements themselves
and to take seriously the possibility that they may be fundamentally unjust
or morally indefensible. If these arrangements are morally defective or
problematic, this undercuts the force and legitimacy of obligations based
on these arrangements.

While I fully agree that present arrangements concerning national sovereignty are morally defective and non-ideal, it does not follow that moral
requirements based on such arrangements lack force or are without
serious moral weight in the way that the objection claims. The argument
given above for differential obligations to citizens and prospective immigrants does not require that one assume the moral legitimacy of existing
national arrangements. Suppose for the sake of argument that it could
somehow be shown that present arrangements in the United States
concerning family structure and parental responsibilities regarding children are morally problematic, and that some quite different, alternative
arrangement would be much better. It does not follow that individual
parents and children who live under present arrangements concerning
family structure and responsibility and who have organized their lives

around these arrangements and created expectations based on them, are justified in regarding moral requirements based on these arrangements as non-weighty matters they can easily dispense with. Non-ideal institutions can give rise to real, weighty obligations. I shall return to this point below, in connection with Rawls' theory.

IV

At this point, I want to step back and briefly consider some more general issues having to do with international distributive justice and the obligations of governments to the residents of other countries – issues which form an important part of the background to both Carens' and Little's chapters. I shall try to explore these issues within a basically Rawlsian or contractarian framework, both because Carens and Little advert at a number of points to this framework and because, independently of this, it is of considerable interest to see what such a framework does or does not imply concerning migration and the obligations of rich nations to poor nations.

Rawls suggests that we assess principles of justice by asking whether they would be agreed to by parties choosing in an original position, behind a veil of ignorance. Obviously, it will make a great deal of difference, in connection with questions of international distributive justice, who the parties to this contract are. Broadly speaking, we may distinguish two possibilities as follows:

1. We may think of the parties to the contract as inhabitants of a particular country, who know this and first use the contractarian framework to choose principles distributing rights and resources within their country. Only after this, do the countries themselves or their representatives come together to choose principles governing relations between states.

2. Alternatively, we can apply the contractual framework globally, thinking of the parties to the contract as all of the inhabitants of the world, supposing that no one knows the country to which he will belong, and asking this group to agree on a set of distributive principles. Obviously, given natural empirical assumptions, this second alternative has much more egalitarian implications than the first. For example, assuming that the parties choose a global version of the difference principle, the second alternative may require extensive transfers of wealth from rich countries to poor countries. And assuming there are empirical grounds for supposing that permitting extensive immigration would make the poorest groups in the world better off, it follows that the parties to a global contract would agree on very extensive rights of entry.

As is well known, Rawls takes the first approach, applying the framework first to individual countries, rather than globally. He has been extensively criticized for doing this – the complaint being that this is an *ad hoc* move, which is inconsistent with the underlying egalitarian spirit of his theory. According to the critics the fact that one is an inhabitant of one particular country rather than another (or a citizen of a rich country rather than a poor country) is a paradigmatic example of the sort of 'morally arbitrary' fact that the method of the original position is designed to abstract from.

I want tentatively to suggest, in what follows, that there is more to be said in favour of the first approach than the critics allow. In doing so, I will in part simply be drawing attention to grounds within Rawls' own theory for taking the first approach. But I think that I will also be drawing attention to some puzzles that arise within contractarian approaches when we try to abstract too much from real world facts about people's actual motivation and non-ideal behaviour.

According to Rawls, the parties in the original position attach a great deal of importance to motivational constraints in deciding which principles of justice to adopt. The principles of justice that the parties choose must be such that they will be motivated to subscribe to them and act in accord with them, once they take up their place in society. Rawls of course appeals to this constraint as part of his argument that the parties would not choose utilitarian principles. It seems to me that parallel considerations can be used to undercut the global application of Rawls' theory contemplated in the second alternative distinguished above, or at least to block certain conclusions that might seem to follow from the global application of the theory.

Consider, for example, the suggestion that the parties to a global contract would agree on very extensive immigration rights (subject perhaps only to the requirement that there be no breakdown of public order). I have already suggested – and I think that both Carens and Little would agree – that there is simply no realistic possibility of an affluent country under a democratic government admitting immigrants on the scale implied by such rights. Such rights are not rights that people in affluent countries would be motivated to act in accordance with or to respect, once they take up their places in such societies. Recognizing this, the parties to a global contract would not agree on such rights. Similar arguments would apply in connection with extensive transfers of wealth from affluent to poor countries.

Some moral and political philosophers are willing to accept the idea that people might have extensive moral obligations even if there is no realistic possibility that most people will ever act in accordance with those obligations, as long as it is in some relevant sense causally possible for people to conform to the obligations. However, this is not Rawls' view, and not, I think, the view naturally suggested by a contractarian approach. Moreover, although I shall not argue the point here, I also think that it is a view which is hard to square with any plausible naturalistic account of the status of morality. If morality is something that we construct, or make up, or agree to, and is somehow grounded in facts that what people want and how people interact together, some such motivational constraint as Rawls' seems unavoidable.

Suppose, however, that one doesn't accept the suggestion that facts about people's motives can influence the actual content of rights and obligations. There still remains a closely related problem with the global use of the contractarian framework contemplated above. Put simply, the difficulty is that as we abstract away from real world facts about actual motives, behaviour and institutions in our characterization of the original position and as we exclude such information from the calculations of the contracting parties, the relevance of the (ideal) principles and institutions that would emerge from such an idealized original position to what we should do in the actual non-ideal world (which is not characterized by such motives, behaviour and institutions) becomes progressively less clear. To illustrate, suppose that we do try to apply the contractarian approach globally, in something like the manner envisioned under the second alternative above. It is perhaps not entirely clear what principles would emerge from such a choice situation, but let us assume for the sake of argument that the principles that emerge will attach a lot less weight to national sovereignty than governments presently do. Perhaps the parties to the contracting situation would agree to a single world government, with no division into separate nation-states, at all. Perhaps the parties would agree to a system of separate states but with rights and prerogatives of sovereignty which are very much weaker than those which nations now claim – a system in which there is free movement of people across borders, and so forth. In this second case, the parties would presumably also insist that each individual nation conform to the requirements of justice, that relations between states be non-aggressive and non-exploitive and that all nations accept some common set of mechanisms for the peaceful resolution of differences.

My question is quite simple: what does a demonstration that all of these arrangements would be agreed to in a properly characterized original position imply about how nations should behave in the actual world, which is very far from conforming to these ideal arrangements? It is not in general a defensible moral principle that if it is obligatory (or even a good thing) to do P under ideal, utopian circumstances, then it is also obligatory (or even a good thing) to do P under the actual circumstances, no matter how far they may differ from the ideal. Nor does it follow that we should assess existing behaviour and institutions by how closely they approximate to this ideal. (This connects up with the point made earlier that our obligations may be quite heavily affected by non-ideal institutions and non-ideal behaviour in the actual world.) To put this point in Rawls' language, our world (and especially that part of our world which has to do with the relations between states, or the relationship between governments and the inhabitants of other states) is not anything like a world of full compliance with the requirements of justice, but very much a world of partial compliance, in which large numbers of people and institutions fail to do what justice requires and in which others, acting against this background of non-ideal institutions and behaviour, acquire obligations which are different from those they would acquire under more perfectly just institutional arrangements.

Choosing from within a global contractarian framework, states would no doubt agree to renounce war as an instrument of national policy and decide to maintain very small, or no military forces. But under actual conditions, in which many states are quite willing to pursue or support aggressive wars, states which wish to behave justly seem to me to be under no obligation to disband armies maintained for defensive purposes and in fact would be quite foolish to do so. Similarly, consider a world of full compliance with the principles of justice, in which both affluent and non-affluent states organize their internal affairs in conformity with Rawlsian principles. Suppose that it could be shown that under such conditions affluent states would provide considerable transfers of wealth and aid to less affluent states. We are still then faced with the question of what this demonstration implies for the obligations of affluent states in the actual world, in which non-affluent states very often (even typically) pursue domestic policies radically at variance with Rawlsian principles. In the real world, as Little emphasizes in his chapter, such transfers will very frequently be appropriated by elites and will not reach needy citizens for whom they are intended. Moreover, in the real world, the failure of non-affluent states to adopt policies and institutions that liberal egalitarians would approve of has in many cases played an important causal role in their present need for aid. Any aid that might be given will be of limited usefulness unless these states are willing to adopt very different political and economic policies. In such circumstances, it seems to me to be very reasonable to insist, as Little does, that aid be given only 'if the public in the donor countries can be assured that [it goes] to countries with reasonably viable general economic policies that show some concern for the welfare of the mass of the people' (see page 54).

Similarly, suppose that it could be shown that in a world of full compliance with the principles of justice, eligibility for social welfare programmes like national health care would not be tied to citizenship or nationality. We are still then faced with the problem of what such a demonstration implies for affluent states with such programmes in the actual world. In the actual world, social welfare programmes linked to citizenship are already in place, and citizens have contributed to them, and obligations and expectations have already been created on the basis of their continued existence. Moreover, in the actual world it is exactly the failure of many non-affluent states to adopt social and economic policies which liberal egalitarians support that creates incentives for the kinds of migration which, under a policy of open borders, threatens liberal egalitarian institutions in affluent countries with collapse. Given these facts I think that (even supposing that the demonstration envisioned above of what justice would ideally require in a world of full compliance could be provided) it is far from obvious that it would be wrong for actual states to limit eligibility for social welfare programmes to citizens or long-term residents, if failure to do so would jeopardize the continued existence of such programmes.

Whether or not one accepts this last claim, it does seem uncontroversial that facts about non-ideal behaviour and institutions are relevant to and will make some difference for, the obligations of citizens in affluent countries. We need to find some way of incorporating the relevance of such facts into our moral and political theories. The theory of how to apply a contractual theory like Rawls' to non-ideal circumstances is very much underdeveloped, but one possible strategy (assuming that it could be followed in a way that avoids incoherence and contradiction) is to try to build facts about non-ideal institutions and behaviour into the background circumstances in which the parties to the contract must choose. Thus, for example, one might try to imagine that the contracting parties choose principles governing relations between states in an original position in which it is known that the world is divided into a number of different states and cultures, with different values and political systems, that these states are largely indifferent to and often actively hostile to each other's interests, that the internal affairs of some of these states approximately conform to liberal egalitarian (or at least liberal) principles, while those of many other do not, that the states differ sharply in wealth and power, that there is no neutral organization capable of enforcing principles governing relations between states, or principles governing international distributive justice and no general agreement among states regarding these principles. Although I shall not attempt to argue for this claim here, I suspect that the most natural way to build these background circumstances into the contracting situation in a way that may avoid incoherence is to adopt something like the two-stage procedure envisioned under the first alternative above (that is, to adopt Rawls' solution). I also suspect that, on any reasonable way of building these background constraints into the contracting situation, the parties will not (for all of the reasons described above) choose principles permitting free movement across borders and will not (for essentially the reasons mentioned in Little's chapter) adopt principles mandating extensive transfer of wealth between countries, although they would endorse more modest principles of foreign aid or disaster relief.

Finally, these remarks go, I hope, some distance towards answering the argument for freedom of movement that attributed to Carens above: the argument that if restrictions on freedom of movement within countries in order to preserve social welfare programmes are unjustifiable, then restrictions on freedom of movement between countries for this purpose must also be unjustifiable. Much of the force of this argument derives, I believe, from the tacit assumption that to respond to it we must show that there is some deep positive moral significance to facts about nationality which ground the above asymmetry, and the suspicion that no response of this sort is available within a liberal egalitarian framework. (Such a response – we might call it the Romantic Nationalist Response – would try to show that there is something highly morally desirable, even ideal about the division of the world's peoples into separate states, typically with distinctive national and cultural identities – presumably on the ground that people have a strong interest in associating only with those who are culturally or ethnically like themselves or can best find fulfilment under such an arrangement.) This is not the response I have attempted to make. Rather, I have tried to show that even if no such positive argument of the sort envisioned by the Romantic Nationalist is available, there none the less may be defensible reasons, having to do with obligations incurred against a background of non-ideal institutions and behaviour, for a different treatment of internal and external migration. Restrictions on entry, in my argument, have the status of non-ideal, second-best solutions to problems of preserving institutions and policies we care about in an imperfect world. In a better world, in which even extensive immigration would not threaten these policies and institutions, my view is that the case for restrictions on entry would be far weaker, even if the result were radically to undermine distinctive national and cultural identities.

I conclude this section by mentioning, but not exploring, a more radical possibility. I have been arguing that if one wants to remain within the framework of a theory like Rawls' while dealing with issues having to do with immigration and economic inequalities between nations, it will be necessary (if one is to obtain results having any relevance to our obligations in the actual world) to build in constraints having to do with the motivation and behaviour of real people and states. But while it seems possible to do this (and while, indeed, relevance seems to require this), one might naturally wonder whether the resulting construction is really consistent with the underlying spirit of Rawls' theory. That theory, after all, is animated by the underlying idea of eliminating or compensating for 'morally arbitrary' differences between people and by the idea that (subject to the constraints of the first, equal liberty principle and the equal opportunity clause of the second principle) social policy ought to focus on making the worse off, whoever they are, as well off as possible. The complications about motivation and non-ideal behaviour introduced above may be unavoidable, but does it not remain true that these animating Rawlsian ideas are at odds with extensive restrictions on immigration? I think that it is indeed arguable that this is the case. However, the conclusion I would draw, if this suggestion is accepted, is not that liberal egalitarianism does after all entail open borders. I would suggest instead that the appropriate conclusion is rather that Rawls' theory is not a good reconstruction of what liberal egalitarians are committed to. An alternative possibility is that we should see the social welfare policies of the liberal egalitarian states as resting not on the single principle of improving the condition of the worse off but rather as resting on a variety of different rationales (having to do with the provision of public goods, with the desirability of various kinds of social insurance schemes and so forth), which in many cases are less universalistic and more closely tied to the existence of particular communities and particular patterns of expectation and cooperation than is Rawls' Difference Principle.[11] Perhaps we should see the modern welfare state as motivated by a concern to eliminate or ameliorate the effects of certain specific kinds of 'moral arbitrariness' (e.g. that one citizen happens to need expensive medical care while another does not), but not as devoted to correcting for *all* morally arbitrary differences (including e.g., all those having to do with one's country of origin) wherever they may occur among human beings. To consider seriously these possibilities is to accept that standard accounts of liberal egalitarian ideals require some fundamental rethinking. I think that one of the merits of Carens' chapter is that it brings home to us the case for such a reconsideration.

V

I would be remiss if I did not conclude this chapter by briefly drawing attention to some empirical facts which have in the rest of this book received relatively little attention but which probably will decisively shape future moral discussion of immigration.

The first is that the populations of most affluent countries are rapidly ageing, with birth rates near or below replacement levels. Most affluent countries (including the United States, Canada, Japan and most of the countries of Western Europe) will face serious labour shortages – particularly

shortages in skilled labour – over the next few decades.[12] The second is
that the populations of many of their non-affluent neighbours (Central
America in the case of North America, and the countries of the Maghreb in
the case of Europe) are growing very rapidly, and face high levels of
poverty and unemployment and very limited economic opportunities. The
situation is thus one in which the interests of (many citizens in) the affluent
countries and the interests of some prospective immigrants appear to
coincide – both can benefit from immigration. Indeed, the economic
incentives supporting immigration on both sides are so strong and access
sufficiently easy that substantial illegal immigration probably will continue to occur regardless of what formal immigration policies the affluent
countries adopt. Completely preventing such illegal immigration would
require the adoption of Draconian measures, including restrictions on civil
liberties, which are inconsistent with liberal egalitarian values. Because of
this, it seems to me that the interesting issue about immigration is not
whether the affluent countries should accept significant immigration –
they will very likely find it is in their interest to do so, and in any case, they
will be unable to prevent it. Nor, for all the reasons described above, is
there a serious question about whether affluent countries should adopt a
policy of open borders. Instead, the interesting and important real life
issues about immigration will have to do with (1) who will come (given
that not all who wish to come will be accepted) and (2) how they will
be treated once they arrive. I would claim that the broad answers to
these questions within a liberal egalitarian framework are that it is not
objectionable to take into account the interests and desires of citizens of
host countries in deciding who to admit (so that, for example, immigrants
with needed skills may be given preference over those who lack such skills)
but that once someone has become (legally or illegally) a permanent
resident with a settled intention to build a life in the host country, it must
be open to him to become a citizen with the same rights and privileges that
other citizens have. The creation of a class of permanent residents who are
restricted from becoming citizens (if they should wish to do so) or any
similar system of differential status among a state's permanent inhabitants
is fundamentally incompatible with liberal egalitarian ideals. I shall not
attempt to argue for these claims here, but I do want to suggest that issues
that fall within the general scope of (1) and (2) above (and particularly in
the case of (1) issues about the control of illegal immigration and, in the
case of (2), issues about exactly how and when one may become a citizen
and about the rights of residents who are not yet citizens) are the issues
concerning immigration which will figure in public discussion over the
next few decades and on which liberal egalitarians should focus their
energies.

Notes

1. Thus, for example, in the United States, *The Wall Street Journal* is a vigorous advocate of extensive immigration – see the editorial of July 3, 1990 calling for a policy of 'open borders'. Other recent prominent advocates of extensive immigration whose political affiliations are identifiably right (or at least centre/right) include Ben Wattenberg and Karl Zinsmeister, "The Case For More Immigration", *Commentary* (April 1990), 19–25 and Julian Simon, *The Economic Consequences of Migration* (Oxford: Basil Blackwell, 1990).

2. Space precludes a detailed discussion of this part of Carens' chapter. I do, however, want to register a very strong protest against Carens' attempts to distinguish Japan's barriers to immigration, which he thinks are based on a legitimate desire to maintain Japanese cultural identity, from Australia's 'White Australia' immigration policies which 'cannot be separated from British imperialism and European racism' (see page 38). To begin with, the claim that racism and ideas about cultural and ethnic superiority play no significant role in Japanese immigration policy is just false. More generally, any proposal which (like Carens') means in practice that there will be two sets of rules governing immigration policy, with Europeans (or North Americans) held to a stricter standard of behaviour than non-Europeans, seems to me to be fundamentally objectionable.

3. For information about unemployment and welfare rates among immigrants see, e.g., George J. Borjas, *Friends or Strangers: The Impact of Immigration on the U.S. Economy* (New York: Basic Books, 1990). While the overall rate of immigrant participation in the welfare system in 1980 was 9.1 per cent (as compared with 8.0 per cent for natives), the rates among different immigrant groups varied from 4.6 per cent (Germany) to 25.9 per cent (Dominican Republic). Among immigrants from India, only 6.0 per cent were below the poverty line in 1980, as compared with 33.7 per cent from the Dominican Republic and 26.0 per cent from Mexico. Unemployment and poverty rates among some Southeast Asian groups (such as Cambodians and indigenous peoples, such as the Hmong) are also reportedly quite high in the United States, although I do not have recent figures. This heterogeneity has been the historical pattern; for further historical information about the very different economic performances of different immigrant groups see Thomas Sowell, *Ethnic America: A History* (New York: Basic Books, 1981).

4. For example, the average income for an immigrant welfare household in the United States was $2,800 in 1980, as compared with per capita GNP in the Philippines of under $700 (Borjas, *Friends or Strangers*, p. 152).

5. For the United States, I have found Borjas, *Friends or Strangers*, to be a useful source of information. A briefer summary of current information regarding the United States can be found in Stephen Moore, "Who Should America Welcome?" *Society* (July/August 1990), 55–62. Jagdish Bhagwati, "Behind the Green Card", *The New Republic* (May 14, 1990), 31–9, also contains helpful discussion.

6. See, e.g., Borjas, *Friends or Strangers*, pp. 74–96.
7. See Gary Burtless, ed., *A Future of Lousy Jobs?* (Washington, D.C.: The Brookings Institute, 1990).
8. See Wattenberg and Zinsmeister, "The Case for More Immigration," p. 20.
9. See, for example, Borjas, *Friends or Strangers*, pp. 150–62.
10. It is worth underscoring a point that it is implicit in the preceding remarks. In thinking about the costs and benefits of immigration to host countries, we should keep in mind that depending upon the characteristics of the immigration these costs and benefits can be very unequally distributed. The presence of large numbers of unskilled immigrants may benefit prospective employers of such workers, i.e. owners of large farms looking for agricultural workers or affluent homeowners looking for domestic workers. It also may benefit consumers in the form of lower prices for various products. However, it may be much less clear that it will on balance benefit less well-off citizens, who may compete with the newcomers in employment and for access to social welfare services. Rather than thinking of immigration as involving a simple conflict between the interests of the immigrants (which favour open borders) and interests of the host country (which favour stringent restrictions on entry) we need to realize that a permissive immigration policy will benefit some citizens and quite possibly impose serious costs on others. More generally, liberal egalitarians need to consider the distributional consequences of various immigration policies, as well as their overall impact on aggregate welfare.
11. Something like this conclusion is suggested by Brian Barry's recent article "The Welfare State Versus the Relief of Poverty," *Ethics*, vol. 100 (1990), 503–29, although I do not mean to claim that he would endorse the use to which I put this argument.
12. For a good discussion of the situation in Western Europe, see the *New York Times*, Sunday, July 22, 1990, p. 1.

Libertarian Perspectives

Libertarianism and the transnational migration of people

Hillel Steiner

When I was a young boy, growing up in Toronto during the post-war years, my parents owned a summer cottage in a small community about 45 miles north of the city on the shores of Lake Simcoe. The community consisted of around fifty families, each with its own cottage on its own plot of land. It also included a children's day camp and a common beach, the use of which was restricted to members of the community and to hired camp staff (who were not members of the community). The previous owner of the tract of land occupied by the community had sold it off in lots to the cottagers on terms that constituted them as a collective decision-making body for certain purposes.

Although I cannot now remember (if indeed I ever knew) many of the terms of sale, I do know that they included a liability to contribute to whatever the collectivity judged to be the cost of maintaining common amenities like the roads, the beach and the facilities of the day camp. More pertinently, they also included a collective power to veto any proposed sale of a cottage to an outsider. What I do not recall was the sort of majority required for such a veto nor whether a veto gave rise to a communal obligation to purchase the cottage in question nor, if so, how that purchase price was to be determined. Assuming for the moment either that there was no such obligation or that it involved a price less than that of the vetoed purchase, this community is describable as one enjoying an absolute legal power to restrict immigration and a relative legal power to restrict emigration by levying what amounted to a tax on it.[1]

One libertarian response to this legal arrangement is to find it morally perfectly acceptable. (Perhaps many non-libertarians would find it similarly so.) For while libertarians firmly reject almost all legislated restrictions on how one may dispose of one's person and property, they are equally firm in their rejection of any legislated restrictions on the range of restrictions one may oneself incur contractually. Although you are not at liberty to incarcerate me in your broom closet without my consent, that consent is sufficient as well as necessary to give you that liberty. This principle – freedom of contract – thus underwrites at least the restriction on emigration from that cottage community. Persons complaining of such restriction needed only to refer to the terms on which their cottages were purchased to be reminded that it was self-incurred. Their self-incurred character is indeed a reason commonly employed by states to justify emigration restrictions on their own citizens. We shall look at such claims presently, along with the libertarian attitude to them.

What about the cottage community's immigration policy? Does it violate anyone's libertarian rights? Here we get into much deeper water, as far as libertarian principles are concerned. For the immigration question raises directly an issue which merely hovers in the background of the emigration question: namely, are the cottagers' legal titles morally valid? Do they conform to libertarian rules constituting property rights? The familiar first step in answering such questions is to investigate the moral basis of the previous owner's (the cottage's vendor's) title since its moral validity, in conjunction with the unforced nature of its transfer to the cottagers, are necessary and sufficient to vindicate their titles. (It is probably relevant to mention that each cottager's title covers not only his/her plot and cottage but also something presumably best conceived as a non-detachable share in the common amenities of the community, i.e. beach, roads, day-camp site, equipment and buildings.) And vindication of their titles would serve to justify the community's immigration policy since any immigrant who was not an approved cottage purchaser would necessarily be a trespasser and thereby a violator of rights.

Was the previous owner's title valid? Again, the libertarian will want to know whether the title anteceding it was itself valid and whether its transfer to the previous owner was also unforced. It is thus not difficult to see that the validity of the cottagers' titles can be generally described as turning on their having a pedigree of successively antecedent valid titles terminating in an ultimately antecedent, or original, valid title.

It is here that the water gets deeper and that libertarians divide. For clearly the conditions vindicating non-original, or derived, titles cannot apply to original ones. Original titles have no antecedents nor, therefore, are they created (as derived ones are) by an owner's exercise of the power to transfer title. The conditions validating original titles are necessarily different from those validating their derived successors. What are these conditions?

Some libertarians have argued that they are ones which are satisfied by what we may call a 'first come, first served' rule: a rule that assigns ownership of unowned things to those persons who (initially) appropriate them from nature.[2] Such persons acquire entirely unencumbered titles to these things and possess the liberty and the powers to dispose of them – including to transfer them – as they wish. The titles thereby transferred carry only such encumbrances as their successive owners choose to incur.

Other libertarians, correctly in my view, reject the 'first come, first served' rule as being inconsistent with the libertarian foundational rights of self-ownership and/or equal liberty: rights created under that rule are incompossible (i.e. incompatible) with such foundational rights.[3] Accordingly, they regard any original title as encumbered by a proviso designed to render it consistent with each person's self-ownership and/or entitlement to equal liberty. Moreover, since these foundational moral rights are vested in *all* persons, regardless of their temporal/generational location, that proviso-based encumbrance remains attached to each title successively derived (through transfer) from an original title. It vests obligations in a title's current owner correlative to rights in all its current non-owners. The content of the proviso – and hence, of these rights and obligations – is a matter of difference among such libertarians, all of whom none the less take their cue from Locke's 'enough and as good' formula.

Perhaps the most straightforward version (and, I think, the one which fits the most plausible interpretation of the foundational rights) is that long advocated by Henry George and his intellectual disciples: namely, each person's entitlement to an equal portion of the value of natural resources and thus a correlative obligation in owners of such resources to surrender that amount.[4] George called this proposal the 'single tax' since, like most libertarians, he believed that all other taxes confiscate things which justly belong to their possessors. Moreover, his economic theory led him to believe that *laissez-faire*, conjoined with his tax's egalitarian distribution of the pure rent element in natural resource owners' income, would work to eliminate poverty and considerably reduce social inequality by providing both a guaranteed universal basic income and the incentive structure to render economies more competitive and productive.[5]

We need not concern ourselves here with whether George's faith in his proposed remedy for major social ills is justified. What is of more immediate interest is his underlying Lockean principle: that natural resources – compendiously construed as territorial sites by most Georgists – fundamentally belong to all persons equally. It is this principle that generates each person's entitlement to an equal share of their value. And since, despite George's own silence on the issue, there are no grounds for denying the *global scope* of this entitlement, its bearing on questions of migration is at once direct and complex.

Perhaps its most obvious probable impact would be to decrease the demand for entry into wealthier societies. Since average per capita land values in such societies are more likely to be higher than in poorer societies, the global application of the single tax should result in an on-balance redistribution of wealth from the former to the latter. And presumably this would greatly tend to reduce a principal motivation for that aforesaid demand.

Second, of course, there is the plain historical fact that almost no jurisdictions in the world do levy or have levied the Georgist tax, much less have they been engaged in the global redistributions it mandates. For libertarians who regard morally valid land titles as thus encumbered, this fact poses a serious challenge to any charge of trespassing that landowners might individually or collectively bring against immigrants. And in thus impairing landowners' titles, this fact might further be taken, *inter multa alia*, to void emigration restrictions like the one we found operating in the cottage community, since that restriction derived from the contractual sale of a similarly impaired title.

Indeed even libertarians who do not regard valid original titles as proviso-encumbered and who therefore affirm the justness of unencumbered land ownership – that is, libertarians who subscribe to the 'first come, first served' rule – would be bound to acknowledge that, as a matter of historical fact, most current land titles have not descended from original ones through a series of unforced transfers. American Indians continue to have valid property rights which remain neither restored nor restituted nor recognised. And similar stories can be told about most of the owned territory of the world.

Third, however, and of greater theoretical interest, is the question of how libertarianism would regard migration restrictions in a world where land titles were *not* morally impaired. It is the sad fate of virtually every moral and political doctrine to be called upon to deliver judgements in given circumstances which, on its own basic principles, constitute a 'second-best' situation. The result of such deliverances, more often than not, is some proposal that embarrasses those principles by advancing certain types of morally valid right at the expense of other types, whereas in a 'first-best' world all these rights would be compossible.

In the world as it is, it is probably statistically true that most libertarians strongly oppose legislated restrictions on transnational migration. Why? Because as a matter of on-balance empirical judgement – and apart from the ubiquity of impaired land titles – such restrictions are seen as defending neither contractual agreements nor property rights. It is true that arguments supporting these restrictions are sometimes cast in terms of their having these functions. But frequently they possess this characteristic only by virtue of some background state policy which libertarians equally oppose. A common example is the argument justifying the debarment of would-be immigrants who fail to satisfy some standard of medical fitness, on the grounds that the cost of their treatment would be borne by state-supplied medical services. Of course, no libertarian would object to a private medical insurance company's insistence that new subscribers satisfy such a standard, the difference being that the restriction is in this case contractually incurred. *— with contracts anything is legitimate*

Libertarians are disinclined to see legislated restrictions, on what people jointly and individually may do with themselves and their property, as contractually incurred. Nor would they easily be persuaded that migration restrictions protect property rights. Though they are more than ready to believe that many legislated restrictions do, and are designed to, enhance the *value* of some people's rights at the cost of devaluing others' rights, if not of violating them outright. This is certainly the standard libertarian analysis of most restrictive migration policies. Since the role of the libertarian state is strictly confined to the enforcement of individuals' moral rights which consist exclusively of property and contractual rights, migration restrictions aimed at protecting the *value* of property rights – let alone broader cultural values[6] are entirely beyond its rightful authority. Protection of such values (the worth of which libertarianism in no way denies) is quintessentially a private concern – if it were not, what conceivably could be? – and, as such, must be left to the private and voluntary efforts of individuals and groups. And where it is not, there are usually strong grounds to suspect that the state has non-neutrally favoured one domestic interest at the expense of another. That is, there are strong grounds for suspecting that the general social harm alleged to be consequent upon repealing migration restrictions – and which is *ipso facto* not incurred by the migrants themselves – is confined to only part of the domestic population who expect to be disadvantaged by their presence and does not accrue to other parts who foresee the social intercourse fostered by that presence as enhancing their own cultural or economic well-being. Closed shops, whatever may be said in their favour, are not commonly thought to be of general social benefit. Here, as in so many other cases, arguments for legal restriction that invoke the danger of socially harmful consequences cannot avoid being question-begging if the population over whom harms and benefits are being summed simply excludes some of those who would be affected by the restriction.

In a world of morally *un*impaired land titles, there is a sense in which the libertarian would countenance immigration restrictions. That sense is identical to the one in which trespassing is widely regarded as justly prohibitable. For in such a world states would not violate individual rights by appropriating or expropriating land. Consequently, all land titles would be private ones and an unwelcome foreigner would *ipso facto* be no more unwelcome than an unwelcome fellow resident. If I am willing to lease, sell, or give away space to other persons and am under no contractual obligation to refrain from doing so, the state has no authority to establish whether they are insiders or outsiders before permitting me to do so. Conversely, if I am unwilling to do so, the state has both the power and the duty to prevent their entry into my property. It utterly lacks any authority to billet them in my home or factory or to confiscate my resources for their material support.[7] The same holds true in respect of the cottage community where the choice to allow or deny entry rests with the community by virtue of the contractual obligations severally undertaken by each of its members.

What about emigration in such a world? For libertarianism, the only acceptable grounds for restricting emigration are those which more generally justify certain forms of detention. Where people's contractual obligations cannot be discharged unless they remain within their national jurisdiction, a libertarian state is mandated to prevent their departure. Presumably the same mandate would extend to cases of people facing legitimate legal proceedings where there was good reason to believe that their emigrating would frustrate that process. Libertarians tend, however, to be extremely sceptical of such arguments when they are offered in defence of many current instances of emigration restriction. In the case of cited contractual or quasi-contractual obligations, such restriction often extends well beyond what could reasonably be demanded to effect their discharge: state-supplied occupational training, particularly where no other source of training is legally permitted, does not plausibly warrant an indefinitely long period of post-training indentured service. And being the subject of legal proceedings for an offence which violated no one's moral rights justifies no detention whatever.

Beyond these considerations, however, there is a conception of trans-national migration envisioned by libertarianism that is far more radical than what is commonly entertained in discussions of its restriction. For on libertarian principles, imperfectly adhered to by Locke in this regard, the territorial claims of nations are justified by *and derived from* the territorial claims of individuals. Locke's own initial account of how political jurisdictions are formed by consent suggests that a nation's territory consists of and is co-extensive with those of the several landowners who join together, perhaps with others, to constitute its government. Libertarians agree. But they are thus disappointed with Locke's later apparent endorsement of the practice of 'Commonwealths not permitting any part of their Dominions to be dismembered'.[8]

In thereby denying landowners the right of secession, Locke succumbs (as have so many others) to the mysterious charms of what we might call the 'theory of magic dates'. Prior to a magic date, a landowner along with all his/her belongings may permissibly enter into or exit from any consolidated arrangement with one or more others for the joint protection of their rights by an authorised agency. But after a magic date, any such arrangement must be one which is morally binding in perpetuity. (The theory is even more often applied to territorial jurisdictions established by conquest.) Hence the sole permissible form of transnational migration thenceforth open to landowners involves the removal of themselves and only their *moveable* belongings from their 'own' landed property. There is, on this theory, a fundamental moral asymmetry between the conditions for conjoining a piece of territory with others into a nation-state and the conditions for disjoining it from them.

The 'theory of magic dates' is notoriously incomplete: it offers no explanation of why there should be a plurality of such dates in human history nor any formula for locating them. But even if these deficiencies could somehow be made good, it is clear that any categorical prohibition of arrangements permitting secession flies in the face of basic Lockean – and libertarian – property right principles. Of course, landowners can contractually bind their assignees (those to whom they sell or give their land titles) not to secede. And it is a further and fascinating question – one which considerably exercised classical liberal writers – as to whether the freedom of contract principle licenses property owners in general contractually to bind their assignees to bind their assignees in turn. But even if such entailed obligations are permissible terms of contracts, they are still not the mandatory ones prescribed by the 'theory of magic dates'. Transnational migration, through territorial secession and either political independence or (contractual) integration into another existing political jurisdiction, remains a libertarian moral possibility.

There can be little doubt that, as a matter of empirical fact, the historical advance of classical liberal or libertarian principles was accompanied and on balance aided by the development of the strong nation-state. The flourishing of these principles and the universal human rights they imply was bound to be enhanced by the supercession of pre-liberal local and tribal jurisdictions and their integration into larger cosmopolitan ones, thereby dissolving many racially and ethnically discriminatory restrictions which previously had enjoyed the status of law. But while the historical debt of liberal principles to the nation-state is thus indisputable, it is not infinite. And it has certainly not been shown to be so great as to warrant compromising those principles for the sake of maintaining unaltered that particular institutional form. Twentieth-century experience is ample testimony to the fact that the untrammelled sovereignty of the nation-state is not an invariable guarantee of respect for individual rights.

In sum, libertarianism's attitude to transnational migration follows straightforwardly from its view that national boundaries possess no less – and no more – moral significance than the boundary between my neighbour's land and mine. Neither I nor any collectivity of which we are both members can claim a non-contractual power to prevent her or him from allowing, or compel her or him to allow, another person on to her or his property. And we similarly lack any non-contractual power to prevent her or him removing themselves and all their property from our jurisdiction.

Notes

1. Here and throughout this chapter I take immigration and emigration respectively to involve the assumption and abandonment of *residence* within a particular legal jurisdiction. In this respect, the communal power to veto a cottage's sale is not strictly a restriction on emigration inasmuch as summer cottages are, by definition, not primary places of residence for their owners.
2. There is some dispute and probably some ineliminable vagueness about the scope of what counts as an act of appropriation. Locke's 'labour-mixing' formula tends to be favoured, despite its acknowledged lack of invariable applicability (John Locke, *Two Treatises of Government* (1690), ed. Peter Laslett (Cambridge: Cambridge University Press, 1960). In any event and since this difficulty has little immediate bearing on the problem at hand, perhaps we can be satisfied to construe acts of appropriation as acts of initial using. See Anthy Fressola, "Liberty and Property," *American Philosophical Quarterly*, 18 (1981), 315–22.
3. See Hillel Steiner, "Capitalism, Justice and Equal Starts," *Social Philosophy and Policy*, 5 (1987), 49–71.
4. Henry George, *Progress and Poverty* (London: William Reeves, 1884).
5. Using Federal Reserve Board figures, one Georgist has recently calculated an American per capita pure rent figure of $4,000 per annum; see Alfred F. Andersen, *Liberating the American Dream* (New Brunswick, N.J.: Transaction Books, 1985), 152–54.
6. Cf. Michael Walzer, *Spheres of Justice* (Oxford: Oxford University Press, 1983).
7. That is, beyond what they, like any non-immigrants, may be entitled to from the single tax.
8. Locke, *Two Treatises of Government*, T.II, chap. VII, sec. 117. Here, as in several passages in his extensive discussion of property rights (chap. V), there is a rather unexpected shift from prescriptive to descriptive language at the point where Locke reports some pertinent prevailing practice which violates his previously propounded principles but which he none the less appears unwilling to condemn.

—— 7 ——

The migration of money – from a libertarian viewpoint

Deepak Lal

The term 'libertarian' needs some elucidation. The position which was occupied by classical English liberalism has had to be renamed; at least in the United States, as J. Schumpeter noted:

> the term [economic liberal] has acquired a different – in fact almost the opposite meaning – since about 1900 and especially since 1930; as a supreme if unintended complement, the enemies of the system of private enterprise have thought it wise to appropriate its label[1]

Hence as F. A. Hayek, the clearest and most important modern votary of classical English liberalism notes:

> In the United States, where it has become almost impossible to use 'liberal' in the sense in which I have used it, the term libertarian has been used instead. It maybe is the answer but for my part I find it singularly unattractive. For my taste it carries too much the flavour of a manufactured term and of a substitute.[2]

I agree and hence along with Hayek will continue to use the term liberal, in its original eighteenth- and nineteenth-century sense.

It is in this Hayekian sense, namely of the liberalism of 'Burke, Macaulay and Gladstone . . . Tocqueville and Lord Acton', and not 'the rationalistic Continental liberalism or the English liberalism of the utilitarians' that I shall be interpreting the libertarian position. Hayek in his *Constitution of Liberty*, provides a clear statement of the scope of legitimate government activities in his chapter on 'Economic policy and the rule of law'. I set out this position in Section I and also briefly outline the ethical viewpoint which underlies economic liberalism. This allows me directly to answer the question whether it is ever appropriate for a country to restrict or promote either the inward or outward flow of capital from the viewpoint of economic liberalism. This is our task in Section II.

95

I

Like J. S. Mill,[3] Hayek distinguishes 'between the coercive measures of government and those pure service activities where coercion does not enter or does so only because of the need of financing them by taxation'.[4] Thus the government can provide various services if it sees fit, as long as it does not exclude their provision by private agents. Whilst accepting that, there is 'a real danger to liberty if too large a section of economic activity comes to be subject to the direct control of the state. But what is objectionable here is not state enterprise as such but state monopoly.'[5]

As Hayek makes clear, the cornerstone of the liberal position is non-discrimination between different economic agents. This implies that: 'a free system does not exclude on principle all those general regulations of economic activity which can be laid down in the form of general rules specifying conditions which everybody engaged in a certain activity must satisfy.'[6] Though the resulting general, non-discriminatory government interventions (regulations) may be unwise from the viewpoint of economic efficiency because they 'reduce overall productivity', they will not infringe that stability of expectations necessary both for economic growth and to preserve individual liberty which is engendered 'by a permanent legal framework which enables the individual to plan with a degree of confidence and which reduces human uncertainty as much as possible.'[7] For such general measures of government intervention the liberal position would be that: 'The appropriateness of such measures must be judged by comparing the overall costs with the gain; it cannot be conclusively determined by appeal to a general principle.'[8]

Thus a general *ad valorem* tax on capital inflows/outflows (the so-called equivalent of the optimum tariff to be discussed in Section III) which does not discriminate by economic agents (by nationality, sector, creed, etc.) would not be against liberal principles. It would have to be judged by its efficacy in subserving the proposed objectives of the government. It is in this sense that the 'non-discrimination' principle of the economic liberal is exactly like the application of the rule of law. The discretion, if any, which the application of general rules necessitate (which necessarily cannot be adumbrated to meet every future unforeseen contingency), should be that found in the common law.[9]

The justification for this 'non-discrimination' rule is both ethical – questions of justice and liberty – but also narrowly economic as it is likely to be most conducive to promoting that wealth of nations which at least since Adam Smith has been a self-proclaimed aim of economics as a practical 'science'. What, however, *is* ruled out on liberal principles are discretionary control of prices and quantities:

because they cannot be achieved by merely enforcing general rules but, of necessity, *involve arbitrary discrimination between persons*. . . . The exercise of all controls of quantities [and prices] must, of necessity, be discretionary, determined not by rule but by the judgment of authority concerning the relative importance of particular ends. . . . To grant such powers to authority means in effect to give it power arbitrarily to determine what is to be produced, by whom and for whom. [emphasis added][10]

Again the grounds for opposing these discretionary measures are both ethical and economic.

The liberal principle of non-discrimination also implies that governments 'cannot determine the material position of particular people or enforce distributive or "social" justice'.[11] For such end-patterned distributivist policies must conflict with liberty in a fairly minimal sense. As R. Nozick has memorably put it:

Any patterned distribution can be upset by people's voluntary actions in exchange and hence no end-state principle or distributional patterned principle of justice can be continuously realized without continuous interference with people's lives. . . . The socialist society would have to forbid capitalist acts between consenting adults.[12]

But this does not mean that government action to redress absolute poverty would be unjustified on liberal principles. This has been granted by Adam Smith, Milton Friedman and Hayek,[13] to name three leading liberal thinkers. Friedman justifies government action to relieve absolute poverty on the grounds that it is like a collective good. He writes:

I am distressed by the sight of poverty; I am benefitted by its alleviation; but I am benefitted equally whether I or someone else pays for its alleviation; the benefits of other people's charity therefore partly accrue to me. To put it differently, we might all of us be willing to contribute to the relief of poverty, *provided* everyone else did. We might not be willing to contribute the same amount without such assurance.[14]

Thus *laissez-faire* is not a correct characterization of the economic liberal's position, as I hope the above discussion makes clear. The fundamental principle is of non-discrimination. What is the justification of the 'non-discrimination' principle? John Gray, in an important and highly perceptive book on Hayek[15] has provided an answer. As he notes, the ethical foundations of Hayek's refurbished classical liberalism are a 'synthesis of Kant's requirement of universalizability in practical reasoning with David Hume's account of the content and basis of the rules of justice'.[16] They contrast for instance with those of another powerful contemporary libertarian voice, namely that of Nozick, whose entitlement theory is in direct lineage from Locke.[17] From Hume, Hayek has adopted an indirect or system utilitarianism to judge the 'whole system of rules or practice',[18] which is combined with the Kantian test of universalizability to yield the priority of liberty under the rule of law. Thus as Gray sums up:

> By interpreting the demands of universalisability in the framework of the permanent necessities of human social life . . . we derive Hume's laws of nature. . . . In Hume, as in Hayek, the laws of justice are commended as being the indispensable condition for the promotion of general welfare i.e. their ultimate justification has a utilitarian component. But in order to achieve this result, neither Hayek nor Hume need offer any argument in favour of our adopting a Principle of Utility. Rather, very much in the spirit of R. M. Hare's reconstruction of utilitarian ethics,[19] Hayek's claim is that an impartial concern for the general welfare is itself one of the demands of universalisability. A utilitarian concern for general welfare is yielded by the Kantian method itself and is not super-added to it afterwards. Hayek's thesis, like Hume's, is that a clear view of the circumstances of human life shows justice to be the primary condition needed to promote general welfare. But, like Hare and Kant, he thinks concern for both justice and the general welfare to be dictated by universalisability itself.[20]

One implication of the resulting maxim of the priority of individual liberty under the rule of law is that:

> the rule of law must in treating citizens anonymously and equally be indifferent to the inequalities in man's initial endowments and material fortunes. Aiming to equalise these latter would in fact involve treating men differently and unequally and could not avoid producing many serious inequities.[21]

The most eloquent account of the incompatibility of patterned concepts of justice and liberty is of course by Nozick. Both Hayek and Nozick reject (as did most of the classical economists including Marx), the distinction that J. S. Mill[22] introduced that the efficiency (production) and distributive aspects of an economic system can be separated. But unlike Nozick, Hayek's theory of justice whilst being procedural is not based on any assertion of fundamental human rights. Also unlike Nozick's entitlement theory which allows the rectification of past injustices in the creation of current entitlements, Hayek like Hume 'accepts the existing pattern of entitlements as historically given and does not seek to overturn them in the interest of any principle of rectificatory justice'.[23] This would seem sound to any economist for whom the principle that 'bygones are bygones' is almost a fundamental economic principle.[24]

II

The first consequence of applying the liberal principles outlined and justified in the previous section to capital flows is that exchange controls and other related quantitative and hence discriminatory practices are against liberal principles.[25] As Friedman puts it:

> There is much experience to suggest that the most effective way to convert a market economy into an authoritarian economic society is to start by imposing direct controls on foreign exchange. This one step leads inevitably to the rationing of imports, to control over domestic production that uses imported products or that produces substitutes for imports, and so on in a never-ending spiral.[26]

Friedman also noted that exchange controls were to 'the best of my knowledge invented by Hjalmar Schaat in the early years of the Nazi regime'.[27] If exchange controls are ruled out on liberal principles (and on grounds of economic efficiency – see below), is there nevertheless a case for controls on capital movements, of the general non-discriminatory sort that is allowed by liberal principles? These must be judged by their effects on economic efficiency.

The economic case for free capital movements can be simply stated.[28] It is exactly analogous to the case for free trade in commodities. The removal of barriers to foreign trade in commodities and assets expands the feasible set of consumption possibilities (both current and future) for every country. It does so by providing an indirect technology for transforming domestic resources into the goods and services that yield current and future utility to consumers.

The optimal tax argument

This argument is based on assuming perfect capital markets, which in turn implies that neither the borrower nor lender has sufficient monopoly or monopsony power to influence the terms on which it can borrow or lend. If it does, then on grounds of *national* economic welfare, it may be prudent to levy an optimum 'tax' (like the optimum tariff for commodities) on the relevant capital flows.[29] It has been argued by A. C. Harberger [30] in the context of the recent debt crisis in developing countries that as most developing countries faced an upward sloping supply curve of syndicated bank credit, they should have levied an optimal tax on such borrowings to equate its tax inclusive average cost to the higher marginal cost.

Such a tax, whilst possibly maximizing the well-being of the 'nation' imposing the optimal tax could nevertheless (by restricitng capital flows) damage the well-being of other nations, and cosmopolitan 'welfare' could be lower. Thus a general 'optimal' tax of this sort would not go against liberal principles, as long as our concern is purely the well-being of *our* nation. If, however, our liberal concern also encompasses the well-being of the individuals in other countries then both on moral and prudential grounds the 'optimal tariff'-type argument for restricting free capital mobility would also be unjustified. The moral ground follows directly from the Kantian principle of universalizability which implies that it would be immoral to follow the 'beggar thy neighbour' policy of restricting capital inflows on optimum tax grounds.

The prudential argument against such a tax is partly that if the foreign country retaliates, national welfare may be lower than without the tax. This view is strengthened if the pervasive *ignorance* surrounding the determinants of the supply and demand schedules for foreign capital are recognized. I know of no robust empirical estimates of the supply function of foreign capital for any country. As Hayek has emphasized,[31] it is planners' hubris to assume that the knowledge required for their constructivist purposes can be obtained at low cost. In reality much of the relevant knowledge cannot be obtained (except at prohibitive cost) by the centre, especially when we consider the 'optimal' taxation of foreign capital inflows.

To see this it is useful to look at the issues involved from a more disaggregated (and realistic) viewpoint. In a liberal state the capital stock will be owned by private agents.[32] The actual flows of capital therefore will consist of trade in future income streams from assets located in different countries. Thus suppose that citizens of two countries engage in mutually agreeable trades until each group ends up 'owning' all of the other's physical assets. This foreign ownership of the country's assets does not diminish the country's capital stock or remove it from the country. It means only that, as a result of national and foreign individuals' portfolio preferences, the ownership of assets has been altered. In the process of adjustment the relative prices of different assets may have changed – leading to distributive effects, which of course on the libertarian position are not of concern to the authorities. At any point in time most of a country's capital stock is physically fixed and cannot be shipped out (except in economists' models with perfectly malleable capital goods) so its productive capacity will not be altered. The only question is: who has the rights to the income stream that is generated by its capital stock? If nationals are willing without coercion to exchange their rights from local assets for those from foreign assets, both sides to the bargain have presumably gained. Hence from an economic liberal's viewpoint there is no reason for coercive taxation on the basis of some incommensurable social utility for restricting (or promoting) these flows. Moreover, as the supply of capital is based on unknowable (by the authorities) future expectations of individuals about the relative profitabilities of their investments in different locations and jurisdictions, any estimate of the future supply of foreign capital, which is required to estimate the optimum tax, also cannot be derived. Thus even if desirable on grounds of social utility the optimal taxation of foreign capital will be unattainable.

The final argument against the taxation of capital flows on 'optimal tax' grounds, is based on the empirical fact that there is no international framework for enforcing individual property rights as is commonly found within most countries. This implies that there will be special forms of risks and uncertainties attached to foreign as opposed to domestic lending, particularly in the major form of foreign capital flows between developed and developing countries in the last two decades: sovereign lending. Though there are various forms of penalties – withdrawal of trade credit, moratorium on future lending, sequestration of foreign assets – which could influence a sovereign state's decision to default on its foreign debt, these penalties are less onerous than those available to creditors in domestic financial markets. Nor is there an equivalent of bankruptcy at the international level. This means that a sovereign borrower is only likely to continue to service its foreign debt as long as the expected utility from the *sovereign's* income stream if it repays is greater than if it defaults. The sovereign's net income must include the implicit costs of riots, *coup d'états*, etc., if it raises the burden of domestic taxation explicitly or implicitly (say through inflation) to obtain the funds to repay its foreign creditors. This foreign risk attached to foreign lending implies that credit will be rationed in international capital markets, with lenders unlikely to extend credit (provide capital) to levels that would exist if contracts were internationally enforceable.[33] Thus in the presence of sovereign risk, 'long before a country's ability to pay would become relevant, its willingness to pay constrains its access to credit'.[34] But this implies that the amount of foreign capital will be *below* that which would exist in the case of perfect capital markets (in which by assumption there is no sovereign risk). Hence, the level of capital flows is *already* likely to reflect the 'optimal tax'-type restrictions being suggested by some observers. I suggest it is impossible, in principle, to determine whether the actual level of capital flows exceeds or falls short of the optimum level derived from our simple social utility maximizing economic models. Prudence, therefore, dictates we let well alone.

If there are no moral or prudential grounds for the optimum tax-type case for government intervention in international capital markets, what other arguments for public intervention are there that fall short of the detailed exchange and capital controls which are clearly unjustified on liberal principles? Three cases are of contemporary relevance. They all concern relations between developed and developing countries, two of which are related to the ongoing 'debt crisis'. The first in the latter sub-set concerns the question of capital flight; the second, so-called 'debt-forgiveness' of the sovereign loans of the most highly indebted countries and the third concerns official foreign aid.

Capital flight

Let us consider 'capital flight'. Capital flows may be motivated by three broad types of considerations: fear of domestic political or economic crisis; differences in rates of return at home or abroad, net of tax differentials; and expectations of exchange-rate movements. All three types of flows can be financed not only from current savings, but also from idle cash balances and sales of domestic bonds, equities and physical capital assets.

It is the fear of politically motivated flows that has perhaps been most important historically in creating a climate of opinion favourable to capital controls. Haberler has pointed out:

> [It was the] politically induced capital [flow] . . . from Hitler-Europe to the US during the last years before the outbreak of the Second World War which strongly influenced Keynes's views on capital controls. He said: 'There is no country which can, in the future, safely allow the flight of funds for political reasons or to evade domestic taxation or in anticipation of the owner turning refugee. Equally, there is no country that can safely receive fugitive funds.'[35]

The reasons given by Keynes if taken as justification rather than as explanations for the restriction of flight capital can hardly be accepted on liberal grounds. But a modified case could be made about the 'injury' such capital flight causes to the other citizens of the country, such that a *general* prohibition on liberal grounds would be justifiable.

Usually the argument is put in terms of managing the balance of payments. As Keynes, the progenitor of the so-called 'adjustable peg' system of exchange-rate management under Bretton Woods recognized, the system depended upon maintaining controls on short-term capital flows. This restriction was necessary because an 'adjustable peg' exchange-rate system offers a one-way gamble to speculators and can thus push an otherwise 'equilibrium' exchange rate into disequilibrium on the basis of some transient 'news'. But as became clear during the operation of the Bretton Woods system, in a world of growing interdependence and freer foreign trade, the controls on short-term flows cannot prevent the speculation that threatens countries whose pegged rates are seen by the market to be out of line. It is also difficult to separate short- from long-term capital flows. Finally, seemingly speculative flows could be generated by the 'leads and lags' resulting from normal hedging by traders. It was in part to counteract the inevitable instability and unviability of the 'pegged' exchange-rate system in the face of the one-way speculative gambles it afforded, that the world moved in the 1970s to a system of floating exchange rates, however dirtily managed.

Under a floating exchange-rate system capital flows do not need to be controlled; rather the system depends for its efficiency and stability on the freedom and volume of such capital flows – in particular those which are based on the speculative motive. There is no reason, therefore, any longer, unless one wants to resurrect the Bretton Woods system (but why?) for capital controls to manage the balance of payments. Moreover, under floating exchange rates no major diminution of its general welfare would result from a country's citizens choosing massively to move out of the domestic currency. For such a movement would cause the currency to depreciate, imposing what is in effect a heavy capital levy on the fleeing capitalists! The only cause for concern in the recent flight of capital out of many Latin American countries following internal economic disorder is the terms on which this was effected. Thus, for instance, Argentina is reputed to have 'flight capital' parked in the world's financial centres almost equivalent to its public debt. But much of this flight of capital took place during the so-called 'TABLITA' system of exchange-rate adjustment. Under this system the government pre-announced its exchange rate for the future. As this nominal exchange-rate depreciation was targeted to be less than that of domestic inflation (on the erroneous grounds that the nominal exchange rate's movement rather than that in the consumer price index would condition inflationary expectations) the real or effective exchange rate appreciated, giving those moving capital out of these countries a capital bonus!

Nor has the flight of capital from Latin America caused its economic malaise. The chain of causation runs the other way – from public policy-produced economic collapse, generated by hyperinflationary financing of burgeoning fiscal deficits, to the wholly justified actions of private agents seeking to protect their past savings (against the unauthorized liquidation implicit in hyperinflation) by switching their assets into a more stable medium of exchange. What is more, as recent studies of capital flight have shown,[36] when economic conditions become more stable the 'flight capital' returns. As such the mobility of capital is in practice one of the more important means of imposing constraints on governments from undertaking those predatory actions that liberal principles forbid.[37]

There is a variant of the 'capital flight' argument which has been used by some 'liberals' (in the American sense) to argue against the free mobility of capital. This is based on the argument that such capital mobility makes Keynesian-type demand management and the domestic legislation of social goals – such as labour standards, etc. – more difficult if not impossible.[38] This is true. But on liberal principles much of this economic action is misguided, and its demise can hardly be lamented nor the agent of its destruction reproved.

Foreign aid

Next, we examine the arguments, not for the prevention of capital flows, but for the public transfer of capital, often on concessional terms to poor countries. This is sometimes presented as being ethically justified either on the distributive grounds that it improves the world income distribution, or on the grounds of poverty alleviation, i.e. flowing from our moral duty to help the poor. There is no prima facie case on liberal principles for the former (distributive) but there could be for the latter (poverty alleviation) justification for such official assistance by rich countries to poor countries.

The latter statement, which refers to countries – and hence the usual form of such transfers, immediately blunts its moral standing. For though there may be a duty to help poor people there is none on liberal principles to help poor countries. It is only if it can be shown that foreign aid *does* alleviate the poverty of *poor people* in developing countries that there could be a moral case for it. However, the most recent and detailed empirical study of such transfers by an economist morally committed to them concluded that, foreign aid 'appears to redistribute [income] from the reasonably well off in the West to most income groups in the Third World *except* the very poorest'.[39] Though this can be taken to provide reasons for exhortations to aid donors to design their policies better to reach 'the poor',[40] the contingent fact that despite twenty years of experimentation, aid still does not reach the poorest in developing countries, should take the edge off some of the moral fervour surrounding the advocacy of foreign aid.[41]

International property rights

There is an important hitherto unresolved question lurking behind our discussion of the economic liberal's case for free movement of capital (and its fruits, profits and interests – subject to any taxation which is neutral between domestic and foreign sources of capital). The question arose in the context of sovereign risk when discussing the debt crisis, and it concerns the nature of the international 'society' of nation-states.

The sanctity of private property rights is an indissoluble part of the principle of individual liberty for economic liberals. Most Western economies, by and large, embody these property rights as part of their legal systems. Apart from the moral justification for this legal protection for private property, its enforcement across a number of countries greatly facilitates the movement of capital between them, as it reduces the political risk. Most developing countries, however, have eschewed such legal protection for national and most certainly foreign owners of capital. This has raised the political risks, particularly of sovereign lending.

How should liberal states react to the illiberal economic interventions concerning their nationals' property 'rights' in foreign countries? Here the nature of the international 'society' of states is important. With justice, Hedley Bull characterized the extant conglomeration of nation-states as an 'anarchical society'.[42] This raises the image of a Hobbesian state, in which each state would seek its own advantage at the expense of another. Lacking any world society, such action by individual states cannot be condemned on moral grounds, as discussed above for the case of an 'optimal tax' on capital flows. But in the face of illiberal policies concerning capital flows in other countries, should *any* country restrict capital flows on prudential grounds? As we saw, even in the 'optimal tax' case, prudence might dictate otherwise. Whilst certainly, if the country concerned has little or no monopoly/monosony power in trade in either goods or capital then despite the restrictions imposed by other countries, unilateral adherence to free trade would still be optimal from the viewpoint of the general welfare of our country.

This argument may however, appear to be too static. Even in a Hobbesian state, as Axelrod has shown,[43] a policy of tit for tat, followed by the 'rational' agent in an iterated non-cooperative multiperiod Prisoner's Dilemma game, can lead to the evolution of the mutually beneficial cooperation, which in our case would imply establishing a legal system for the protection of international property rights, and hence the enhancement of free international capital mobility. That such international cooperation has evolved in our anarchical international society is attested to by some commonly accepted international conventions against piracy[44] and various contagious diseases.

May such conventions evolve in the current anarchical world system of nation-states concerning international property rights? To judge these prospects it is useful to examine the historical evolution and dissolution of an international order guaranteeing international property rights. The great nineteenth-century booms in foreign lending were prompted by the extension of norms of conduct based on European capitalist individualism – in particular the sanctity of private property rights – to much of the Third World, through the expansion of *Pax Britannica*, and its influence on the local legal institutions even of many independent states, as in Latin America. A strict set of legal rules were established through a number of commercial treaties between European states.[45] The legitimacy of these nineteenth-century rules was not challenged until the Soviet and Mexican revolutions, and the explicit introduction of *etatist* policies by Turkey (under Ataturk) as a means of national economic development. Since then, there has been a gradual erosion of public acceptance of the sanctity of private property rights when faced with social policies designed to promote general – usually nationalist – prosperity.

There was a partial restoration of these international property rights which underpinned the nineteenth-century economic order with the establishment of *Pax Americana* after 1945. But it has not successfully withstood the explosion of economic nationalism, following the decolonization and the formation of numerous Third World nation-states determined to assert their rights of national sovereignty against any purported international property rights.

As direct foreign investors provide more local hostages to fortune, they have borne the brunt of the deleterious effects of this disintegration of the legal order. Moreover, most governments of developing countries, being both nationalist and dirigiste, have sought to regulate, tax or nationalize particular foreign investments on grounds of national social utility rather than out of any general antagonism towards private property as such. This has meant that the United States has been unable to identify expropriation of foreign capital with ideology (communism or socialism), as the nationalization of companies in the late 1960s and early 70s by right-wing regimes in the Middle East proved.

This inexorable erosion of the old standards of international property rights might, however, be ending. With the recent emergence of Third World multinationals, the importance of many OPEC countries as portfolio lenders and the United States becoming the world's largest debtor, the old distinction between the divergent interests of developed capital-exporting countries interested in protecting international property rights, and of Third World capital-importing countries keen to circumscribe them, is becoming less valid. In future the interests of developed and developing countries may converge and lead to an increasing acceptance of rules protecting international property.

Debt-forgiveness

It is in this context that we should also judge the recent actions, as well as those being proposed for government action by the governments of developed countries to resolve the so-called debt crisis. The latter crisis is largely due to the unwillingness to pay of a number of large debtors, particularly in Latin America.[46] This unwillingness to pay is linked to the domestic problems these countries face in raising the requisite resources for debt service and converting them into foreign exchange. These problems in turn are due to their endemic fiscal problems and dirigiste trade control systems which have created repressed and inflexible economies. The fact that the twin global shocks of high interest rates and a world recession in the 1980s did not lead to a debt crisis in many equally heavily indebted South-east Asian countries suggests that domestic rather than external factors explain the incidence and point to the cure for the debt crisis. This is not the place to rehearse the domestic policy requirements for the 'debt crisis' countries to regain international credit worthiness. What we are concerned with is the need, if any, for international *public* action to resolve the crisis.

At first it was argued that the governments of the creditor countries needed to intervene to prevent defaults which would have injured the money centre banks (located in these countries) which run a vast international inter-bank credit market. Any consequent bankruptcy of these banks would have led to a collapse of the international banking system. Developed country governments were then asked to act as lenders of last resort to prevent this banking 'panic'. There was little merit in this argument,[47] as has been borne out by subsequent history. A move which would clearly have been equivalent to the indirect subsidization of the losses incurred by Western banks on their sovereign lending at the expense of Western taxpayers, was resisted by their governments. As a result, over time the money centre banks absorbed the losses on their imprudent sovereign loans by setting aside larger reserves against losses. The shareholders of these banks as well as their managers bore the cost (as they should) of their failed gamble. There clearly was no danger and patently is none at present of a world banking collapse following on from the defaults of the major 'debt crisis' countries.

More recently, therefore, a different tack is being taken by those who still wish to use Western taxpayers' money to subsidize indirectly the shareholders of the imprudent lenders. It is now argued that money should be given to the debtors, particularly the Latin American, to enable them to extinguish their debt, for otherwise the demonstrable inability to pay of their recently instituted democratic governments will lead to an authoritarian backlash. This political 'debt-forgiveness' argument clearly would require public action by Western governments.

On liberal principles it would be desirable to aid other countries to maintain liberal economic and political regimes. If empirically it can be shown (and it must be emphasized it has not) that foreign aid alone would prevent these countries from becoming illiberal, a case could be made for such aid. But this would be a case, for instance, for the US government openly to aid these countries through USAID, at the same time leaving it up to the countries themselves to deal with their creditors, rather than to continue the present situation of the US government trying to arrange a 'deal' between the debtors and the creditors.

There is, however, grave cause for concern about the 'moral hazard' involved in such public action in bailing out either the creditors or the debtors from the consequences of their past actions. As noted above, there are strong theoretical and empirical grounds for the view that it is not the ability but the willingness of these countries to pay which is in question. Mexico, after all, has large reserves of oil which it could partially trade for the extinction of its debt if it changed its policies on foreign ownership of natural resources. Moreover, if the past imprudence of Third World governments is to be subsidized by Western taxpayers this penalizes those governments (including some of the poorest, e.g. India) which did not indulge in improvident foreign borrowing and, most seriously, creates an incentive for future imprudence on the part of *all* Third World sovereign borrowers.

Despite the possible current political attractions of the various schemes for 'debt-forgiveness'[48] therefore, the moral hazard argument against it would suggest that on liberal principles the correct public stance for Western governments could be to adopt the position taken by Britain in the nineteenth century in the face of spectacular defaults on foreign bonds. In a famous circular of 1848 Palmerston said: 'The British government has considered that the losses of imprudent men who have placed mistaken confidence in the *good faith* of foreign governments would provide a salutary warning to others.'[49]

Alternative routes towards global financial integration

Whilst there is no case therefore on liberal principles for redressing the consequences of voluntary 'private' actions through public means, might there not still be a case for some international regulation of international flows of money on the grounds that it is necessary to provide the information required for prudent private action, and to prevent fraud. Or, putting it differently, has the recent movement towards deregulation of domestic and international money markets at least in the OECD countries gone too far?[50] This is an important subject for the future, and we can do more than treat it rather cursorily. Prevention of fraud and dissemination of information as would be provided by an international system of common law would undoubtedly be something liberals would support. This so-called 'integration' and 'harmonization' of 'national' laws and practice concerning movements of money, and the regulation of the domestic banking system could, however, come about in two radically different ways leading to two very different types of integrated 'world' economies. The first may be labelled the 'social-democratic' American liberal vision, the other the libertarian or classical English liberal vision.

The content of the former has been clearly set out by C. Kindleberger, who writes: 'My instinct and my reading of history . . . suggests we should head the other way [away from decontrol and deregulation]: to a fixed exchange rate in the fullness of time, i.e. one world money, and to co-ordinated monetary policies, i.e. a single monetary policy for the world.' But he notes 'I must confess I see no easy path to such an outcome, nor any likelihood of an early achievement of it, but this seems to me first best, and the target for which we should aim.'[51] This aim and the means to achieve it are well known as this has been the conventional economist's view of economic integration *under public auspices*, i.e. through some form of planning.

The second 'libertarian' vision is less well known, but it has been clearly set out first by Hayek[52] and subsequently in important work by Ronald Vaubel[53] and most recently by George A. Selgin.[54] The argument is based on questioning the utility of a government monopoly of money. Basing itself on the experience of free banking episodes in Scotland and the United States in the nineteenth century, this neo-liberalism questions the self-serving arguments advanced by governments that national control of the money supply was required for monetary stability. White,[55] in particular has shown that, contrary to popular presuppositions the Scottish free banking system was not unstable, and was only 'taken over' because of the self-interest of the Bank of England. So the new proposal is to abolish the government's monopoly of money. Issuers of competing currencies would (unlike governments) have to limit the amount of paper they issue to maintain its value. This would end the 'political' management of national monies which can be held responsible for much of the destabilizing fluctuations that government monopoly of money has led to during the last century.[56] Thus as with the provision of commodities, the supply of money too should be governed by competitive self-interest. As Hayek puts it, 'in a world governed by pressures of organised interests, we cannot count on benevolence, intelligence or understanding but only on sheer self-interest to give us the institutions we want. The insight and wisdom of Adam Smith stand today.'[57]

We cannot go into the technicalities of the arguments (pro and con) for the removal of the government's monopoly of money in any particular country. What is relevant, is that in a world of floating exchange rates and with no exchange controls, in effect the world's citizens (at least in developed countries) would have competing currencies in which they could denominate their assets. This is already happening at a rapid rate with the so-called 'securitization' of world capital markets. All that is required to 'denationalize' money internationally is for the removal of the provision that each country's 'money' is the only legal tender within its own jurisdictions.

As Hayek envisages, in the free competition between currencies that would result, a 'single' or 'dominant' currency would emerge to provide the 'world' money required for international integration. This process of competitive harmonization can be contrasted with the planned harmonization envisaged by the liberals of American hue, by analogy with another 'form' of international social integration that has occurred, namely in the field of language. Hayek's 'spontaneous order' has always emphasized that many social institutions have arisen out of the competition of different traditions. The current international domination of English in scientific, commercial and even official discourse is indubitable. Yet this has emerged spontaneously out of the competition of different languages, an eloquent contrast being provided by the failure of that arch Fabian socialist planner George Bernard Shaw's rationalist plan to create and propagate the perfect international language – Esperanto!

The same contrast between integration based on a spontaneous or planned order, underlies the current problems surrounding the processes and differently interpreted forms that the commonly accepted aim of European integretion should take. The first, outlined in her unfairly maligned Bruges speech by Mrs Thatcher, the second as embodied in the Delors Report. The former envisages an end state of otherwise sovereign nation-states, competing with each other, but with no barriers to any economic transactions between them; the second envisages a harmonization of national economic policies and even outcomes (through the 'social' dimension) under the aegis of an imperial bureaucracy.

It is obvious which conception liberals should support. In the field of European monetary integration the logical position for the advocate of a liberal policy is not a planned European monetary system (EMS) which is merely a variant of the 'adjustable peg' Bretton Woods scheme and hence inherently prone to instability and breakdown. Nor is a gold standard-type system run by a European Central Bank feasible unless European nation states are extinguished. But a system with free competing currencies in which one or maybe two will emerge as a result of competitive choice by its consumers as the European currency, is both feasible and desirable.

In a world of free money as well as free trade, it is impossible to predict which 'currency' would become the international currency. But I am willing to make an educated guess. There is a little island in the Pacific which is comprised almost entirely of phosphatic rock. It is the sovereign nation of Nauru. This rock being extremely valuable as fertilizer, the islanders have become immensely wealthy (owning large parts of Sydney) by literally digging and selling their 'land'. Very soon the island will disappear. What economic activity can the Naurians turn to? I have a suggestion. With no 'land', nor any other 'national' economic activity available to them, they will be ideally suited to living off the seignorage that the issuance of an internationally acceptable paper currency will provide. As this (in future) could be their only source of income, they will have a natural interest in maintaining the seignorage obtainable by keeping the supply of 'Nauras' stable; more so than the high and mighty dollar. Might we then not all find ourselves in the brave new liberal world of free money and free trade on a competitively chosen Naurian standard?!

Notes

1. J. Schumpeter, *A History of Economic Analysis* (New York: Oxford University Press, 1954), p. 394.
2. F. A. Hayek, *Constitution of Liberty* (London: Routledge, 1960), p. 401.
3. J. S. Mill, *Principles of Political Economy* (Harmondsworth: Pelican, 1970) bk. V, chap. xi, sec. 1.
4. Hayek, *Constitution of Liberty*, p. 222.
5. Ibid., p. 224.
6. Ibid. In modern philosophical terms, as J. Gray has noted (*Hayek on Liberty* (Oxford: Blackwell, 1984)), this Hayekian position on the primacy of the rule of law, has been subject to much criticism, but he provides a defence of Hayek's position.
7. Ibid., p. 222.
8. Ibid., p. 224.
9. Thus Hayek writes:

> If the law cannot always name the particular measures which the authorities may adopt in a particular situation, it can be so framed as to enable any impartial court to decide whether the measures adopted were necessary to achieve the general effect aimed at by the law. Given this 'rule of law' based form of government 'the coercive powers of government still serve general and timeless purposes, not specific ends. It must not make any distinctions between different people'. Ibid., p. 227.

10. Ibid., pp. 227–8.
11. Ibid., p. 231.
12. R. Nozick; *Anarchy, State and Utopia* (Oxford: Blackwell, 1974), p. 163. Also see D. Lal, "Distribution and Development: A review article", *World Development*, vol. 4, no. 9 (1976); and D. Lal, "Markets', Mandarins and Mathematicians," *The Cato Journal*, vol. 7, no. 1 (Spring/Summer 1987).
13. A. Smith, *The Wealth of Nations*, bk. V, chap. 2; M. Friedman, *Capitalism and Freedom* (Chicago: Chicago University Press, 1962, pp. 190 & ff; and Hayek, *Constitution of Liberty*, pp. 257 & ff. Hayek writes:

> All modern governments have made provision for the indigent, unfortunate, and disabled and have concerned themselves with questions of health and the dissemination of knowledge. There is no reason why the volume of these pure service activities should not increase with the general growth of wealth. These are common needs which can be satisfied only by collective action and which can be thus provided for without restricting liberty. (p. 257)

But he warns that this relief of poverty can slide into the desire 'to use the powers of government to insure a more even or just distribution of goods' (p. 259).

14. Friedman, *Capitalism and Freedom*, p. 191.
15. Gray, *Hayek on Liberty*.
16. Ibid., p. 8.
17. Nozick, *Anarchy, State and Utopia*.
18. Gray, *Hayek on Liberty*, p. 59.
19. R. M. Hare, *Moral Thinking* (Oxford: Clarendon Press, 1981).
20. Gray, *Hayek on Liberty* pp. 65–6.
21. Ibid., pp. 72–3. For a detailed critique of egalitarianism see J. Raz, *The Morality of Freedom* (Oxford: Clarendon Press, 1983) and the collection of essays in W. Letwin, ed., *Against Equality* (London: Macmillan, 1983).
22. Mill, *Principles of Political Economy*.
23. Gray, *Hayek on Liberty*, p. 76.
24. Any lay doubters of this maxim should visit the recent excavation in the old city in Jerusalem, which have unearthed layer upon layer of strata representing the bones of those who were killed and decimated by the temporarily dominant secular and spiritual power in the region during the seemingly endless cycle of man's inhumanity against man in Palestine. Any believer in rectificatory justice would need the wisdom of Solomon (which of course would be disputed because of its implicit bias given *his* racial origins!) to work out the requisite rectification of historic entitlements in the Levant. It is surely much better as a maxim of practical reason to accept (at least in most cases) that bygones are bygone!
25. Parts of this section are based on two of my earlier articles in D. Lal, *A Liberal International Economic Order: The International Monetary System and Economic Development*, Princeton Essays in International Finance, no. 139 (Princeton, N.J.: Princeton University Press, 1980); and "International Capital Flows and Economic Development," *Public Policy and Economic Development – Essays in Honour of Ian Little*, ed. M. Fg. Scott and D. Lal (Oxford: Clarendon Press, 1990).
26. Friedman, *Capitalism and Freedom*, p. 57. These judgements have been validated by the experience of numerous developing countries since World War II. See I. M. D. Little, *Economic Development* (New York: Basic Books, 1982); D. Lal, *The Poverty of "Development Economics"* (Cambridge, Mass. Harvard University Press and London: IEA, 1983, 1985).
27. Friedman, *Capitalism and Freedom*, p. 57.
28. See D. McDougall, "The Benefits and Costs of Private Investment From Abroad: A Theoretical Appraisal," *Economic Record* (1960); M. Kemp, "The Gain From International Trade and Investment: A Neo-Hecksher-Ohlin Approach," *American Economic Review*, vol. 56 (1966); R. Jones, "International Capital Movements and the Theory of Take Offs and Trade," *Quarterly Journal of Economics*, vol. 81 (1967).
29. See R. Jones, "International Capital Movements . . ."
30. A. C. Harberger, "Welfare Consequences of Capital Inflows," *Economic*

Liberalisation in Developing Countries, eds A. Choksi and D. Papageorgiou (Oxford: Blackwell, 1986).

31. F. Hayek, "The Use of Knowledge in Society," *American Economic Review*, vol. XXXV, no. 4 (September 1945), pp. 519–30.
32. Most, but not necessarily all – as for instance Mill in his non-authoritative functions of governments allows them to set up enterprises in *competition* with private ones. What the liberal position rules out is public monopoly as well as the creation of private monopolies by public decree. See J. S. Mill, *Principles of Political Economy*.
33. See J. Eaton, M. Gersowitz and J. E. Stiglitz, "The Pure Theory of Country Risk," *European Economic Review* (June 1986).
34. Eaton et al., "The Pure Theory. . . ," p. 499.
35. G. Haberler, "The Case Against Capital Controls for Balance of Payments Reasons," *Capital Movements and their Control*, ed. Alexander K. Swoboda (Leiden: Sitjhoff, 1976), p. 74.
36. See, for instance, J. T. Cuddington, "Capital Flight: Estimates, Issues and Explanations," *Princeton Studies in International Finance*, no. 58 (December 1986). Also see the essays in D. Lal and M. Wolf, eds., *Stagflation, Savings and the State* (Oxford: Oxford University Press, 1986).
37. Thus, as one recent analyst of Latin American capital flight (by no means a liberal!) concludes:

    over expansive monetary and fiscal policies, an incompatible exchange rate policy, and a repressive set of financial policies designed to divert resources toward the public sector will cause widespread distortions and imbalances even in the short run. Capital flight is an important symptom of these policy-induced distortions. While attacking this symptom directly by imposing capital controls may be essential in a crisis, it hardly represents a long run antidote for destabilising exchange rate, fiscal and financial policies. Without capital controls, the threat of capital flight might impose much needed discipline on policy makers. (Cuddington, "Capital Flight . . .")

38. See Howard M. W. Wachtel, *The Money Mandarins: The Making of a Supranational Economic Order* (New York: Pantheon Books, 1986); and my review of this book in D. Lal, "By Land or by Sea, the Merchant Shall Inherit the Earth," *The World Economy*, vol. 11, no. 1 (March 1988).
39. P. Mosley: *Overseas Aid* (Hemel Hempstead: Harvester Wheatsheaf, 1987).
40. This of course is Mosley's conclusion!
41. The sharpest critic of foreign aid has been Peter Bauer. Many of his prognostications concerning the irrelevant if not downright harmful effects of foreign aid have been borne out by the post-war history of the Third World. See his *Dissent on Development* (Cambridge, Mass.: Harvard University Press, 1976) and *Equality, The Third World and Economic Delusion* (London: Weidenfeld & Nicolson, 1981).
42. Hedley Bull, *The Anarchical Society* (New York: Columbia University Press, 1977).

43. R. Axelrod, *The Evolution of Co-operation* (New York: Basic Books, 1984).

44. Although the recent vogue of air-hijacking by state terrorists suggests that the acceptance of this prudential convention by most states is by no means universal.

45. See C. Lipson, *Standing Guard – Protecting Foreign Capital in the 19th & 20th Centuries*, University of California Press, 1985.

46. See Lal and Wolf, eds, *Stagflation, Savings and the State*, for detailed analysis of the debt crisis; also Lal, "International Capital Flows. . . ."

47. For a statement of this position see W. R. Cline, *International Debt: Systemic Risk and Policy Response* (Washington, D.C.: Institute of International Economics, 1984). A refutation of this case is in Lal, *The Poverty of Development Economics*, American Edition, 1985, appendix 1. Also see Lal, "International Capital Flows. . . ."

48. The case for such forgiveness is stronger in the case of the African debtors, in large part because this debt is owed to public agencies in the West, who can therefore, if they choose, forgive this debt, particularly as the loans were provided on *political* grounds. For other reasons why debt-forgiveness is not even necessary for the other Third World debtors see Lal, "International Capital Flows. . .".

49. Cited in Lipson, *Standing Guard*, p. 44. The moral hazard argument against bailing out imprudent private agents was clearly put by Herbert Spencer (cited in Lipson, ibid.) who said: 'The ultimate result of shielding men from the effects of folly is to fill the world with fools.' H. Spencer, "State Tamperings with Money and Banks" in his *Essays: Scientific, Political and Speculative*, vol 3 (London: Williams and Norgate 1891), p. 354.

50. This is why C. Kindleberger poses the question in his *International Capital Movements* (Cambridge: Cambridge University Press, 1987), chap. 4.

51. Kindleberger, *International Capital Movements*, p. 62.

52. F. A Hayek, *Choice in Currency: A Way to Stop Inflation*, Occasional Papers no. 48 (London: Institute of Economic Affairs, 1976); F. A. Hayek: *Denationalisation of Money* (London: Institute of Economic Affairs, 1976).

53. R. Vaubel, "Free Currency Competition," *Weltwirtschaft Archiv*, vol. 113 (1977), p. 435–59; R. Vaubel, "The Governments' Money Monopoly: Externalities or Natural Monopoly"? *Kyklos*, vol. 37, no. 1 (1984), 27, 58.

54. G. A. Selgin, *The Theory of Banking* (Totowa, N.J.: Rowman & Littlefield and the Cato Institute, 1988).

55. L. White, *Free Banking in Britain* (Cambridge: Cambridge Univesity Press, 1984).

56. The most spectacular being the Great Depression, which despite continuing controversy is seen to have been the result of mismanagement of the US money supply (allowing an unreasonably large contraction) by the Federal Reserve Board. See M. Friedman and A. Schwartz, *A Monetary History of the United States* (Princeton, N.J.: NBER 1963).

57. Hayek, *Denationalisation of Money*, summary.

8

Commentary: Magic associations and imperfect people

Onora O'Neill

Magic associations: Hillel Steiner on libertarianism and transnational migration of people

Hillel Steiner's chapter is at one level a self-conscious commentary on the difficulty of bringing pristine libertarian theory to bear on our actual world, and in particular on problems of transnational migration. The 'Lockean' libertarian theory that he espouses operates with an austere, yet highly controversial, set of initial categories: the individual, rights or entitlements, among them pre-eminently rights to property and contract. Even the category of the state is regarded as derivative, if not questionable: anarchist libertarians regard states as invariably unjustifiable; other libertarians justify only a minimal state with powers to enforce liberties of the person and rights of property. Given its starting point, libertarian thinking is likely to reject all claims on behalf of nations or nationality, cultural identity or the continuity and integrity of communities. What count are only the rights of individuals, including rights to move, associate, reside and work, and finally rights of citizenship. The central question raised by Hillel Steiner's chapter is whether we can grasp and discuss these rights in ways that are relevant and helpful in our actual world, if we abstract from the national, cultural and community considerations that libertarian thought self-consciously bypasses.

Steiner begins his discussion of libertarianism and transnational migration by sketching an analogy between immigration/emigration questions and questions of access to a vacation 'community' within a state jurisdiction, where property owners agree to exclude outsiders, to contribute to shared expenses and to allow the 'community' a veto on proposed sales. He represents this example as a community with absolute power over immigration and relative power over emigration.

How good an analogy is this? How good a model of transnational migration does it offer? There are certain striking disanalogies. First, the 'community' Steiner describes operates within and under the jurisdiction of a state, from which its powers in many ways derive. Second, the power of this 'community' to control 'immigration' is only its power to exclude trespassers from private property, in accord with state law, and its power to veto sales. It has no power to exclude police or other state officials, to screen the visitors any one member of the 'community' invites, or to exclude them. Third, the 'community' has no powers whatsoever to prevent 'emigration'; residents, as Steiner notes, were not required to stay in their vacation cottages all year – or at all; there were merely restraints on the sale of these cottages. Prima facie it seems unlikely that close examination of a case in which the issues of immigration and emigration control do not arise will shed much light on a world in which states control both.

However, the motivation for Steiner's starting-point is easily appreciated. If one holds, as libertarians do, that property rights are prior to and indeed (part of) the foundation of whatever (minimal) state powers can be justified, then it is tempting to look for the pure case of property rights and freedom of contract without state powers. Perhaps it is because the actual example of a vacation 'community' is not really adequate to these purposes that Steiner reverts to more familiar libertarian terrain, abstracts from all state powers, and imagines a 'Lockean' state of nature in which moral rights precede the state. This purer image of entitlement is used to weigh the cottage owners' moral title to their cottages. Steiner concludes that current titles will only be as good as the original titles from which they derive (assuming justice in transfer).

Here he distinguishes two libertarian positions. The first, which he rejects, regards original titles as morally unencumbered – established by the principle 'first come, first served', and capable of engendering current titles which are equally unencumbered. Because he thinks rights of equal liberty more basic than property rights, Steiner argues for a second, Georgist position which views original, and so later, titles as encumbered by obligations to compensate those excluded from original appropriation.

At first thought such an obligation to compensate looks as if it might have tremendous implications for the poor, and so for the pressure for access to the territories and markets now protected by state immigration restrictions. However, on reflection it is not so clear that libertarian thinking would lead in the direction of a universal system of compensation for all the poor. The compensation is, after all, owed for exclusion from original appropriation and applies irrespective of temporal and generational location. However, not all of those who are poor at a given time are so because excluded from inherited shares deriving from original appropriation. Some may be poor because they made bad choices in managing their resources. On libertarian principles they chose, or at least chose to risk, this outcome so are owed no compensation. Compensation for exclusion from inheriting the fruits of original appropriation is not equivalent to compensation for present poverty. It would be interesting to see just what it amounts to. I suspect that it is impossible to determine what such compensation should amount to, and see no reason for thinking that it will secure a universal basic income, although it might have some striking redistributive implications and so reduce some incentives to migrate.

Steiner finally returns to a purer world in which original titles are not encumbered, hence derived titles are absolute if justly derived and states may enforce only the rights of property and contract. Here, he insists, legislated restriction on transnational migration would be rejected by libertarians as violating rights of the person. The only legitimate restrictions on movement would be the enforcement of trespass laws and the detention of rights violators. It is not crucial to libertarian thinkers if a massive repeal of immigration and emigration restrictions would lead to massive social change, or harm, or the dismembering or disintegration of states, traditions or communities. Landowners have rights of secession if states and their authority are derivative from the acts of individual right holders; states have no rights to integrity when individuals choose to dissociate. Nations, traditions and communities have no rights at all.

Given individual rights to immigration, emigration and secession, the supposed sanctity of actual states can only be seen as reflecting a superstitious worship of 'magic dates', at which certain associations of individuals consolidated into states. The only legitimate restrictions on movement and association are those imposed by individual owners on access to their property or their company. These, of course, may be legion; in a world without public provision or public spaces they could be infinitely more restrictive than immigration and emigration constraints now imposed by states.

I confess to confusion. Steiner begins with a vacation 'community' which is highly dependent on a wider association, from which its powers derive. Its members rely on and accept a world in which ownership is not the condition of access; they got to their cottages by public roads paid for out of public funds; they relied on state enforcement of laws against trespass and violence and on state control of immigration to that wider association. This 'community' was wholly subordinate in its determination of rights of movement or abode, and in no way determined rights of work or citizenship. Then we are asked to imagine that the property rights which may exist within a sub-community are foundational and that everything else flows from them.

When we are invited to abstract from the actual world and to assume that individuals with rights are primordial, we take a version of the 'foundational myth' of the cottage 'community' with us – alias the 'Lockean' State of Nature. Instead of a spurious 'theory of magic dates', we are then to rely on an equally spurious 'theory of magic associations' – magic because their members do not regard any such membership as constitutive of or important for who and what they are or can do, any more than cottage owners need treat this as their sole source of identity and affiliation. They are fully formed independent persons whose liberty rights are of paramount importance to them, who view matters of nationality and community merely as matters of preference rather than identity. For 'magic associates', the access of new members or the departure of others, even the fragmentation of the association by secession of territories, are as it were, merely commercial matters of trade.

In a possible (?) world of 'magic associates' (sometimes known as Abstract Individuals) the libertarian way of making issues of transnational migration vanish would, it seems to me, be quite plausible. For the libertarian world is after all one without nations, traditions or communities except as these enter into the preference structures of individuals. The 'states' of a purely libertarian world are not nation-states; they are not sovereign states; they are only voluntary associations among consenting property owners. In this world it is not hard to magic away the problems of immigration and emigration. However, is this conjuring trick relevant to our world?

In his final paragraphs Steiner notes that there has been a symbiotic relationship between liberalism (including its libertarian versions) and the development of strong nation-states. Yet he seems to me to underestimate the significance of this connection. In a pre-liberal world, social identity might be given by tribe or kin, it might not depend on those who share a sense of identity being collected in a single or an exclusive territory. Because liberal principles undercut reliance on pedigree and origin as the basis for recognizing who count as our own, and who as outsiders, liberalism had to find some alternative basis for identifying who counts. Pre-eminent among these ways are the differential rights with respect to a given state that citizenship confers. To the extent that other indicators of shared membership are lost – national, cultural and communal ones in particular – these differential rights within a jurisdiction are all that is left to distinguish 'members' of different states. If there are states, their boundaries must possess a moral significance *other* than that of 'the boundary between my neighbour's land and mine'.

Liberalism can, of course, be expressed as a series of claims of universal scope: human rights, equality of respect, toleration of pluralism. But these universal principles have to be embodied in contexts that are historically and territorially determinate. Associates under liberal principles must recognize *certain* others as governed not only by the same principles, but by the same particular embodiment of those principles – they must, for example, be able to recognize some others as fellow-citizens, or as fellow-countrymen. Perhaps the goal of liberalism is a world state in which no distinction is drawn between insiders and outsiders, and all limited associations are reduced to the level of voluntary associations that libertarians would countenance. And yet the world state, with its risk of accumulated might, seems to me far from the pristine libertarian vision. Libertarians who prefer a *plurality* of states must acknowledge that their citizens will need to recognize and act differently towards those who are their fellow-citizens. This recognition will have to be based on discernible characteristics, including *at least* differential entitlements within a given jurisdiction. But if there are differential entitlements for different individuals, then accession and secession cannot be matters of individual choice. Just as we cannot abolish the distinction between legitimate and illegitimate births unless we abolish marriage, so we cannot abolish distinctions between citizens and non-citizens unless we abolish the plurality of states. Whether a plurality of states must be a plurality of nation-states, or of states whose citizens are linked by other common bonds, such as minimal 'constitutional patriotism' (*Verfassungspatriotismus*), seems to me an open question. However, it is a question that we need to address, and not to magic away.

Imperfect people in perfect markets: Deepak Lal on the migration of money – from a libertarian viewpoint

In the complex battle for the liberal inheritance, Deepak Lal campaigns for a position that he prefers to call not libertarian, but liberal. Certainly his libertarianism is very different from Hillel Steiner's, or from Robert Nozick's. Lal rejects coercion and discrimination between agents, but does not make a principle of the elimination of state regulation of economic activity. Hence while he rejects forms of 'American' liberalism, that purportedly *aim* at redistribution or equality, he does not follow other libertarians in their campaigns to condemn state aid to the poor. His views on the migration of money parallel these: It would be wrong to restrict the flow of capital, to force transfer of capital on concessionary terms, or to forgive indebtedness incurred by ill-judged sovereign lending or borrowing. On the other hand it *might* be acceptable to forgive the debts of African nations on political grounds, if this could be done without damage to international property rights. Lal's arguments for these positions are intricate and sophisticated; I shall comment quite selectively, mainly on his Hayekian starting-point.

Lal claims that non-discrimination between persons is fundamental to his version of liberalism/libertarianism, and that the principle of non-discrimination (universalizability) entails a form of indirect or system utilitarianism. This startling claim has been maintained by R. M. Hare in his *Moral Thinking*, receives libertarian endorsement and Hayekian blessings from John Gray and has been shown up as quite implausible by a number of writers, including specifically Philip Pettitt.[1] This is fortunate for would-be libertarians, who would hardly welcome commitment to the full rigours of utilitarianism!

Debates about non-discrimination in many areas have made it abundantly clear that it is a weak formal notion. Non-discrimination demands that like cases receive like treatment; but the principle does not forbid differentiated treatment for unlike cases.[2] What is forbidden is only differentiation on an irrelevant or inappropriate basis – and once we acknowledge this, the debate is on. Is ability to pay an appropriate basis for differentiated tax assessment? Is national origin or citizenship an appropriate basis for differential access to rights of work or residence? Is it a relevant basis for differentiated rights to travel or migration, or for financial acts? It is not enough to say that 'the non-discrimination principle of the economic liberal is exactly like the application of the rule of law': the rule of law often differentiates between, and perhaps sometimes legitimately differentiates between, different types of economic agent. Economic agents are, after all, an extremely heterogeneous array of natural and artificial persons, and while discrimination between like cases would no doubt be condemned by virtually anyone, liberal, socialist or other, I cannot see that we get much, or perhaps any, guidance about identifying the important categories of cases by appealing to non-discrimination. No doubt arbitrary interference that treats like cases in unlike ways defeats stable expectations and is unjust, but this is hardly the issue between different positions in political theory.

In particular, it does not follow from commitment to non-discrimination that governments cannot justly determine patterns of distribution. It follows only that they cannot do so by methods such as arbitrary seizure. There are multitudes of ways of regulating by stable and known procedures that in fact reliably achieve and preserve stable end-state patterns. Lal recognizes this point within a libertarian context in distinguishing Hayekian concern for stability with non-arbitrariness from Nozick's supposedly Lockean belief that all taxation beyond the needs of the minimal state violates rights. What Lal needs to show is why his particular non-arbitrary libertarianism is to be preferred to Nozick's, or, say, to non-arbitrary social democracy, or a non-arbitrary conservatism. In ruling out arbitrary discrimination, we do not automatically converge on Lal's form of liberalism/libertarianism.

This explains why Lal cannot discard the arguments that supposedly derive a (selective) utilitarianism from the very principle of non-discrimination. Non-discrimination alone will not do enough work for his purposes. Yet the utilitarian principle cannot be squeezed out of universalizability: optimal results cannot be derived from 'Kantian' beginnings. Indeed, a synthesis of Hume and Kant is unlikely to be internally coherent, since they rely on radically different conceptions of human freedom and action.

That apart, Lal's more specifically libertarian claim that we can move from the formal requirement of equal freedom for like cases (which is all non-discrimination requires) to his conclusions about international flows of capital seem to me unconvincing. Of course, this does not show that these conclusions are unconvincing – and Lal offers subsidiary efficiency arguments for many of them. However, since efficiency arguments are of indeterminate ethical weight outside utilitarian reasoning, their importance is unclear – unless Lal can offer more than the implausible arguments of Hare and Gray to back his contention that utilitarianism follows from universalizability or non-discrimination.

This is not to say that a Hayekian position is without attractions of various sorts; it may be even nicer if it is not forced to appear in utilitarian disguise. What follows is rather that the arguments to establish why stability is important, and how it is to be ranked against other goals, and hence which stabilities are most important, must be worked out more thoroughly. Appeals to stability – or to efficiency – cannot be treated as fundamental.

My comments on the more strictly economic sections of Lal's chapter will be brief. His discussion is detailed, and some aspects of it exceed my competence. In particular, I cannot assess the weight of various claims about the relative efficiency or inefficiency of different ways of controlling, or not controlling the flow of capital. I can only note that even if all his claims were borne out, the ethical significance of appeals to efficiency remains open. Efficient solutions might sometimes be gruesomely unjust; which is not to say that efficiency is irrelevant to considerations of justice.

Lal's most interesting general contention in this part of his chapter is that for capital movements, unlike the movements of people, national boundaries have already been in part eroded. (Perhaps they have also already been partly eroded for those people who belong to a small international elite with wealth and expertise.) This greater erosion of boundaries to the movement of money means that the relation of theory to actuality is quite different here. It may be fanciful to think away all the implications of difference of citizenship; it may be quite realistic to think away barriers to the movement of money.

Some of Lal's most interesting conclusions seem to me to reflect this real difference more than any Hayekian foundations. He does not argue that controls on the movement of money are intrinsically unjust on Hayekian grounds, so much as he indicts them either for impairing economic efficiency as defined by perfect markets, or as ill-defined in the actual world. Both protectionism and barriers to the free movement of capital reduce the feasible set of consumption possibilities, provided that no borrowers or lenders have monopoly or monopsony power to influence the terms of loans. Accepting that this is so, it seems to me that our hardest problem may be to judge when markets in the actual world meet – or come close to meeting – these 'perfect' conditions. Many will agree that the conditions are not met in certain markets (cf. village moneylenders), and that they are ill met in many others. There are a lot of hard cases, and it is about these that Hayekian liberals and their liberal and socialist critics will disagree.

Lal acknowledges the importance of the 'distortion' of 'perfect' markets by differentials of power, but then rather oddly treats such cases as nonstandard. His illustrations of his position are more benign, indeed pious, than testing. For example, he points out the harmless effect of free movement of capital when the 'citizens of two countries engage in mutually agreeable trades until each group ends up "owning" all of the other's physical assets'. In this happy case no power advantage has been gained, and all parties have gained, or at least freely risked incurring any loss they suffer. The crucial question, it seems to me, is the extent to which this benign example can serve as paradigmatic for actual international movements of capital. In these matters we cannot, as Bernard Williams has put the matter, rest too much on the fragile structure of the voluntary. Transactions whose outward face is that of acts between consenting adults may be deeply structured by inequalities of power.[3]

Lal's last set of arguments against the control or even the taxation, of international capital flows invoke empirical considerations about the consequences of intervention and of non-intervention. There is some tension between the two types of consideration that are here advanced in tandem. The first type points out that restrictions on international capital flows do not have all the good effects that some of their protagonists aimed for, and may have harmful effects. For example, public international transfers of capital have tended not to help the very poorest. The second type points out that international capital flows are, or are becoming, hard to identify – new forms of 'denationalized' money make it hard to assign nationality to stocks of capital. These types of consideration coexist rather uneasily: to the extent that money is denationalized, the first type of consideration appears to need reformulating. If capital knows no frontiers, taxation 'to redress absolute poverty', which Hayekian libertarians such as Lal do not reject within a state, should also take a transnational form. The internationalization of capital may render the specific question of the justice of transnational flows of capital obsolete, but replaces it with the underlying question of the justice of protecting, or alternatively exposing, the poorest to the impact of capital movements.

One of the most appealing features of Lal's Hayekian liberalism/ libertarianism is the realistic view it takes of the imperfect character of human knowledge and the unavailability of perfect information. These thoughts are basic to the arguments against central planning. However, just because such imperfections are rather persistent, a Hayekian position cannot place much faith in standard theories about perfect markets. In particular, if utilitarianism cannot be extracted from non-discrimination, as I have indicated it cannot, Hayekian recognition of human imperfection will entail only moderate enthusiasm for market arrangements, and only selective concern for efficiency.

Notes

1. R. M. Hare, *Moral Thinking* (Oxford: Clarendon Press, 1981); John Gray, *Hayek on Liberty* (Oxford: Blackwell, 1984); Philip Pettitt, "Universalisability without Utilitarianism," *Mind*, 96 (1987), 74–82.
2. See Onora O'Neill, "Justice, Gender and International Boundaries," *British Journal of Political Science*, 20 (1990), 439–59.
3. Bernard Williams, *Ethics and the Limits of Philosophy* (London: Fontana, 1985); O'Neill, "Justice, Gender and International Boundaries."

Marxist Perspectives

9

Marxism and the transnational migration of people: Ethical issues

Chris Brown

This chapter examines ethical issues posed by the migration of people from the Marxist perspective on human affairs. This subject is remote from the mainstream concerns of that perspective, and it will therefore be necessary to unpack and rework most of the terms to be found in the title of this text. The first section will examine, very briefly, the complex nature of the tradition(s) of Marxism and their generally uneasy relationship to ethics. The second more substantial part of the chapter will attempt to explain why the usual terms employed to discuss problems of migration have little in the way of purchase when it comes to Marxist thought, and will suggest one or two ways in which ethical problems posed by migration have been and/or could be formulated within the tradition. The final section will examine some occasions when writers within the mainstream of Marxism have found themselves forced to come to terms with these issues, with a view to elaborating both their methods and their conclusions.

The traditions of Marxism and the problem of ethics

All worthwhile ethical traditions are complex, potentially self-contradictory and resistant to easy summaries, but it is none the less particularly difficult to pin down the ethical tradition of Marxism. In the first place, the term Marxism has in its hundred year plus history stood for a number of directly contradictory positions; in the late twentieth century it has become a meaningless term, assuming substance only when qualified, while even 100 years ago Marx himself realized what was happening to his name when, famously, he denied himself the title of Marxist. From this complex of meaning it is perhaps helpful to identify and isolate some coherent strands before proceeding to stipulate a definition that will be employed in the remainder of the text.

First, viewed in terms of the history of Marxism as a doctrine it is possible to identify three distinct stages which are termed here, following Kolakowski, the period of the Founders, the Golden Age and the Breakdown.[1] In the mid-nineteenth century the founders, Marx and Engels, formed one strand of a slowly emerging socialist movement, offering to this movement a political economy that purported to lay out the laws of motion of capitalism and the reasons for its inevitable collapse. In the golden age of the Second International, lasting from around 1890 to 1914, Marxism was the official doctrine of the most advanced and successful socialist movements in Europe. No longer simply an economics, Marxism was now seen as an overarching perspective on human affairs that could plausibly be expected to offer a view on virtually all aspects of human existence. In the period of the breakdown following the onset of war in 1914 and the Bolshevik revolution of 1917, Marxism fragmented, with Marxist-Leninist thought in Russia becoming increasingly remote both from in its origins and from socialist thought in Western Europe, a gap which was intensified by the rise of Stalin and the gradual acceptance of the institutions of pluralist liberal democracy by the Western social democrats.

The result of this breakdown is that in the late twentieth century several different variants of Marxism can be identified; three seem most important – Soviet Marxism, Third Worldist 'neo-Marxism' and Western Marxism. Soviet Marxism has been for most of this century the dominant mode of Marxist discourse, but is now undergoing extensive self-criticism and has lost most of its influence outside the area of 'really-existing' socialism.[2] Third World 'neo-Marxism', a revolutionary doctrine focused on the problems of development and underdevelopment, is in most respects antithetical to Marx's own conceptions of society and economy but still claims to be in the Marxist tradition.[3] Western Marxism – for the most part a movement to be found in the academy rather than the party – claims to build on the traditions of the centre and left of the Second International in descent from Luxemburg, Gramsci and, possibly, Lenin and Trotsky, but certainly not Stalin.[4] When the term Marxism is used in this chapter without qualification, it will be to this latter that the term refers; thus Marxism will be seen in the light of the Second International tradition (the 'classics') as represented today by individual Western Marxists rather than by the ideologists of the East or the South.

This attempt to stipulate a meaning of core Marxism is fraught with difficulties; in practice it will prove difficult to avoid a wider usage of the term and, certainly, the input of 'official' Marxisms to the development of the doctrine cannot be wholly set on one side. However, with respect to the key issue of the relationship between Marxism and ethics no restrictive delimitation is required. Virtually all variants of Marxism share a common reluctance to engage in sustained ethical thought and a common suspicion of morality as conventionally defined. This distancing stance is even more pronounced when it is international ethics that is at issue, in so far as this involves the combination of a suspect mode of discourse – ethics – with a dubious level of analysis: the international. The latter complex of problems will be discussed in the next section of the chapter, but before proceeding to look at the difficulties involved in conceptualizing migration issues some general comments on Marxist ethics are needed.

The distinctive feature of mainstream Marxism has always been its claim to provide an understanding of society that is materialist. Engels in *Socialism: Utopian and Scientific* offers stark and oversimplified antinomies, and clearly his highly positivist understanding of science would not be acceptable to all Marxists, but this tract defines with characteristic sharpness the distinction between a Marxist, materialist, scientific, understanding of the world and alternative moralizing varieties of socialism.[5] Marxism is science; it identifies the laws of motion of capitalism and its inevitable downfall in terms purged of ethical content. Capitalism will be replaced by socialism and communism not because the latter are morally superior but because the former's underlying logic drives it to create the conditions for its own destruction. In any event, morality is an ideological by-product of the mode of production; in the words of *The German Ideology*, morality, with religion and metaphysics, is no more than a phantom formed in the brain, a sublimate of material life processes, unable to retain the semblance of independence.[6] Morality is a class phenomenon rather than something transcendant; calls to behave morally generally reflect the interests of the dominant class in society – currently the bourgeoisie – while the claims of a proletarian morality could only be the expression of the real interests of that class, although in this case the universal claims of the proletariat give its interests a wider significance. In any event, right conduct cannot be determined by reference to ethical considerations or moral codes; 'What is to be done?' is a question the answer to which can only emerge out of *praxis*, the theoretically informed experience of the working-class movement and right conduct can only be determined by the ultimate goal of revolution and the creation of communism.

This account of Marxism and ethics, while essentially sound, does contain elements of caricature and requires qualification in two important respects. First, it is now clear that Marx's work rested on a philosophical anthropology, a clear sense of what man ought to be and could be, an essentially ethical conception of humanity's potential for self-development and freedom.[7] This anthropology – which comes through most clearly in posthumously published early writings such as the *Paris Manuscripts* and in his later notes for *Capital*, the *Grundrisse* – is at the heart of Marx's conception of communism as a realm of human freedom, and undercuts to some extent the claim of Marxism to have abolished metaphysics.[8] However, it in no respect undermines the critique of morality as ideology, and in any event these writings emerge from a philosophical tradition – 'left' Hegelianism – which even the most sophisticated of working-class movements have hardly made their own.

More important for this discussion is what Lukes has called the 'paradox' of Marxism and morality.[9] This paradox rests in the fact that while Marxism as a doctrine sets its face against any form of moralizing, taking pride in its cool objectivity, most Marxist writings – and certainly such definitive works as *The Communist Manifesto* and *Capital* – are permeated with an incandescant moral rage generated by the conditions they describe and a like moral fervour on behalf of the cause they promote.[10] Indeed, it would not be unreasonable to hazard that this paradox has been a necessary condition for the growth of support for Marxism; however impressive the intellectual roots of the doctrine may be, the visceral appeal of Marxism has rested precisely in its essentially moral self-identification as the ideology of and for the wretched of the earth.

What this suggests is that within Marxism a number of different moral and ethical elements coexist uneasily. In principle, Marxists reason consequentially and instrumentally rather than morally, judging action on the basis of its contribution to the achievement of an end defined by the objective dialectic of history. However, on closer analysis it turns out on the one hand, that this end – for Marx at least – is actually determined by an ethical conception of man's fate, which certainly cannot be brought within the bounds of science, while, on the other, the cold, consequentialist reasoning in which Marxists take pride is constantly subverted by a rhetoric which is inescapably moral in nature. This paradox seems unavoidable, at least in the sense that those who attempt to suppress altogether one side of the dilemma seem to lose contact with a recognizably Marxist position – as is witnessed by the, very different but equally unMarxist, positions of on the one hand the Stalinists of the Comintern, and on the other of the neo-Kantian social democrats of the Second International.

The problem of international ethics is further bedevilled by the difficulty of coping with the existence of separate communities in an international society from the point of view of a theory of society which must see such phenomena as superstructural rather than basic.[11] This point will be discussed below in the specific context of migration and the meaning of communities, but for the moment it is sufficient to note that there exists within Marxist thinking on the ethical dimensions of international affairs a version of the contradictions identified above. Marxists are cosmopolitans whose account of the nature of human beings divides persons according to class and not nation; the oldest slogan of Marxian socialism calls upon the workers of the world to unite. But at the same time Marxists are revolutionary opportunists, exploiting circumstances as they arise to make the revolution and justifying their actions in terms of their ends. As the history of the relationship between Marxism and nationalism suggests, these two positions do not always coexist easily, and the costs of consequentialist reasoning for the credibility of Marxist cosmopolitanism can be high. The next sections of this chapter will take up these issues in the context of international migration, examining both the theoretical problems Marxists face in conceptualizing the ethical issues generated by this phenomena and the practical difficulties Marxist writers have experienced in coping with its politics.

Marxism and migration: theoretical approaches

From a Marxist viewpoint many of the issues perceived as problems by conventional thought on the ethics of migration either cannot be formulated as such, or can only be seen in a derivative form. The analytical categories employed by Marxists either do not include, or consistently devalue, those most frequently employed in bourgeois thought. Thus, pressing ethical concerns with the state and the community identified as central by writers such as Walzer and Dowty have no effective purchase within a Marxist framework, while those notions that are central to Marxism, such as class, are secondary to conventional, bourgeois thought.[12] That this is so probably causes more damage to Marxist thought than to the moral discourse of the Western mainstream, but cannot for this reason be ignored.

To flesh out these points it may be helpful to offer a brief outline of some of the more important features of Marxist thinking on migration, not in ambitious pursuit of a Marxist theory of migration but simply as a way of finding a starting-point. Migration at its simplest is about the movement of people, over long or short distances, permanently or temporarily, within or across national boundaries, or the boundaries of communities and cultures. Such movements have been characteristic of capitalism since its inception and, unsurprisingly, have featured in general works of Marxist political economy from Marx to Mandel.[13] Moreover, many theorists of migration have come from a Marxist background; there is therefore a great deal of Marxist writing on migration. The point is that this writing tends to conceptualize migration in essentially economic terms rather than in terms which readily transpose into the language generally employed in ethics.

Thus, from a Marxist perspective, initial thoughts on migration focus on the general issue of demand for labour within a capitalist economy. Capitalism is characterized by 'expanded reproduction' which involves a growth in the demand for labour; moreover, the axiomatic desire of capitalists to depress the general level of wages to counteract the alleged tendency of the rate of profit to fall will lead to the formation of a 'reserve army' of labour. For both reasons a continual increase in the workforce is desirable – possibly, actually necessary – and such an increase will be met in part by migration. The supply of migrant labour is created by the dispossession of the potential proletariat, such that they, in common with the current proletariat, have no choice other than to sell their labour power to the capitalist.

This general picture is to be found in outline in *Capital* and subsequent general studies of Marxist political economy, and some of the basic categories employed – such as that of the 'reserve army' – appear to have dominated Marxist thought in the area until quite recently: see, for example, the use of this notion in the seminal study of Castles and Kosack.[14] However, more recent Marxist work has refined these categories quite substantially in response both to the empirical evidence and to recent developments of theory. These refinements come in respect of two main areas. First, the notion of a reserve army of labour has had to be dramatically revised (perhaps out of existence altogether) by the realization that by and large migrant workers are *not* competing with indigenous workers and therefore cannot be seen as depressing wages on the margin.[15] Migrant workers are a source of cheap labour for the capitalist, enabling the latter to pay low wages for certain jobs because the costs of the social reproduction of labour is met elsewhere and because the migrant workforce is generally ununionized.[16] This still involves a relationship between migrant and indigenous workers and an effect on average wages, but the relationship is somewhat more complex than that envisaged by the classical formulation of the reserve army.

Perhaps more fundamental is the re-conceptualization of the spatial, geographic dimension to the distinction between 'inside' and 'outside' the capitalist economy. This distinction is important to Marx's account of the development of capitalism; the shift of workers from non-capitalist to capitalist relations of production originally characteristic of the decline of pre-capitalist agriculture in early modern England serves as a paradigm for later movements, including those crossing state boundaries.[17] However, under the influence of neo-Marxist, 'world-systems' thinking, this notion of a non-capitalist 'outside' providing labour power to capitalism is now widely regarded as suspect; instead much current writing sees the 'world economy' as a whole, with transnational migration as simply one facet of the wider issue of labour control.[18] Such a perspective, unlike the more traditional inside/outside distinction, facilitates the study of a range of different aspects of the role of labour in the world economy such as the phenomenon of 'unfree' labour migration in, e.g. Southern Africa,[19] or the – potentially most interesting issue of all – development of a new international division of labour, which by moving lower-paid work from centres to peripheries or semi-peripheries may in the longer run make some forms of migration wholly redundant.[20]

Now this brief, even caricatured, account of Marxist thinking on migration gives the impression that this thought is essentially functionalist and economistic, seeing the phenomenon of migration from the perspective of the functioning of capitalist economies. This impression is not misleading; although Marxist writers have not infrequently examined migration from cultural or sociological perspectives, at root any Marxist *explanation* of migration is going to be based on economics, and the roles of individuals, states and communities will be seen in the light that passes through economic structures.[21] It is this feature of Marxism that accounts for the difficulties experienced in the attempt to translate the categories generally employed in conventional thought on the ethics of migration into forms that make sense to Marxist discourse. Normative issues are posed to Marxist thought by transnational migration, but within the context of class, not with reference to the individual and/or the state/community.

To think of the ethics of migration in the context of the individual it is necessary to think of the latter as an independent maker of choices about his or her future; it can then be asked whether the individual has the right to make certain sorts of choices, what sorts of networks of obligations and duties surround the making of such choices, and so on. Now, clearly this notion of the individual as a maker of choices does correspond to a certain account of reality, but it does not correspond to a reality that Marxist theory helps to explicate. Very few Marxists would actually hold the full anti-humanist position that individuals are simply bearers of roles within an economic structure,[22] but for the purposes of Marxist economic theory some such assumption is more or less unavoidable, and it certainly makes little sense to ask what kind of rights individuals do, or should have. The notion of the free, self-determining individual is important to Marx's philosophical anthropology, but it is the non-existence of such individuals under existing conditions that fuels his critique of capitalism. The demand that the partially human subjects of capitalism be turned into rights holders may be powerful in terms of political rhetoric, but can only be subverted by the reality of the rule of capital – just as the notion of 'free' labour is subverted by the requirement to sell one's labour power to those who own the means of production. Except in terms of political rhetoric, the notion of the individual cannot be at the centre of Marxist ethical thought.

The position with respect to the state and community is somewhat different in detail but similar in essence. States clearly play a very important role in the political economy of migration; under modern conditions where the migrant workforce is largely separate from the indigenous workforce, the maintenance of this separation is a function of the state.[23] It is the state that in principle regulates the flow of migrant workers and it is the state that determines what political rights migrant workers possess, or, more plausibly, do not possess. The distinction between migrants and indigenous workers is reinforced by cultural and communal differences, and in those cases where migrants are granted political rights (for example in the United Kingdom with respect to commonwealth immigration) such differences may play a key role in maintaining separate labour markets. What this indicates is that membership of a state or community is of central importance, but its political centrality does not translate into normative centrality, a primary ethical focus. The reason for this is again perfectly clear; the state cannot be central to a Marxist ethics because the state is at root a secondary, superstructural phenomenon. Clearly, the sort of formulae employed in the *Communist Manifesto* – the executive arm of the state as a committee for managing the common affairs of the whole bourgeoisie and so on[24] – cannot stand unamended and Marx and Engels themselves, along with later Marxists, have added greatly to the sophistication with which the phenomenon of the state is conceptualized, but the basic point – that the state is not primary while the economic structure is – cannot be avoided without jettisoning the Marxist perspective as such.[25]

Once again, the language of 'rights' is inappropriate. It makes little sense to ask whether states have the right to restrict entry or prevent departures, to 'poach' skilled workers and professionals from elsewhere, or to stop similar people from leaving. Such matters are in the last resort a function of the operation of a capitalist economy and to ask whether states have a right to behave in this way is like asking whether capitalists have a right to make a profit – a perfectly sensible question but only if the terms of reference of the argument are stood on their head. Before looking at an area where normative concerns do have purchase within Marxist thought – the area of class formation and class politics – it might be worth making the point that perhaps the terms of reference of the argument *should* be stood on their head. It may be that the Marxist approach to the state (and to the notion of the individual) is radically flawed precisely because of its functionalism and economism and some such argument will be made below. All that needs to be said here is that if this is so, it should be taken as a reason for leaving Marxism behind rather than as a reason for taking Marxism to be something that it is not. A great deal of radical thought loses coherence because of a reluctance either to abandon Marxism or to accept its implications – a criticism that can be, and has been, laid at the door of, for example, dependency theory.[26]

Ethical aspects of transnational migration cannot be formulated within a Marxist framework using the categories of the individual and the community, but they do have purchase in the context of class. Class is central to any normative analysis with a Marxist bent. It is as a member of a class that is conscious of its true self-interests that an individual gains freedom from the domination of ruling-class ideas, and it is as a class organ that the state and community is formed and operates. Working-class solidarity is a prime moral commitment of Marxists – although as noted above the consequentialist nature of Marxist moral argument raises the important issue of whether such a commitment can ever clash with the deeper aim of creating conditions conducive to revolution, an issue of some relevance to the question of migration.

The unity of the working class is both a premise of Marxism and a practical political objective. It is also threatened by migration, and not by accident. As Castells puts it:

> *the utility of immigrant labour to capital derives primarily from the fact that it can act toward it as though the labour movement did not exist*, thereby moving the class struggle back several decades. A twenty-first century capital and a nineteenth century proletariat – such is the dream of monopoly capital in order to overcome its crisis. [emphasis in original][27]

From a Marxist perspective this fragmentation of labour is deeply damaging to the long-term achievement of socialism and thus to the real long-term interests of migrant and indigenous workers. The problem is that for both groups of workers short- to medium-term interests are tied up with the fragmentation of the workforce. From a 'reserve army'/marginal worker perspective this is clearly true in so far as the general wage level is being held down by the availability of migrant workers, but even on a more sophisticated account of the role of immigrants it is clear that interests do clash. Even if migrant workers are only doing the jobs indigenous workers will not do at the going rate, this simply allows capital to avoid increasing that rate to a point at which indigenous workers would be prepared to work – thus cutting unemployment and generally increasing the bargaining power of labour. Seen from the other angle it is clearly in the interests of indigenous workers to keep migrant workers out of those positions (or sectors) which are currently high-wage and/or high-skilled and/or heavily unionized.

In short, the situation is riddled with contradictions. Berger has caught this nicely when he makes the point that immigrant workers are simultaneously a threat to the bargaining power of the indigenous workers and, themselves, the most exploited of all workers – although, characteristically, he uses the term exploitation in the loose sense rather than with a specifically Marxist meaning and offers no evidence that greater surplus

value is created by migrant workers.[28] The dilemma for Marxist thought
is clear. On the one hand, and at the risk of excessive repetition, it needs to
be stressed that from a Marxist perspective the worker has no country;
workers as a whole are exploited by capital and to accept the notion of a
proletariat defined by its membership of a particular state or community is
to abandon a first premise of socialism. On the other hand, actual class
politics take place within real political contexts in which the differences
between groups of workers may be of key importance irrespective of
the desires of militants. Preserving the political strength of indigenous
working-class movements may involve accepting these differences, but
such acceptance can only undermine the long-run goals of Marxist political action. Politics takes place within specific locations in the face of
particular circumstances, and those Marxist movements which have seen
success in the twentieth century have been those which have, at least at
crucial moments, managed to associate themselves with national causes.
At the same time, when national causes involve overt acceptance of the
division of the working class the dangers of a 'national socialism' in every
sense of the term become apparent.[29]

This last point raises one further issue it is worth discussing before
proceeding to cases. Migration can create two proletariats within one
society, and this obviously presents particular problems, but once again it
should be stressed that Marxism is at root cosmopolitan; whether low-
paid unskilled workers are separated from high-paid, high-skilled workers
by a street or by an ocean has no moral significance even if the political
difference between these two cases is enormous. The problem of migration
is simply one aspect of a wider problem of realizing the long-term interest
in proletarian unity in the face of the many obvious obstacles to this unity,
and in the absence of a political vocabulary that can overcome medium-
term fragmentation by reference to rights and duties.

Transnational migration thus poses formidable problems for the development of effective class politics. How these problems are approached is
difficult to conceptualize in general terms, and at this stage of the argument
it may be helpful to examine actual cases. One of the most interesting of
such cases can be illustrated from texts by the founders of Marxism – the
case of Irish immigration to England in the nineteenth century. The next
section of this chapter will look at some writings on this topic, beginning
with one of the formative works of Marxism and, more briefly, will
examine some other occasions where the issues of class formation and
immigration have given rise to thought-provoking material.

Marxism and migration: texts and cases

Friedrich Engels was the son of a textile manufacturer, and in 1842 was sent to the family firm's Manchester branch, mainly in order to keep him out of harm's way. One result three years later was the publication in Germany of *The Condition of the Working Class in England* (hereafter CWCE).[30] This text was produced before such classic early statements of 'Marxist' doctrine as *The German Ideology* (completed 1846) or the *Communist Manifesto* (1848), but contains in embryo form the most important doctrines of historical materialism; the tone and spirit of the text is fully in keeping with later work.[31] The content of CWCE is encapsulated by its title; it is a reasonably reliable account of the emergence and current status of the world's first industrial proletariat. Its interest for the purposes of this chapter lies in its treatment of Irish immigration. The Irish contribution to the 'English' working class was substantial – maybe a million already in 1842 and an additional 50,000 a year at that time – and although no state frontiers were crossed, cultural and economic differences between England and Ireland were such that the problems raised by Irish immigration can be seen in parallel with more recent transnational migration. The way in which Engels treats this phenomenon is thus of considerable interest.

The low cultural level of the Irish is a subject upon which Engels is prepared to write without reserve; the Irish character – albeit only 'under some circumstances' – is comfortable only in dirt, and the Irishman 'goes in rags, eats potatoes, and sleeps in a pig-sty'. 'Dissolute, unsteady, drunken' Irish workers are incapable of handling work which requires long training or regular application, but for simple less exact work, where brawn rather than brain is required the Irishman is as good as the Englishman. The inevitable result is that in these areas competition is 'gradually forcing the rate of wages, and with it the Englishman's level of civilisation, down to the Irishman's level'.[32]

Although the willingness to call a pig-sty a pig-sty is somewhat out of keeping with modern sensibilities, the situation Engels describes in CWCE is one that has resonances throughout the last century and a half and, suitably bowdlerized and refined, many of Engels's descriptions, along with his account of the logic of competition, could be transferred to contemporary circumstances without too much difficulty. Nor for that matter did it require great analytical skill to see what was happening in English cities as a result of Irish immigration – Engels himself quotes other authors who have come up with similar accounts of the issue. What is interesting is the normative dimension of Engels account, partly for what it says, partly for what it does not say.

Taking the latter point first, what it does not say is anything that could be construed as a rights-based account of the problems posed by Irish immigration. Whether the Irish have a right to be in Manchester, or the English have a right to exclude them simply does not arise as an issue – and this not because of the lack of a cross-border dimension to the problem. The situation is quite simply described:

> The rapid extension of English industry could not have taken place if England had not possessed in the numerous and impoverished population of Ireland a reserve at command. The Irish had nothing to lose at home and much to gain in England. . . .[33]

Given the general absence of controls on movement, the possession of this reserve has nothing to do with Ireland's quasi-colonial status; it is the relative poverty of Ireland that is crucial, and Engels specifically makes the point that this distress would not be alleviated by repeal of the Act of Union – although this was a judgement that Marx and Engels later qualified somewhat (see below). Irishmen come to England because – on estimates quoted by Engels – 27 per cent of the population of Ireland were destitute, paupers depending on public or private assistance to survive. This poverty is both a source of their degraded condition and their prime motivation for coming to England. Their acceptance in England is a function of the needs of capital: the wishes of communities are neither here nor there.

How then does Engels approach the problem? – by examining the impact of Irish immigration on the formation and attitudes of the English working class and on the prospects that this class will take its destiny into its own hands. The result of this enquiry is interesting, and instructive, Irish immigration has: 'degraded the English workers, removed them from civilisation, and aggravated the hardship of their lot; but on the other hand, it has thereby deepened the chasm between workers and bourgeoisie, and hastened the approaching crisis'.[34] From the point of view of the overthrow of the system the greater the degradation of the workers the better: 'we can but rejoice over everything that accelerates the course of the disease'. Moreover, the Irish and English workers have much to offer each other:

> The Irish and the English are to each other much as the French and the Germans; and the mixing of the more facile, excitable, fiery Irish temperament with the stable, reasoning, persevering English must, in the long run, be productive only of good for both.[35]

The hot-blooded Irish will provide the spark that will push the phlegmatic but determined English into action.

Leaving aside the outrageous stereotyping, this account of the working class as a melting pot in which the best characteristics of both peoples rise to the surface is attractive and in the best cosmopolitan tradition. It might even be seen as a long-run prediction vindicated by the fact that the last Prime Minister and Chancellor of the Exchequer to come from the British Labour Party were named Callaghan and Healey respectively, although one is bound to say that only the latter conformed even in part to Engels' expectations as to character. The relevant point is that in the context of the mid-nineteenth century Engels is being hopelessly unrealistic, clearly indicating that however sympathetic he may have been to the aspirations of the workers his understanding of their sentiments was that of an outsider. A generation later, in a letter to comrades in New York of 1870 Marx saw the situation in very different terms:

> Every industrial and commercial centre in England now possesses a working class divided into two *hostile* camps, English proletarians and Irish proletarians. The ordinary English worker hates the Irish worker as a competitor who lowers his standard of life. . . . He cherishes religious, social, and national prejudices against the Irish worker. . . . The Irishman . . . sees in the English worker both the accomplice and the stupid tool of the *English rulers in Ireland*.
>
> This antagonism is artificially kept alive and intensified by the press, the pulpit, the comic papers, in short by all the means at the disposal of the ruling classes. *This antagonism* is the *secret of the impotence of the English working class*, despite its organisation. It is the secret by which the capitalist class maintains its power. And the latter is quite aware of this. [emphasis in original][36]

This letter has been quoted at length because it catches so well the dilemmas posed by migration as well as some of the illusions it can generate. Unlike Engels at an earlier date, Marx is well aware that a problem exists, indeed possibly overstates its importance; the problem is that his sense of what can be done about this is no more to the point than was that of Engels a generation before. For Marx the antagonism between Irish and English workers is kept alive by the machinations of capital and specifically by the continuation of English rule in Ireland. His solution is that English workers must support Irish freedom, thus: '[the General Council of the International must] make the English workers realise that *for them* the *national emancipation of Ireland* is not a question of abstract justice or humanitarian sentiment but *the first condition of their own social emancipation*.' [emphasis in original][37] Even disregarding the fact, all too obvious in the twentieth century, that at least some Irishmen do not wish to be emancipated, it is difficult to see why Marx believes that the antagonisms he has described will disappear after Irish independence. It may be that the psychology of the situation would change, but the material differences which cause English workers to regard the Irish as competitors would be unaffected. It is difficult to avoid the conclusion that Marx's realism, so apparent in his description of the problem, deserts him when it comes to the solution.

These texts of Marx and Engels are interesting because they illustrate the dilemmas of migration with such clarity; even though the economic function of immigrant labour may have changed in the last century the moral dilemmas have not, and the difficulties are partly a product of the material circumstances concerned, but equally stem in part from problems generated by the general approach of Marxism to ethical questions. A consistent historical materialist who is a trenchant critic of bourgeois political morality cannot credibly employ bourgeois notions in defence of proletarian values. Marx cannot argue that Irish workers have a *right* to equal treatment or that English workers have a *duty* to treat Irish workers as comrades irrespective of the material conditions that divide them; these arguments simply are not available to him. All he can do is argue that the divisions between workers are artificially created by capital. There is, of course, a sense in which this is axiomatically true for a Marxist, and as a long-run position it can be defended more generally, but in the medium run it simply avoids the issue, which is that there are material clashes that cannot be wished away.

The dilemmas identified in this brief account of Marx and Engels on the issue of Irish immigration to nineteenth-century England have recurred repeatedly in the twentieth century, even though the degree to which migrant workers have posed a direct challenge to the positions of indigenous workers may have changed. The experience of Western European labour movements *vis-à-vis* immigrant workers in the post-1945 period has recreated many of the features described by Marx in 1870, with established workers showing varying degrees of lack of enthusiasm for the arrival of foreign competitors.[38] A general rhetorical commitment to fraternity and equality has not prevented some very unfraternal behaviour – perhaps most notably in the case of the French Communist Party which has attempted to arrest its declining electoral fortunes in the 1980s by engaging in anti-immigrant campaigns of some virulence.[39] Outside of Europe some labour movements have been explicitly racist. The Australian labour unions combined socialist ideology with support for the 'White Australia' policy until the 1970s;[40] the slogan of the Communist Party in the Rand Dispute of 1922 in South Africa – 'Workers of the World Unite and Fight for a White South Africa' – summarized the attitude of that body before it became an organization whose white support was drawn largely from the middle classes.[41]

The South African case raises in the starkest form the consequences of an approach to normative issues that attempts to deny the relevance of morality in favour of a materialist account of right conduct. If a commitment to cosmopolitan values means anything at all then apartheid and other forms of racial discrimination must be rejected; the problem is that of persuading white workers that this rejection is in their interests in the face of all the evidence to the contrary. Consequentialist reasoning cannot perform this task, a fact recognized implicitly by the rhetoric employed by Marxist writers, even if an explicit appeal to standards of morality which transcend class cannot be formulated.

A final illustration of the same problem, although structured very differently, can be found in the emigration policies of the countries of 'really-existing' socialism – the Soviet Union and its East European neighbours. It is notoriously the case that these countries did not allow a general right to leave to their citizens, and in some cases – most particularly along the inner-German frontier and in Berlin – went to extraordinary lengths to prevent unauthorized exits.[42] These restrictions were in part produced by political forces but there seems little reason to doubt that fear of the economic consequences of complete freedom of movement was crucial. Hungary, which had the most liberal emigration policies of Eastern Europe, acknowledges that it was obliged to shape its wages policy in ways that would not be justified otherwise in order to keep its professionals; in the case of the German Democratic Republic the cost of such a policy would almost certainly have been unsupportable.[43]

From a human rights perspective this was, of course, an unacceptable interference with the right to leave that all citizens should possess – a right, incidentally, that the USSR and its allies have accepted in signing the Helsinki Accords – but it is less clear that Marxist thought can find fault with restrictions made necessary by the problems encountered in building socialism if, a big if, this is what these societies are actually doing. Most non-Soviet Marxists would want to criticize these interferences with human freedom, but, again, it is not clear on what basis they do so, given the unavailability of the language of rights. Nor is this simply a problem for authoritarian, Stalinist versions of Marxism; any Marxist/socialist attempt to change in a dramatic way the existing distribution of rewards in society is going to create a category of losers who possess talents needed at home but marketable elsewhere; a regime that was committed to political freedom would find itself seriously restricted by this version of the brain drain. Once again, the long-term proposition that change was in everyone's interest would be in conflict with medium-term realities and the absence of a firm basis within Marxist thought for categories such as rights and duties would make itself felt.

Conclusion

The main theme of this chapter has been that the ethical issues raised by migration do not easily fit within a Marxist framework. A materialist account of the reasons why people move from one location to another must be based on the determining notion of a mode of production. The individual and the community are categories without transcendent meaning; they take their shape from the material conditions that prevail, and cannot be seen as bearers of rights. Persons are defined politically as members of a class rather than as members of a community that is cross-class or non-class in composition. In so far as it makes sense to think of there being ethical imperatives within a materialist conception of social life, then these imperatives must cluster around the task of overthrowing capitalism and replacing it by socialism/communism. As such, moral reasoning is consequentialist, judging action according to its ultimate consequences. The post-revolutionary end state will be one in which the notion of nationality will disappear, and although the notion of rights will still be inappropriate this will be because of the absence of those restrictions of human freedoms which have caused bourgeois writers to look to the notions of rights in the first place.

As has been demonstrated, this position presents real problems for the actual examination of migration issues largely because it assumes away most of the actual problems experienced by migrant communities and host communities. Potential contradictions exist between the interests of hosts and migrants, states and individuals and the resolution of these contradictions within a Marxist framework is fraught with problems. A purely consequentialist approach might mean the abandonment of the universalist perspective that is inherent to the Marxist vision of the future, and yet this cosmopolitanism cannot be defended by reference to rights which are themselves, from a Marxist framework, indefensible. The abandonment of universalism via such notions as 'socialism in one country' has lead into Stalinism, but the alternative stress on legally enforceable rights and duties seems equally as distant from the materialist premises of Marxism as Stalinism is from Marxism's claim to provide a route to human liberation.

There seems no answer to this dilemma from within a Marxist framework. As with the wider issue of Marxism and international ethics, the juxtaposition of Marxism and migration poses questions in both directions, but in particular from the direction of the adequacy of Marxist conceptions of society. Marxist notions of the individual and the community are easy to defend on optimistic assumptions about the real relationship between the two, more problematic when these assumptions come under pressure. Migration is one of the most important sources of such pressure.

Notes

1. Leszek Kolakowski, *Main Currents of Marxism, Vol. I, The Founders, Vol. II, The Golden Age, Vol. III, The Breakdown* (Oxford: Clarendon Press, 1978).
2. Kolakowski, *Main Currents of Marxism, Vol. III*; Stephen White and Alex Pravda, eds., *Ideology and Soviet Politics* (London: Macmillan, 1988).
3. See, e.g., Walter Goldfrank, ed., *The World System of Capitalism: Past and Present* (Beverly Hills: Sage, 1979).
4. Parry Anderson, *Considerations on Western Marxism* (London: New Left Books, 1976); New Left Review, ed., *Western Marxism: A Critical Reader* (London: New Left Books, 1977).
5. Friedrich Engels, *Anti-Duhring: Herr Eugen Duhring's Revolution in Science* (Moscow: Progress Publishers, 1947).
6. David McLellan, ed., *Karl Marx: Selected Writings* (Oxford: Oxford University Press, 1977).
7. Eugene Kamenka, *Marxism and Ethics* (London: Macmillan, 1969).
8. McLellan, *Karl Marx*; Karl Marx, *Grundrisse: Foundations of the Critique of Political Economy (Rough Draft)* (Harmondsworth: Penguin, 1973).
9. Stephen Lukes, *Marxism and Morality* (Oxford: Oxford University Press, 1985).
10. McLellan, *Karl Marx*; Karl Marx, *Capital: A Critique of Political Economy*, vol. I (Harmondsworth: Penguin, 1976).
11. R. N. Berki, "On Marxian Thought and the Problems of International Relations," *World Politics*, 24 October 1971, 1.
12. Michael Walzer, *Spheres of Justice: A Defence of Pluralism and Equality* (Oxford: Martin Robertson, 1983). See also Peter G. Brown and Henry Shue, *Boundaries: Natural Autonomy and its Limits* (Totowa, N.J.: Rowman & Littlefield, 1981); Alan Dowty, *Closed Borders: The Contemporary Assault on Freedom of Movement* (New Haven, Conn.: Yale University Press, 1987).
13. Marx, *Capital*; Ernest Mandel, *Late Capitalism* (London: Verso, 1978).
14. Stephen Castles and Godula Kosack, *Immigrant Workers and Class Structure in Western Europe* (Oxford: Oxford University Press, 1973).
15. Michael C. Howard and John E. King, *The Political Economy of Marx* (London: Longman, 1975).
16. See Manuel Castells, "Immigrant Workers and Class Struggle in Advanced Capitalism: The Western European Experience," in R. Cohen, P. Claus, W. Gutkind, P. Brazier, eds., *Peasants and Proletarians: The Struggles of Third World Workers* (New York: Monthly Review Press, 1979).
17. Marx, *Capital*.
18. Alejandro Portes and John Walton, *Labour, Class and the International System* (New York: Academic Press, 1981); Immanuel Wallerstein, ed., *Labour in the World Social Structure* (Beverly Hills: Sage, 1983).
19. Robin Cohen, *The New Helots: Migrants in the International Division of Labour* (Aldershot: Gower, 1987).
20. F. Frobel, J. Heinrichs and O. Kreye, *The New International Division of Labour* (Cambridge: Cambridge University Press, 1980).

21. See, e.g., John Berger and Jacob Mohr, *A Seventh Man* (Harmondsworth: Penguin, 1975).
22. Louis Althusser, *Reading Capital* (London: New Left Books, 1970).
23. Castells, "Immigrant Workers. . . ."
24. McLellan, *Karl Marx.*
25. G. A. Cohen, *Karl Marx's Theory of History: A Defence* (Oxford: Oxford University Press, 1979).
26. B. Warren, *Imperialism: Pioneer of Capitalism* (London: Verso, 1980).
27. Castells, "Immigrant Workers," p. 363.
28. Berger and Mohr, *A Seventh Man*, p. 146.
29. Ronald Munck, *The Difficult Dialogue: Marxism and Nationalism* (London: Zed Books, 1986).
30. Friedrich Engels, *The Condition of the Working Class in England* (London: Grafton Books, 1969).
31. Friedrich Engels and Karl Marx, *The German Ideology* (1846) and *The Communist Manifesto* (1848).
32. Engels, *The Condition of the Working Class in England*, 1969, pp. 66, 109, 125.
33. Ibid.
34. Ibid., p. 153.
35. Ibid.
36. Karl Marx and Friedrich Engels, *Selected Correspondence* (Moscow, Progress Publishers, 1975).
37. Ibid.
38. Castles and Kosack, *Immigrant Workers and Class Structure in Western Europe*, 1973.
39. Cohen, *The New Helots.*
40. Peter J. Brain, Rhonda L. Smith and Gerard P. Schuyers, *Population, Immigration and the Australian Economy* (London: Croom Helm, 1979).
41. H. J. Simons and R. E. Simons, *Class and Colour in South Africa 1850–1950* (Harmondsworth: Penguin, 1969).
42. Dowty, *Closed Borders.*
43. Ibid., p. 116.

——— 10 ———

Transnational migration of money and capital – a Marxist perspective

Kurt Hübner

The Marxian theory of capitalism is, in essence, a theory of a money-based, private, decentralized economy. Such an economy cannot conceivably develop – domestically, much less internationally – without a credit system or its functional equivalent.

'Taken as an integrated whole', says political-geographer David Harvey, summarizing the dispersed and unsystematic Marxian literature on the subject, 'the credit system may be viewed as a kind of central nervous system through which the overall circulation of capital is coordinated.' Elaborating, he goes on to add that:

- It permits the reallocation of money capital to and from activities, firms, sectors, regions and countries.
- It promotes the dovetailing of diverse activities, a burgeoning division of labour and a reduction in turnover times.
- It facilitates the equalization of the profit rate and arbitrates between the forces making for centralization and decentralization of capital.
- It helps coordinate the relations between flows of fixed and circulating capital.
- The interest rate discounts present uses against future requirements while forms of fictitious capital link current money capital flows with the anticipation of future fruits of labour.[1]

Money is made available in the form of credits through a specific sector of the capitalist economy – the banking system – which from the very start operated on a notably far-reaching, international scale. In the world economy, just as in the national economy, banks are not merely credit brokers. They also issue credits which themselves become accepted as a medium of exchange. When creating such 'credit money' *ex nihilo* bankers are anticipating production which will only be realized sometime in the future. In this way banks and the credit-money which they create can act as levers to the expansion of capital.

The credit system can only serve these purposes though when the free mobility of money and capital – both within national economies and between them – is guaranteed. Within Marxian theory, this mobility is seen as indispensable for capitalist development tendencies to unravel consistently. Arguably, historical developmental processes concur in calling for free mobility of this sort as well.

The expansion of capital, both in space and in value, is expedited by a modern credit system. But it is, of course, now encountering some important limits. These limits to global accumulation have arisen through the institutional separation of the spheres of politics and of economics which characterizes modern capitalism. The most common basis of this separation at the national level is private property. The bourgeois state owes its origins to the need, dictated by the existence of private property, to secure and protect the owners of that property.

On the global level, this separation is manifested in the existence of a multitude of nation-states within the world economy dedicated to economic accumulation and the valorization of capital. This separation is in conflict with itself, inasmuch as political and economic actions are differentiated. While the political space is carved up into many nation-states and political sovereignty is determined by territorial borders the economic space is essentially global. The world market transcends national boundaries. The contradictions of global accumulation and valorization are merely reproduced in the more specific movements of capital within national boundaries.

The world market and the nation-state can most adequately be conceptualized as two *functional spaces* within the same *territorial space*. To persist with the spatial analogy, the nation-state and the world market can be said simply to have different ranges. The functional space of the nation-state is steered by a historical (and an accordingly specific) mode of socio-political regulation, which is itself an expression of the national socio-political order. This mode of regulation embraces various forms of state intervention: in the allocation and distribution of value and product, in the material–technical conditions of production, in the form of industrial relations and in the certification and educational systems. Regulation proceeds, along these lines, by means of power and justice, money and ideology.

The contrasting functional space of the world market is generally determined by the economic principle of the 'law of value'.[2] In terms of the world market, social relationships can be summed up as economic accumulation regimes, interacting with each other by means of the exchange of values in the form of money. In addition to the circulation of money – capital in commodity form – there is also international movement of productive and interest-bearing capital.

The economic integration of all of these global movements taken together constitutes the measuring rod for national economic worth. A nation's standing in this international competition fixes its present wealth (its established accumulation) and its future prospects (its chances of national development). In this sense, one truly can speak of *Sachzwang Weltmarkt* – a dictatorship of world market.[3]

At the same time the global accumulation process confronts various national regimes of economic accumulation and national modes of sociopolitical regulation, which also serve to help or hinder the penetration process. Economically, these national structures take the form of specific national moneys. Within the functional space of the world economy, there exist various national currencies; and every economic transaction across state boundaries involves conversion of one national money into another. These currency conversions take place in foreign exchange markets, which are tied in turn to various international currency systems.

World economic competition is not therefore characterized by a genuine, direct comparison of values. The very processes by which comparisons are made themselves embrace effects derived from national regulatory structures. Included in this are various forms of national fiscal and monetary, structural and technology policies. Thus, the outcome of international economic competition will be settled by political as well as by purely economic means.

In examining how nations (or, rather, various pockets of national capital) are integrated into the world economy, it is clear that differing sociohistorical 'conditions of access' are such as to ensure that neither quantitatively nor qualitatively are all integrated in one and the same way. In terms of world-system theory, the capitalist world economy is characterized by notions of 'centre', 'semi-periphery' and 'periphery' – and the correlative asymmetries in power. This asymmetry is manifest in, among other things, the international hierarchy of national currencies.

The emerging economic configuration is embedded in an 'international mode of regulation', which for a certain period of time safeguards the reproduction of global processes of accumulation and valorization.[4] Such international modes of regulation do not substitute for the national ones; rather, they play more of a coordinating function. In this sense, the world market is not only a place of *economic reproduction*. It is also a place of *political regulation*, conveyed by particular institutions by specific means.

Today these institutions include the International Monetary Fund (IMF), the World Bank and the General Agreement on Tariffs and Trade (GATT), along with structural networks such as the international money and credit system. Historically, decisive significance attached to the role of a hegemonic power which attempted to regulate the global reproduction process. In this context the central medium of regulation was the national currency of the hegemonic nation. When international liquidity was available, it functioned as 'world money' to steer the international circulation processes and served, ultimately, as a medium for international debt contracts.[5]

The vital role of world money in these respects already appears in the writings of Marx himself.[6] He postulated that money on the world market would shed its local outward shape, and that the expression of common social wealth would again come to the fore. For Marx and the money system of his time world money was obliged to take the form of gold: that is how international forms of capital circulation were then conveyed. Labour from different countries should in that case be represented by a certain amount of gold at any given time. Relative values of national currencies would then correspond to the relative quanta of labour expended within those nations – thus extending the 'law of value' to the world market.

Today the decisive functions of money are served by national currencies and on the world market by an international money.[7] Certainly, this world money is not concretely institutionalized, as in the case of gold. Instead, it has to prove itself in competition with other national currencies. The quality of national currency and of world money is ultimately settled in international foreign exchange markets. Transactions there reflect not only international commodity trading but also the internationalization of productive investments, which similarly require conversion from one currency into another. They can also reflect arbitrage, speculation and hedging aimed at exploiting (or insuring against) fluctuations in foreign exchange rates or differentials in interest rates.

The steering function of a hegemonic nation is not limited to the supply of an international means of circulation. In the context of the asymmetrical world market, characterized as it is by national deficits and surpluses of trade, there is also an urgent need for a supply of international liquidity. The hegemonic nation (which must by definition be a 'surplus' country) recycles its currency surplus in the form of capital exports to countries with trade deficits. Deficit countries are in this way enabled to settle their balance-of-payments accounts without resorting to currency devaluation or to reducing their currency reserves.

We must avoid a functionalist fallacy, at this point. The allocation of international liquidity may sometimes arise from the activities of nation-states or supranational institutions, but it need not. It may be purely private actors who determine the supply of international liquidity. Such private direct investment (credit, for example) is contingent upon specific profitability calculations which take no account of the constellation of the national balances of payments. Expected profits, market strategies and interest rates alone shape those decisions.

The resulting international creditor–debtor relationships are from the point of view of world economic reproduction absolutely functional none the less. What is more, they are substantially legitimate:

> The justice of the transactions between agents of production rests on the fact that these arise as natural consequences out of the production relationships. The juristic forms in which these economic transactions appear as willful acts of the parties concerned, as expressions of their common will and as contracts that may be enforced by law against some individual party, cannot, being mere forms, determine this content. They merely express it. This content is just whenever it corresponds, is appropriate, to the mode of production. It is unjust whenever it contradicts that mode. Slavery on the basis of capitalist production is unjust; likewise fraud in the quality of commodities.[8]

The perceived 'justice' of economic transactions, as seen from this systemic perspective, does not necessarily accord with the criteria of individual participants in the process, however. From the point of view of a nation-state the transnational migration of money and capital can be viewed differently. National accumulations will be decreased with the export of productive capital and increased with its import. In the case of direct investment abroad, a one-time export of a fixed amount of funds will yield repeated dividends in terms of profits to be repatriated; the general tendency is hence towards improvement in the current account balance of, and an increase in economic accumulation in, the investor country. Through a foreign credit loan countries (or, rather, national capital) can be extended over and above the limits of their national financial markets; and they can resort to bolstering the internal accumulation process using international savings.

If, however, consumption or non-productive activities are financed with these credits, then this will produce a burden on the recipient's balance of payments. Similar effects arise from transactions undertaken by wealthholders, oriented towards changes in exchange rates, differential interest rates and liquidity preferences. These transactions are generally short-term and contribute substantially (or would, in a pure market system, anyway) to the volatility of interest and exchange rates. To the extent that such transactions are prevalent, real (i.e. productive) economic processes can be blocked or at least hindered.

Limits on foreign debt, in the form of various financial credits, are determined solely by the respective national capacities of payment and of transfer. In every credit relation, credit must, from the point of view of the debtor, be such that interest and principal payments may be financed from the flow of earnings. That is the so-called 'contributory problem', put to the debtor in every credit relation. The solution to that problem is endangered whenever: (a) the credit is used unproductively; (b) the credit-financed investment project does not live up to expectations; (c) interest charges go up drastically during the term of the credit, thus undermining the profitability of the project.

Beyond all those more specific problems, one further factor remains the same for all international credit relations. The debt-service sums raised domestically must be transferred internationally in the form of international currency. The capacity to effect that transfer is determined, macroeconomically, by the structure of the current account. It depends upon there being a surplus in the current account which is at least equal to the sum of debt service, even after costs of imported commodities and of services necessary for reproduction have been deducted.

In foreign debt relationships there naturally are limits on creditors as well as on debtors. Where creditors are private banks they clearly depend on the steady servicing of credits: the interest payments represent their main source of income; and if interest payments are repudiated, then the banks as private profit organizations would themselves falter. Banks here serve as a domestic analogue to the international creditor–debtor relation, inasmuch as possibilities of credit creation there too depend upon deposits of economic actors who demand interest payments in exchange for the loan of their money.

International credit relations pose the threat of another more distinctive sort of potential crisis, however. Because credits must be serviced in international currency the credit contracts are locked into a kind of 'insecurity gap'. There are various changes in the international economic constellation – changes in commodity prices, currency prices or interest rates, quantities produced, or whatever – which are beyond the influence of either debtors or creditors but which can none the less reduce or even eradicate the surplus of currency, generating a general crisis of credit internationally.[9]

To make these rather general statements more concrete, consider the case of the international debt crisis of the 1980s. What were the reasons for this? One reason was that in spite of more flexible regimes since the early 1970s there has been an increasing polarization of national current accounts, leading to an extremely high demand for shifts of capital from surplus to deficit countries. One pole comprises Japan and the Federal Republic of Germany (FRG), which were able to realize huge surpluses in their current accounts; the other pole consists mainly of the countries of the Third World, together with the United States.[10]

This polarization is explained, above all else, by different national positions in the international economic competitive hierarchy. This is especially true for the countries of the Third World. But it is also true for the United States. Since the early 1980s it has been obvious that the United States had lost its superior competitive position relative to Japan, the FRG, and even a number of newly industrialized countries (NICs). The result has been a deficit in the US trade balance of some $750 billion. The drastic overvaluation of the dollar during the early years of the Reagan Administration explains only a minor part of this deficit. Various empirical studies attribute the deficit much more to the fact that many sectors of American industry fell out of the international restructuring race.[11] The net import of capital reflects this declining international competitiveness of US industry, making the United States into the biggest debtor in the capitalist world economy.

The group of Third World countries, on the other hand, owe their deficit to a strategy of *indebted industrialization*, wherein high imports of capital goods and consumer goods were financed by importing capital. In the early and mid-1970s, this was a highly rational strategy: the long-term real interest rates in the international money and capital markets were extremely low (and sometimes even negative) due to the large supply of interest-seeking money from OPEC countries and the private sectors of the advanced capitalist countries.

In this phase of development, private enterprises invested surplus liquidity in international money and credit markets, even when the interest rates were comparatively low – indicating a high degree of uncertainty about future accumulation strategies, and therefore a high degree of liquidity preference. This liquidity was demanded first of all by less-developed countries (LDCs) without oil reserves in order to pay climbing oil bills and, of course, to meet the rising demand for capital goods and new technologies. The total external debt of Third World countries (and also the countries of the socialist camp), which was financed by private banks, grew rapidly in the course of the early 1970s.[12] In a second phase, starting in the early 1980s, drastically changed economic conditions in the world markets combined with high interest rates and amortization caused the current account of this group actually to turn negative.

Orthodox analyses blame rising interest rates on the US Federal Reserve Board (the Fed) fighting inflation since the late 1970s. Recall, though, that the Fed has empirically proven unable to supervise or monitor loans, unable to regulate the growing competition among commercial banks, thrift institutions and investment banks, and unable to control the widespread financial innovations that have occurred. In the light of such facts it seems implausible that monetary authority could prove any more effective in controlling the behaviour of the interest rate.[13]

We are now operating in a situation where conventional extrapolations of economic decisions are destroyed and the global current account structure generates a high demand for international credit. In such a situation the interest rate is largely market-determined. High demand for credit on the part of illiquid Third World countries and the United States, together with rapid changes in portfolio decisions, are what boosted the interest rate to new heights in the early 1980s.

The consequences for the indebted countries has been dramatic. As the IMF summarizes the situation:

> High interest rates on world financial markets, together with the increased share of debt [which is] subject to variable rates, contributed to a further increase in the average interest rate on external debt, which reached almost 10 percent. At the same time, the value of exports and GDP of the capital-importing countries stagnated under the impact of the world recession. As a result, debt and debt service ratios rose substantially, while the large volume of short-term debt relative to export earnings contributed to an increasing incidence of liquidity problems, as creditors became reluctant to roll over their short-term commitments to a number of countries.[14]

The growing external financing requirements of debtor countries were further increased by the huge outflows of domestic capital fleeing disastrous internal economic development or simply looking for 'safe havens' for concealing wealth. In any event, the creditization of structural current account deficits became a lucrative activity within the private banking systems, which underwent rapid transnationalization since the 1970s.

This development involves an important change in the international mode of regulation. As an agency supplying deficit countries with international liquidity, the IMF has been supplanted by private banks, which are now the ones who set the needed volume of international credit in motion. The IMF has become, in effect, the lender of last resort to LDCs if private markets are unwilling to lend or to accept the risks involved. With the open outbreak of the international debt crisis in 1982 the IMF accepted its new role of the 'safeguard of the international debt economy', acting as the fire brigade in case of debtor insolvency.

The international debt crisis, triggered by the Mexican repudiation of debt payments in 1982, is not the mere result of overbanking and macroeconomic policy failures on the part of the debtor countries. It has to be seen as the result of combined crises: a crisis of national development models in the Third World, an accumulation crisis of the global economy and a crisis of US hegemony.[15]

The outbreak of the international debt crisis was, at root, due to the emergence of the United States as the largest capital importer of the world market. That inflow of capital could only be accomplished by a more-than-proportional rise in US interest rates, relative to those of its competitors. This strengthening of existing market tendencies was neatly accomplished by the Fed. The result was a 'crowding out' of the Third

World countries and the origin of a crisis of liquidity, which was rapidly transformed into a persisting crisis of solvency. National defaults have only been evaded by rescue operations and rigid austerity programmes imposed by the IMF and the World Bank.

What has happened since 1982 could be alternatively described in the following terms. Analytically, what has happened is that the United States has used its remaining seigniorage as a political resource to stabilize its regime of economic accumulation, to the disadvantage of the indebted countries of the Third World. Such results of world market transactions do not measure up particularly well against the self-proclaimed criteria of capitalism.

Notes

1. David Harvey, *The Limits to Capital* (Oxford: Basil Blackwell, 1982), p. 284.
2. For more detail, see E. Altvater, *Sachzwang Weltmarkt: Verschuldungskrise, blockierte industrialisierung, ökologische Gefährdung – der Fall Brasilien* (Hamburg: VSA Verlag, 1987), pp. 79ff.
3. See Altvater, *Sachzwang Weltmarkt*.
4. This thesis is by no means undisputed in Marxist discussions. Lipietz, for example, explicitly rejects the term 'world regime of regulation', saying, 'The complementarities and antagonisms that exist between national economies remain unstable, constituting little more than partial and random *configurations*' (A. Lipietz, *Mirages and Miracles* (London: Verso, 1987), p. 41). Not only the theorem of hegemonic stability and international regime has been called into question; so too has the need for regulative structures in world economy. Recall the classicists' discussion of the gold standard as an international currency system, as a mechanism for steering the international division of labour.
5. Compare to that E. Altvater and K. Hübner, "The End of the American Empire? Monetary and Real Apects of the United States' Hegemonial Crisis," *Political Regulation in the Great Crisis*, ed. W. Väth (Berlin: Sigma, 1989), pp. 43–70.
6. Karl Marx, *Capital* (London: Progress Publishers, 1970), vol. 1, pp. 156ff.
7. See G. Reuten, "The Monetary Expression of Value and the Credit System: A Value-Form Theoretic Outline," *Capital & Class*, no. 35 (1988), pp. 121–41.
8. Karl Marx, *Capital* (New York: International Publisher, 1976), vol. 3, pp. 339ff.
9. See M. H. Wolfson, *Financial Crisis: Understanding the Postwar U.S. Experience* (Armonk, N.Y.: M. E. Sharpe, 1986).
10. For just one example, the OECD estimates that over 80 per cent of the $161 billion deficit in the 1987 US current account was financed by Japan ($87 billion) and the FRG ($44 billion). See Organisation for Economic Co-operation and Development (OECD), *Economic Outlook* (June 1988).

11. See, e.g., the so-called Cuomo Report, *A New American Formula for a Strong Economy* (New York: Simon and Schuster, 1987).
12. During the ten-year period 1973–82 external debt grew at a compound annual rate of 20.5 per cent, while the value of exports grew by 16 per cent and nominal GDP by 12.5 per cent. See IMF, *World Economic Outlook* (Washington, D.C.: IMF, 1986), p. 87.
13. L. Rapping, *International Reorganization and American Economic Policy* (Hemel Hempstead: Harvester Wheatsheaf, 1988), p. 115.
14. IMF, *World Economic Outlook*, p. 87.
15. See E. Altvater and K. Hübner, "Ursachen und Verlauf der internationalen Schuldenkrise," *Die Armut der Nationen: Ein Handbuch zur Schuldenkrise von Argentinien bis Zaire*, ed. E. Altvater, K. Hübner, J. Lorentzen and R. Rojas (Berlin: Rotbuch Verlag, 1987), pp. 14ff.

11

Commentary: Citizenship exploitation, unequal exchange and the breakdown of popular sovereignty

Philippe Van Parijs

The right attitude towards such bulky artefacts as the Marxist tradition is not one of dutiful conservation but of ruthless recycling. There is nothing wrong, therefore, in chopping up unwieldy lumps, in discarding stultifying mental pollutants, in using the latest intellectual technology to reshape – sometimes beyond recognition – dislocated parts, nor in letting the rest rot into oblivion. This is, at any rate, the attitude I shall adopt, both in discussing Chris Brown's and Kurt Hübner's chapters, and in widening the landscape beyond the aspects of the Marxist heritage on which they have focused their attention.

Four 'Marxist' stances

Is it ever legitimate to restrict the transnational mobility of people and money? Faced with this sort of question, it is possible to find ammunition in the Marxist tradition to substantiate four distinct – indeed mutually exclusive – stances.

1. The task and achievement of Marxism is to unveil the laws of history. This provides no room whatever for raising ought-questions or engaging in ethical debates. As Marx himself puts it in a famous passage, notions of right and wrong merely reflect the current mode of production. They do not provide standards for judging it. True, this does not prevent a Marxist from talking about the migration of people and money, nor indeed from asking whether such migration is 'necessary'. But he will then be asserting, for example, that immigration was needed to satisfy metropolitan capitalism's needs for additional labour power, or that capital exports serve the 'function' of counteracting the tendency for the

rate of profit to fall. Both Brown and Hübner briefly mention this first approach, but neither believes, obviously, that much time should be wasted on it. Rightly so.

2. There *is* room for ought-questions, but at the most basic level, there is *no specifically Marxist answer*. For Marxism – or whatever there is in Marxism that is still usable – is not a normative system, but an analytical framework. When discussing matters such as the migration of people and money, therefore, Marxists – such as Hübner in the bulk of his chapter – do have policy recommendations to make on the basis of an analysis that can claim to bear some relation to Marx's admittedly sketchy remarks on the subject. But these recommendations take for granted policy objectives that are no different from those of a 'global realist' for example – as when Hübner argues that some solution must be found to the current debt crisis.

3. There *is* room for ought questions, and there *is* a specifically Marxist answer to them: we ought to fight for a socialist revolution, itself a precondition for the ultimate achievement of full communism. But on such short- or medium-term issues as the migration of people and capital, ethical considerations are *trumped by instrumental considerations*. Whether a claim, an action, a policy is right or wrong is entirely determined by whether it helps society along towards the socialist revolution, for example by strengthening working-class solidarity. As several quotations adduced by Brown neatly illustrate, appeals to the *raison de classe* have here displaced any claim to fairness or morality.

4. Lastly, there *is* room for ought questions, and there *is* a specifically Marxist answer to them: socialism leading to communism. Moreover, the same ethical considerations which warrant the choice of this long-term aim *also provide guidance for the ethical discussion of more immediate issues* such as migration of people and money.

In the remainder of this chapter I shall say no more about the first stance, because I believe it is absurd, nor about the second stance, because it does not construe Marxism as an ethical tradition. I shall hardly say more about the third stance, because I agree with Brown that it is blatantly untenable. But the reason why it is blatantly untenable, is not that it is purely consequentialist – global utilitarianism might be untenable, but not blatantly so – nor that there is an inconsistency between the cosmopolitan commitment of people favouring universal socialism and the narrowly nationalistic recommendations often required by the tough-minded pursuit of socialism in one country: *reculer pour mieux sauter* is part of the stock and trade of strategic thinking. What is disturbing about this third stance at work is rather, more specifically, that it ruthlessly justifies sacrificing the interests of any number of current proletarians – for example, the potential Irish immigrants who should be kept out if the solidarity of the English working class is to be salvaged – for the sake of a hypothetical future event the fruits of which none of them is likely ever to enjoy.[1]

It is thus on the fourth stance – left unexplored by both Brown and Hübner – that I shall concentrate in the rest of this chapter, both because it leads most naturally to connections with the other traditions discussed in this volume and because I find it more congenial than the first three. The fact that this fourth stance does not square with some, or even most of what Marx had to say on the subject, and hence that it may not be 'recognizably Marxist', is of decisive importance to the exeget, but of hardly any interest to the recycler. For one to be entitled to call Marxism what is being recycled, it is enough that some aspect of some self-described Marxist tradition serves as one major source of inspiration. This condition, I believe, is uncontroversially fulfilled in the following discussion.

Exploitation

Among Marxist notions with ethical connotations exploitation is second to none in either theoretical or practical prominence. According to the conventional definition a group of people *is exploited* (*exploits*) if it contributes more (less) labour value – i.e. socially necessary labour – to production than it appropriates – or, more generally, than it can (must) appropriate – through its income. The notion of labour value which plays a central role in this definition raises a number of serious conceptual difficulties which have jettisoned the respectability of the conventional notion of exploitation. This is one of the reasons why John Roemer has undertaken to provide an alternative definition that would make no use whatever of the notion of value.[2] Another reason is that the alternative definition seems to him to capture better the ethical intuition behind the notion, which makes it particularly relevant to our present purposes.

Roemer calls his definition the 'property-relations definition' of exploitation and characterizes it in game-theoretical terms. No game theory is required, however, to understand the intuition underlying it. A group is *capitalistically exploited* (*capitalistically exploits*) on Roemer's definition if it would be better off (worse off), other things remaining unchanged, if wealth were equalized. There is capitalist exploitation, in other words, if the unequal distribution of the means of production or, more generally, of alienable wealth causally affects the distribution of income or, more generally, of material welfare. This notion can easily be extended beyond the case of capitalist exploitation by considering other types of assets. Roemer speaks of *feudal exploitation* to refer to the effect on income distribution of the fact that some people own or partly own other people. And he speaks of *socialist exploitation* to refer to the income-distributive effect of the unequal distribution of skills. The fundamental Marxist ethical imperative then consists in abolishing in turn these various forms of exploitation – first feudal, next capitalist, finally socialist. There is no reason, however, why the list should stop here: any other factor that affects the distribution of material welfare can in principle be used to define a new dimension of exploitation.[3]

This takes us straight to the heart of our subject. In a borderless and frictionless world market economy one may be able to argue that only endowments in wealth and skills will affect the equilibrium distribution of rewards. But if capital is less than perfectly mobile, and if people are not free to move to the areas where job prospects and wage rates are highest, then a third type of asset may affect the distribution of income more powerfully than wealth and skills. Depending on which country you are a citizen (or, sometimes, just a resident) of, your expected income can vary dramatically. I shall accordingly say that a group is *citizenship-exploited* (a *citizenship-exploiter*) if its expected income would go up (down) in the event that citizenship were equalized, i.e. if no special prerogative were attached to being a citizen of any particular country. Like feudal exploitation citizenship exploitation pulls the distribution of income away from what it would be under pure market conditions, where only productive assets (wealth and skills) elicit differential rewards.[4] The Marxist ethical imperative requires that this form of exploitation too should be abolished. This generates at least a prima facie presumption in favour of anything that erodes the differential advantages attached to citizenship, most obviously the free movement of both people and capital.

Let us now sharpen this conclusion by briefly scrutinizing the widely used notion of 'unequal exchange'. Drawing more or less explicitly on Marx's elliptic remarks about the 'commercial exploitation of poor countries by rich countries', various authors have tried to analyze the relationship between developed and less-developed countries as a systematically unequal exchange of goods.[5] This may conceivably be due, first of all, to systematically asymmetric *departures from perfectly competitive conditions*[6] If metropolitan firms can take advantage of monopolistic or monopsonic positions to a larger extent than peripheral firms, the true value of goods travelling from the periphery to the centre will systematically exceed that of the centre-produced goods against which they are being traded. It is debatable whether such asymmetry is an intrinsic feature of the relation between rich and poor countries. It is one, in any case, which theoreticians of unequal exchange have tended to assume away by postulating perfect competition.

On a second interpretation, the inequality in the exchange derives from *unequal capital intensities*. Take a situation in which international trade is perfectly competitive, while capital and labour are not free to move across borders. The countries with a higher (lower) capital/labour ratio will then maximize their income by specializing in more capital-intensive (labour-intensive) production, and the equilibrium prices will be such that the socially necessary labour incorporated in the goods imported by the capital-rich country will exceed that incorporated in the goods it exports. The control over more dead labour makes it possible for one country to appropriate through competitive trade more labour value than it gives away, i.e. to exploit its trading partner according the conventional definition recalled in the previous section.[7] Arguably, this second picture offers a somewhat better approximation of what is actually going on between rich and poor countries, even though one must bear in mind that for present purposes natural resources must be assimilated to capital. One essential feature of the picture, however, is the lack of free movement for labour and capital, a feature explicitly ruled out in standard statements of the theory of 'unequal exchange'.

This leads to a third interpretation, where *differences in wage levels* are given the key role. In Arghiri Emmanuel's original formulation, capital is assumed to move freely across borders in such a way that the rate of profit tends to be equal all over the world.[8] Since capital is perfectly mobile, one can no longer expect rich countries to systematically specialize in capital-intensive activities, and poor countries in labour-intensive activities. Labour, however, is not similarly mobile, and this lack of mobility – so Emmanuel believes – makes it possible to have very different wages for equally productive labour. Competitive trade with unequal wages is bound to generate unequal exchange, now understood as departure from the exchange of goods embodying equally precious bundle of factors, not necessarily from the exchange of equal amounts of socially necessary labour.

Unfortunately, this third interpretation is inconsistent. As Roemer has neatly shown, there is a strict isomorphism, in a frictionless world, between capital mobility and labour mobility.[9] Whether you let capital free to move and confine labour within closed borders, or free labour and confine capital, in *either* case *both* the rate of profit and the wage rate will be equal at equilibrium all over the world. In this sense, the international capital market and the international labour market are perfect substitutes, functional equivalents. The real world, of course, is far from frictionless in the required sense. In particular, movement of capital and labour is not fully determined by a straightforward maximization of expected profits or wages. But as frictions enter the picture and hinder either the free migration of money or the free migration of people, *both* the tendency towards a uniform rate of profit and the tendency towards a uniform wage rate are attenuated.

In this light, Emmanuel's assumption of perfect capital mobility and
equal rates of profit appears plainly inconsistent with his assumption of
unequal wages. Yet there is one way of reconstructing the analysis so
as to restore consistency. It consists in assuming – contrary to Emmanuel's
own explicit statements – that differences in wage levels are matched by
differences in labour productivity.[10] There is then no tension left between
equal profit rates and unequal wages. Productivity differences need not be
due to 'intrinsic' features of the various countries' labour power. They may
be related to physical circumstances (the fertility of the soil, the climate) or
to cultural conditions (the work ethic, the relation to time) which account
for the fact that the 'same' labour power is unequally productive in
different contexts. (There may or may not be in addition an 'efficiency-
wage' positive feedback: those who get lesser wages because they are less
productive are also less productive because of the poorer living conditions
under which they have to live because of their lesser wages.) Such differences are compatible with perfect capital mobility, and also with 'open
borders' for labour, but not with perfect labour mobility: something must
durably prevent workers from taking advantage of the open borders, by
moving to places where physical and cultural conditions make for both
higher productivity and higher wages. This may simply be the fact that
wages are not the only thing in the world they care about, and that
attachment to their native place and culture may make them forgo a
significantly higher money income.

If differences in wages match differences in productivity, one can safely
predict that with a given capital content more labour will be embodied in
the goods exported by the poor countries than in the goods against which
they are traded at competitive prices. But not only does this 'unequal
exchange' fail to qualify as an exchange of unequal amounts of labour
value: less productive labour corresponds to a lesser amount of socially
necessary labour. It can no longer be construed either as an exchange of
goods embodying unequal amounts of precious factors: less productive
labour is economically less precious than more productive labour. Poor
countries, therefore, are not cheated by 'unequal exchange' under this
third interpretation (appropriately reconstructed). It is not only the case
that poor countries gain (in welfare terms) from this exchange, possibly
more than their trading partners; that making the exchange more 'equal'
in terms of amounts of embodied labour may be counterproductive, as rich
countries may find it advantageous to turn to the next best home-produced
substitute; but also that making the exchange more 'equal' in this sense
would make it less fair on any sensible evaluation of what is being
exchanged.[11]

It does not follow, of course, that there is no unfairness associated to the
coexistence of high- and low-wage countries. But this unfairness is best

expressed not as unfair exchange or commercial exploitation between the two sets of countries, but rather as an unequal distribution of assets, here of whatever it is that accounts for the systematic differences in labour productivities.

What are the implications of this rather abstract exercise prompted by the so-called theory of 'unequal exchange' for the Marxcist standpoint on the transnational migration of people and money. First, if citizenship exploitation is defined in terms of job prospects and wage levels (for people with a given productivity), we have seen that in a 'frictionless' world economy it could be abolished by *either* the opening of borders to the migration of money, *or* the opening of all borders to the migration of people. Now, it has often been pointed out (e.g. in the chapters by Joseph Carens and James Woodward) that a massive uprooting of people under the pressure of economic necessity does not sound like a terribly clever way of attempting to deal with international economic inequalities. The good news encapsulated in Roemer's isomorphism is that at least in a 'friction-less' economy there is no need for this painful process because there is a perfect substitute for it. This is not a massive altruistic transfer of resources in the form of 'development aid', but the unconstrained movement of money in search of higher profits. This sounds particularly good news today, as we keep hearing that money is becoming increasingly slippery and that its movements are ever harder to control (see e.g. Susan Strange's chapter), so that – whether we like it or not – borders are more open than ever to the flowing of money.

In the real world, 'frictions' will of course prevent capital movements from getting rid of citizenship exploitation altogether. Paramount among them is the 'political risk' associated with investment in 'unstable' countries. Lower equilibrium wage rates will prevail in those countries in which firms will need a higher rate of profit or lenders a higher rate of interest to offset the risk of expropriation, destruction, labour unrest, default, etc. But as more 'artificial' obstacles to capital movements are removed a country's marginal gain from increased stability (or, more generally, from investor-friendliness) will grow, and hence also its incentive to reduce political risk. This will strengthen the tendency towards a uniform rate of profit and uniform wage rates, thus further reducing citizenship-based inequalities without any need for the migration of people.

A second implication of the above discussion is that even if citizenship exploitation were completely abolished (whether through free capital migration or through free labour migration) the unfairness inherent in a world capitalist economy would not be eradicated. Removing all obstacles to the transnational migration of money (or people) would allow workers in poor countries to share in the benefits currently enjoyed by workers in rich countries by eroding all those wage differentials that are not the reflection of unequal labour productivities. But of two countries with equally large workforces, one would keep appropriating a larger share of the world product because of the superior wealth held by its citizens (be it lent or invested abroad) or because of the superior productivity of its workforce (whether due to its skills or to environmental conditions). The forms of exploitation intrinsically linked to capitalism, therefore, would remain undiminished.

On this basis, it is tempting to infer that it is not such 'imperfections' of the world capitalist economy as the existence of closed borders that constitute its 'fundamental' injustice. But we must beware of not being carried away by sheer rhetorics. Nothing in what has just been said rules out that citizenship exploitation may be more relevant than wealth-based or skills-based exploitation in either or both of the following senses. Citizenship status may exert a *quantitatively more powerful* influence on the distribution of material welfare than wealth status or skill status. Moreover, reducing the material advantages associated to citizenship (by letting money out, admittedly not by letting people in) may also be *more feasible*, or less counterproductive, than reducing those associated to wealth or skills. There are circumstances, therefore, under which the Marxist ethical imperative, construed as the abolition of exploitation, should assign priority to the promotion of international capital mobility (to get rid of citizenship exploitation) over the struggle for socialism (to get rid of wealth exploitation).

Popular sovereignty

I have assumed so far that the reason why Marxists favoured socialism is that it would enable us to get rid of capitalist exploitation, itself an instance of a broader phenomenon of expoitation, which the central Marxist ethical principle tells us must be abolished. Some Marxists could meaningfully argue, however, that what underlies their commitment to socialism is not their concern with exploitation but their concern with popular sovereignty. *Popular sovereignty* can be defined as the actual capacity to implement a democratic polity's preferred choice among technically feasible options.[12] It is obviously limited by the private ownership of the means of production. Suppose, for example, that it would be technically possible to introduce tougher norms of environmental protection or work safety at a slight cost in terms of average income, and that this is what a majority would like to happen. The negative effect on profits that would result from such measures, however, may trigger off private capital flight or a domestic investment strike on such a scale that the price to be paid for the measures (in terms of national income) becomes prohibitive.

A democratically preferred and technically feasible option is thus made unfeasible by the response of private capital owners. Some, such as Deepak Lal, may rejoice at this welcome discipline, but not those who find popular sovereignty an important objective. Under public ownership of the means of production – so the pro-socialism argument goes – this shrinking of society's feasible set would be avoided, popular sovereignty would be enhanced.

If popular sovereignty is the aim, other measures falling short of or going beyond the nationalization of the means of production are equally legitimate. If socialism is not possible, or if introducing it would be counterproductive, the democratic will's room for manoeuvre may be expanded by hindering the exit of capital, perhaps by imposing exchange controls or a tax on repatriated profits. And once socialism has been introduced one may further expand this room for manoeuvre by hindering the exit of skilled labour, perhaps through a stingy rationing of exit visas or through the compulsory reimbursement of what the state spent on an emigrant's education. We can now see that the implications for the transnational migration of people and money is exactly the opposite of the one that emerged from the perspective explored in the previous section. If what matters is the abolition of all forms of exploitation, including citizenship exploitation, there is a strong presumption in favour of open borders. But if what matters is the protection of popular sovereignty, there is an equally strong presumption against them. Are the underlying perspectives inescapably inconsistent, or is there a possibility for reconciliation?

My own view is that the two perspectives are contradictory if the objectives they focus on – the abolition of exploitation, the protection of popular sovereignty – are conceived as aims in themselves. But unlike the abolition of exploitation, I do not believe that popular sovereignty can sensibly be defended as more than an instrumental objective, if only because it clashes by its very nature with individual sovereignty: the more the individuals' room for manoeuvre is shrunk – e.g. by restricting the free choice of occupation, of working time, of residence, of religion, etc. – the less constrained the popular will. Nevertheless, I do believe that popular sovereignty is an important consideration and one that plays a key role in what I regard as the only cogent justification for socialism (if there is one). What needs to be protected, however, is not popular sovereignty *tout court*, but the collective capacity to pursue such a specific substantive aim as everyone's real freedom to lead her or his life as she or he wishes. If the pursuit of this aim is necessarily thwarted by the private ownership of capital, then we have a strong case for at least a partial socialization of the means of production.[13]

Let us return in this light to the transnational migration of people and money. To deal with this issue it is obviously of decisive importance to

know who 'everyone' is in the above formulation of the substantive
objective for the sake of which popular sovereignty can legitimately be
protected at the expense of some aspects of individual freedom. If 'everyone' is just everyone inside the borders of some country or federation of
countries, then the argument for closed borders is straightforward: if the
viability or the deepening of the European (or Canadian or Wisconsin)
social-democratic model is helped by obstacles to human inflow or monetary outflow, then such obstacles are evidently legitimate. But if the
'everyone' whose real freedom one is concerned with covers every member
of mankind – as it must, if consistency with the condemnation of citizenship exploitation is to be re-established – then the justification of closed
borders, if there is one, needs to take a more subtle form. The effective fight
against inequalities in both wealth and job assets in rich countries requires
the introduction of social transfers, indeed, arguably, of social transfers of
an unconditional (non-work-related) kind. The viability of such transfer
systems in one country is likely to be contingent upon some restriction on
the emigration of money and is bound to be contingent upon a major
restriction on the immigration of people: there is no way in which such
systems could survive if all the old, sick and lazy of the world came running
to take advantage of them. The reduction of domestic wealth or job
exploitation, it seems, clashes head on with the reduction of citizenship
exploitation.

I suggest the following combined strategy as a workable compromise
among the two sets of considerations. Let money (and technology) out
towards the low-wage countries, only making some trouble when the
country concerned does not respect trade union rights or democratic
decision procedures. A gradual erosion of citizenship exploitation can be
expected, while mechanisms for the erosion of both wealth and job
exploitation inside the poorer countries are being fostered. As a result the
economic and political pressure for the immigration of people will
decrease, ultimately to the extent that closing the borders would be
pointless. In the meanwhile, however, do not let people in too easily from
poorer countries – because capital migration is a less painful process,
because the least advantaged, being less mobile, are not likely to benefit,
and above all because it would undermine any serious attempt to equalize,
be it locally and partially, wealth and job assets.

Such local equalization, it may be argued, can be justified even by
reference to those with least real freedom in the world. For it demonstrates
that a strongly redistributive economy is more than a fancy dream, and it
thereby provides a tangible model both for redistributive strategies in each
country and for an admittedly very remote first-best fully individualized
transfer system on a world scale which would provide each citizen in the
world with her or his share of the value of aggregate material wealth and

jobs. Does this sacrifice too much of the interests of the least advantaged in today's world for the sake of pursuing an uncertain long-term goal?

Notes

1. See Jon Elster, *Making Sense of Marx* (Cambridge: Cambridge University Press, 1985), 117–18.
2. John E. Roemer, *A General Theory of Exploitation and Class* (Cambridge, Mass: Harvard University Press, 1982), part III.
3. See Philippe Van Parijs, "Exploitation and the Libertarian Challenge," ed. A. Reeve, *Modern Theories of Exploitation* (London and Beverly Hills: Sage, 1987).
4. The analogy between feudal serfs and citizens of poor countries, emphasized by both Ann Dummett and Joseph Carens, is thereby given a systematic framework.
5. Karl Marx, *Theorien uber den Mehrwert Vol. 3* (1863) (Berlin: Dietz, 1960), 106.
6. This interpretation is akin to the notion of international exploitation elaborated, for example, by Serge-Christophe Kolm, "L'exploitation des nations par les nations," *Revue Economique*, 20, 851–72 and R. N. Cooper, "A New International Economic Order for Mutual Gain," *Foreign Policy* 26 (1977), 66–120.
7. John E. Roemer, "Unequal Exchange, Labor Migrations and International Capital Flows: A Theoretical Synthesis," ed. P. Desai, *Marxism, the Soviet Economy and Central Planning* (Cambridge, Mass.: MIT Press, 1983).
8. Arghiri Emmanuel, *L'Échange Inegal* (Paris: Maspero, 1975).
9. Roemer, *Marxism, the Soviet Economy and Central Planning*, ibid, sec. 3–4.
10. Emmanuel, *L'Échange Inegal*, ibid, 205 and 351.
11. Brian Barry, "Justice as Reciprocity," *Democracy, Power and Justice: Essays in Political Theory* (Oxford: Oxford University Press, 1989).
12. See Adam Przeworski and Michael Wallerstein, "Popular Sovereignty, State Autonomy, and Private Property," *Archives Européennes de Sociologie*, 27 (1986), 215–59.
13. This issue is discussed at length in Erik O. Wright, "Why Something like Socialism is Necessary for the Transition to Something like Communism," *Theory and Society*, 15 (1986), 657–72; Robert J. van der Veen and Philippe Van Parijs, "Universal grants versus socialism. Reply to six critics," *Theory and Society*, 15 (1986), 723–57; Gérard Roland, "Why socialism needs basic income, why basic income needs socialism," ed. A. G. Miller, *Proceedings of the First International Conference on Basic Income* (London: B.I.R.G., 1988), 94–105; Philippe Van Parijs, "Basic Income Capitalism", *Ethics*, vol. 102 (April 1992).

Natural Law Perspectives

12

The transnational migration of people seen from within a natural law tradition

Ann Dummett

Most forms of political argument today deal with the proper form and function of the state and the rights of citizens. Classical Marxism has been concerned primarily with the class struggle, which cuts across national borders. Natural law arguments differ from both these forms; they do not assume so much. The law of nature is what governs a *universal, natural order* in the world at large.

The concept of such an order is a difficult one for many people in the twentieth century to imagine, for historicism and relativism have created world-pictures on very different models. However, over the last 2,000 years in Europe, natural law arguments have been continually in use for or against monarchy, slavery, democracy and the behaviour of states towards each other. Edmund Burke called natural law 'that law which governs all laws', and this is its abiding character. It is supposed to be a standard by which legal institutions, positive laws, court judgments and individual actions can be judged. This standard says what is right and just for everyone. Natural law, while the highest form of law in principle, is the humblest in apprehension: every human being, in any form of society, is supposed to be informed of it by reason and conscience.

In medieval Europe, the primacy of natural law was taken for granted, and no authority was entitled to obedience which was not assumed to derive its power therefrom. But the concept was not a Christian creation: Cicero and later Roman jurists based their arguments upon a universal, natural law. Outside Europe, similar concepts are found in Hindu and Taoist systems of thought. With the rise of the modern state, however, and with the readiness of many political thinkers to find new theoretical justifications for the *Realpolitik* of rulers or the exaltation of the nation-state, positive laws came to be justified by having their origin in the sovereign authority of each political unit (whether this authority was a single person, an oligarchy, or the sovereign people in a republic). Today, state authorities usually take for granted that their own determination of the good of their own political units must be their moral guide. *Salus populi* (their own 'populus' and nobody else's) *suprema lex*. As the British Home Secretary, Edward Shortt, put it in 1919: 'Where it is a choice between our own safety and the safety of our people and the infliction of hardship upon an alien, then that hardship becomes necessary and ceases to be unjust.'[1] There could hardly be a more explicit rejection of a natural law concept of justice.

It is no accident that Shortt's words were spoken in a debate on an immigration measure: the Aliens Restriction (Amendment) Act 1919. For it is in its immigration laws that a state most starkly asserts the primacy of state interest over universal principles of justice. If the words 'an individual citizen' were substituted for 'an alien' in the above passage, the sentiment would instantly be recognizable as totalitarian. As it is, only the crudity of its expression may startle the liberal. This is because modern political philosophy habitually keeps its discussion of justice, rights and obligations within the bounds of a particular state: it is concerned with relationships within that state. (What it has to say about external relations is normally confined to the state's relations with other states: in effect, inter-government relations.) Such theories take for granted that they are dealing with a model of a particular society as a closed unit, as a politically self-sufficient system. So, even if theorists accept a doctrine of universal human rights – as did the framers of the American constitution and their revolutionary contemporaries in France – they take the crucial step of adapting it for use within such a closed, self-sufficient system: universal rights become expressed as citizens' rights. This is not to say that such theorists do not care what happens to anyone outside their own society; they may be eager to see everyone in the world enjoy the same rights, but they see the attainment of this goal in terms of their ideal model being adopted by every political unit in the world. Many practical politicians today take for granted that universal human rights must be established by persuading all states to adopt the 'Western' democratic model of political theory; then, everything in the garden will be lovely.

But the supposition that a political society is a closed system, though it may be an essential convention to adopt in considering a just form of internal government for a society, is only a convention. Its limitations are obvious in the contemporary world. Millions of people are living outside their own states. In every country, there is a body of resident non-citizens who are excluded from the same rights as their citizen neighbours. Some works of political philosophy, and some state constitutions, make provisions for the rights of resident aliens, but do so on the assumption that these rights will properly or inevitably be less than citizens' rights. No contradiction is perceived between this assumption and a belief in universal human rights. I believe there is such a contradiction, and it is usually disregarded simply because the accepted conventions of political philosophy are so strong, and because nationalist sentiments, and jealousy of the state's independence of action, are so pervasive in our own time.

What is an alien? Someone who, by an accident of birth, born in the wrong place or to the wrong parents, is not a citizen. Unequal treatment on the grounds of other accidents of birth, such as skin colour or sex or even, within the confines of a state, 'national' in the sense of 'ethnic' origin, is rightly condemned. Just as nobody can choose a colour, nobody has a free choice of citizenship. Nationality, or sometimes statelessness, is acquired at birth, and those who seek to change their national status cannot do so at will; they are completely dependent upon the decision of state authorities whether, and on what conditions, they will be granted a new one. In most states, one of the conditions of naturalization is a period of residence in the territory. To meet this condition the alien must first have gained legal permission to enter and remain in the territory under the state's immigration laws. At the point of entry, the alien's rights, instead of being merely second-class, are non-existent. 'Few principles of international law are more clearly established than the rule that the admission of aliens is at the discretion of each state.'[2] As in public international law, so in political theory and political practice: an alien is not considered to have a right to enter any state's territory. (The right of asylum is, in origin, not a right belonging to an individual refugee but a right of the receiving state to grant asylum.)

In the world of the mid-nineteenth century, it would not have been necessary to discuss an alien's *right* of entry because there was *in fact* an opportunity to enter many countries freely. An emigrant could go somewhere, perhaps not to Japan or Tibet, but certainly to the United Kingdom, the United States and numerous other countries. Without breaking any law one could buy a ticket or work a passage, change one's name, look for any work in a new country and become a permanent resident. Then, as now, states had an acknowledged discretion to refuse entry to, or deport aliens, but there was a general presumption that aliens might come and go freely unless there was a special reason for restricting them – as in the case of a terrorist. Today, the presumption has shifted: no alien may enter unless there is a special reason for admission. Even countries like Australia, Canada and the United States, which maintain a mood of welcome for approved immigrants, assume that all entrants must be scrutinized and that many applications for residence will be refused. Every state has an immigration control system to deal with all comers – visitors, students and temporary workers as well as aspirants to settlement. Nobody is free to move at will.

A sort of international class structure has been created. The rich and highly skilled are its aristocracy: most countries want them, and they can move fairly easily. The employees of international organizations and multinationals are its middle class; they can move in the course of their work and are usually politely treated. But the world's poor, no longer chained to the soil of a feudal demesne, are now chained to their countries of origin because nobody wants them as immigrants. If they are forced to move, as refugees, they often enter limbo: they are shuttled between different countries, put into prison camps delicately called reception centres and may remain uncertain for years on end whether or where they will find a home. If they move from economic necessity, but cannot gain legally approved entry to a new country, they become 'illegals', permanently insecure and often afraid to seek health care, schooling for their children or welfare payments in case they are banished. If they are admitted legally to do the dirty or low-paid jobs that citizens do not want, they are often – as in several West European countries, for instance – granted only temporary residence which must be renewed and they may not be allowed to have their children or spouses join them or to claim to receive the same pay and benefits as citizens.

An adherent of the natural law tradition finds this situation blatantly unjust. For, in this tradition, it is from the fact of being human, not the fact of being a citizen, that rights arise. The principles of justice to be satisfied are found not in any state's laws but in 'that law which governs all laws'. It is a view found in the preamble to the UN Universal Declaration of Human Rights which begins:

> Whereas recognition of the inherent dignity and of the equal and inalienable rights of all members of the human family is the foundation of freedom, justice and peace in the world. . . .[3]

The United Nations Charter had already made clear that the protection of the individual was a proper matter for international concern. After World War II there was a significant shift away from the former presumption of international law – that it was concerned with relations between states and that states were its only subjects – towards a concern for universal human rights and the duty of states to cooperate in upholding them. Numerous UN instruments have defined states' duties towards all the individuals in their jurisdictions, irrespective of citizenship; so have many localized international agreements. For example, those states which have ratified the European Convention on Human Rights and Fundamental Freedoms, and bound themselves to accept the jurisdiction of the European Court of Human Rights at Strasbourg, have to guarantee not just to their own citizens but to everyone within their respective jurisdictions the right to a fair trial if accused of a criminal offence (under detailed specifications); the right to family life, to privacy, and so on. It is allowed that on certain matters, such as the franchise or employment in the public service, rights may be reserved to nationals, but this is a concession to states' universally acknowledged areas of independence, and is not a prohibition on extending such rights more widely (as some countries, e.g. Sweden and the Netherlands, have begun to do). Any individual, in a member-state, can go to the European Court with a claim against a government; if the case is upheld, the government is bound to conform to the Court's decision. The process is slow and cumbrous, and can only be begun when an aggrieved individual has exhausted domestic remedies, but it has proved highly effective. It represents a movement in political thinking as well as in legal procedure; the acceptance that an individual's rights against a state do not arise from citizenship only.

Can we extend the argument, in terms of modern international law, to arrive at the establishment of an individual human right to move between different states' territories? I believe we can. No such right at present exists in international law, and the actual behaviour of state authorities seems to be moving rapidly in the opposite direction from a movement to create it, as barriers against Third World refugees and 'economic migrants' are reinforced. None the less, the steady progress over the last forty years of legal and political thinking in a natural law tradition towards guarantees for the human rights of every individual has started an impetus towards formulating a right to migrate. To begin with, it is acknowledged that freedom of movement is a human right, but international Declarations and agreements confine it within political boundaries. That 'Everyone has the right to freedom of movement and residence within the borders of each state' is asserted in Article 13(1) of the Declaration of Human Rights and similar provisions are repeated elsewhere in other instruments; also in Article 13: 'Everyone has the right to leave any country including his own.' The International Covenant on Civil and Political Rights (1966) and the Fourth Protocol to the European Convention affirm that, 'No-one shall be arbitrarily deprived of the right to enter his own country.' If we take all these provisions together, it is obvious that they are assuming freedom of movement within and across borders to be aspects of a natural right to free movement. International instruments stop short of asserting a right to *enter* any state for a practical, not a logical, reason: the insistence of state authorities on their own discretion to admit or refuse aliens. Logically, it is an absurdity to assert a right of emigration without a complementary right of immigration unless there exist in fact (as in the mid-nineteenth century) a number of states which permit free entry. At present, no such state exists, and the right of emigration is not, and cannot be in these circumstances, a general human right exercisable in practice.

This is only one example of an obvious *lacuna* in international law where agreed propositions have stopped short of saying what the assumptions they rest upon seem to impel them to say. Such stopping short usually represents strong disagreements between governments about how far to go in acknowledging some need or principle: there are political objections by some states' authorities to assuming new, specific obligations themselves which they would be willing to see other states assume. Or it may represent a narrow view of a question perceived in the light of a particular situation. 'Everyone has the right to leave any country including his own' is an example of both processes. The United States and some other Western Countries objected strongly to the emigration controls imposed by the USSR and other East European states after the war, and took for granted that emigrants permitted to leave those countries would be received without difficulty in the West. While this general principle was endorsed by many other governments, the need to ensure some right of immigration was either thought unnecessary or was regarded as an unacceptable encroachment on states' discretion. But if we are concerned with universal human rights, we have to look beyond such limited situations, involving only a few states. If there is a universal right to emigrate, it belongs to Haitians, Turks and Sri Lankans as much as to Russians and Czechs. It is also a right that persists over time, so that if (as does not look impossible at present) the USSR and virtually all East European countries were to open their borders for exit, and millions of people were sudddenly to leave, the good faith of those who denounce emigration controls but uphold immigration controls could be put to a severe practical test.[4]

Belief in 'state sovereignty' is the objection most often advanced against free immigration. Alan Dowty, in *Closed Borders* puts it thus:

> the right to leave does not imply the corresponding right to enter a particular country. Whatever the argument over the authority of the state to block emigration, there is little dispute over its right to limit *immigration*. The two issues are not symmetrical: departure ends an individual's claims against a society, while entry sets such claims in motion. Control of entry is essential to the idea of sovereignty, for without it a society has no control over its basic character.[5]

Now this is a political, rather than a legal, view of sovereignty or, rather, it defines sovereignty in terms of a state's powers over the character of a society (presumably its social, cultural or demographic character; perhaps its moral and political character). Professor Dowty assumes that 'society', through the mechanism of the state, ought to be able to control its own 'basic character', and that an outsider has no claim against its decision. By others, however, state sovereignty may be defended in a more legalistic way, in terms of legal competence to pursue completely independent action. In international law terms, a state's sovereignty means its internal powers over its own affairs; so far as other states are concerned, its status is better described as 'independent' than as 'sovereign'. The world is a collection of independent states, each exercising sovereign jurisdiction over its own territory. But, as earlier paragraphs will have made clear, international law's recognition of this independence, and internal sovereignty, does not imply that any state can behave arbitrarily in either internal or external affairs. That a state has discretion to admit or refuse aliens does not mean that a state can exercise its discretion without regard to just principles. The *standards set* by international law require a state to acknowledge obligations to other states, to universal human rights and to 'that law which governs all laws'. Thus it is possible to say that a state is sovereign and independent, while also criticizing it for acting unjustly, by these standards. In other words, it is not a knock-down argument to say that a state is 'sovereign' when defending immigration control; one must still ask whether immigration control in general, or any particular form of it, is just or unjust.

Professor Dowty's argument is not based on universal human rights but on the collective right of a political society to determine its own character. Michael Walzer, in *Spheres of Justice*, analyzes this concept: 'The primary good we distribute to one another is membership in some human community.' His main theme is distributive justice, and on his theory of this kind of justice depends his defence of entry restrictions. If the state did not restrict entry, he argues, other units, perhaps neighbourhoods, would do it for themselves. Alternatively, the world would become a place of 'deracinated men and women' without cohesion: 'The distinctiveness of culture and groups depends upon closure.' Therefore, closure must be permitted somewhere:

> At some level of political organisation, something like the sovereign state must take shape and claim the authority to make its own admissions policy. . . . But this right to control immigration does not include or entail the right to control emigration . . . The restraint of entry serves to defend the liberty and welfare, the politics and culture of a group of people committed to one another and to their common life. But the restraint of exit replaces commitment with coercion. So far as the coerced members are concerned, there is no longer a community worth defending.[7]

He concludes that the right to leave a country does not generate a right to enter any other. He suggests an analogy between clubs and states: clubs can bar admission to membership but cannot bar withdrawals from it. However, a migrant might well reply that anyone can live without a club, but not without a home.

I think the large assumptions made in this argument are clearly contradicted by facts. It is simply not true that the distinctiveness of culture and groups depends upon closure. Of course it depends what one means by 'culture'. The 'culture' of the modern United States, in anyone's sense, has depended upon openness; it is the creation of a remarkable mixture of peoples. Islamic culture has nothing to do with territorial closure. And there is certainly a sense in which German culture would be very different if Jews had never migrated to Germany: what music, what science, what poetry would have been lost? Indeed, many countries' 'group distinctiveness' is a creation of mixture and movement. As to politics and welfare, these can be threatened (however one characterizes the threat) by a state's own citizens: home-grown terrorists, demagogues and drug dealers cannot, however, be refused entry; they have to be dealt with in some other way.

Professor Walzer does not argue, however, that societies *must* be closed, but that they must have the right to impose closure when such imposition is morally defensible. I do not think that his communitarian ground, quoted above, is a morally defensible position. But the question whether a state should have a right in principle to refuse entry, is a more difficult one. Walzer may be said to be applying natural law principles when he says, 'To say that states have a right to act in certain areas is not to say that anything they do in these areas is right'.[8] Putting it another way, he is applying a well-known principle of liberal politics: if I have a right, I may not use it in such a way that I damage the rights of others. On this basis, Professor Walzer criticizes certain immigration policies, such as the old 'White Australia' policy, and the United States' immigration laws of the 1920s. But this criticism does not invalidate the principle that a state has the right to refuse entry in *some* circumstances. Is this an acceptable proposition? Or do natural law principles, a belief in universal human rights and the acknowledgement that states can owe duties to people who are not their citizens, lead us to say that movement should be completely uncontrolled by states?

Joseph H. Carens argues in 'Aliens and citizens: the case for open borders'[9] that borders should in general be open. Citizenship in Western liberal democracies is the modern equivalent, he says, of feudal privilege: 'an inherited status that greatly increases one's life chances'. The argument in favour of free migration is therefore strongest, in his view, when applied to the migration of poor, Third World people to these Western democracies. While Professor Walzer argues a case for distributive justice, with the emphasis on distribution within a state's borders, Professor Carens wants an international form of distributive justice. He also argues on the basis of universal human rights. He concedes that in the last resort, if migrants were to arrive in such enormous numbers that they threatened public order or national security, a state's duty to preserve public order could then justify some restriction. His argument is radically different from Professor Walzer's but, when the crunch comes, the legitimacy of state controls is allowed.

I think Carens' view can be justified in the terms of natural law principles (and, perhaps, liberal principles) in this way. Suppose we grant that everyone has the human right of freedom of movement across borders. This right can be exercised so long as it does not damage the rights of others. If, and only if, the exercise by great numbers of people of their right to move threatened the fundamental human rights of other individuals, the right to move could be limited and this limitation could properly be imposed by state authorities which have a duty to preserve human rights within their jurisdictions. On this view, the *collective* interest of a receiving society could not be weighed against the individual's right to move, in the sense that the interests of an economy, a culture of a theory of the nation could not be advanced against the right. Only the infringement of recognized individual human rights could justify exclusion. From the point of view of the present argument, this position is a good one because it would be congruent with accepted standards in international law. One could apply the principle (a highly important one in the jurisprudence of the European Court of Human Rights) of proportionality. A state would be bound to impose restrictions on a right (in this case, the right of free movement) only to the degree proportional to the end to be served. It could not say, 'I am doing this on grounds of national security', for example, unless it could be shown just how the number of immigrants concerned would damage what international law recognizes to be a 'national security' consideration and were to keep its restrictions within the bounds necessary only to serve this particular end.

One could apply this idea to certain individuals, as well as to large numbers of people, in these international law terms. There is a model of inter-state free movement, already functioning, which does this. In the European Community, the national of any member-state has freedom of movement in all member-states, and these member-states have bound themselves not to refuse a Community national except on the grounds of public order (*ordre public*), public health or national security. These grounds are circumscribed by Community law, and the European Court at Luxembourg has given a number of judgments interpreting them. In *Van Duyn* v. *Secretary of State for Home Affairs*, for example, the Court had to consider the case of a Dutch woman member of the Church of Scientology who had been refused entry to the United Kingdom on the ground that her entry would not be conducive to the public good in the United Kingdom. While the exclusion of this particular woman was upheld, the Court made clear that the British Home Secretary could not define the public good, as regards a Community national's entry, in any way except the definition of *ordre public* in the Community's law. Here is a working example of an international tribunal ruling on the particular immigration laws of states. This system does not detract from the independence of states, for the countries concerned have voluntarily bound themselves to accept the laws of the Community and the jurisdiction of the Luxembourg Court. Would it not, then, be possible for the same thing to happen on a world scale?

The question of movement of large numbers, within the European Community, has not been an issue. So much stress has been laid on the right to freedom of movement for Community nationals that if several million French people were suddenly to go to Germany, for instance, they would have an unassailable legal right to do so. But while, on one side, we can see the EC as a model of international movement, there is another side from which it looks more like a super-state, an area whose internal borders are open (as they will literally be in 1993) but whose external borders have tight controls over all non-EC entrants. At present, racism in member-states is causing pressure to tighten these controls more. If we are considering a general human right to move, on the part of all human beings to go anywhere, we have to consider what the practical consequences of its exercise might be and how they could be tackled so as to respect human rights in general.

When discussing rights, it is important to stand back from the situations particular to certain times and places, and test one's theory against a variety of circumstances. Too often, discussion of migration is rooted in the particular concerns of some of the people, some of the time. The governing classes in rich European countries are afraid, for several reasons, of large-scale immigration from poor countries. They fear hostility to their respective parties from racist voters; they want to avoid increased welfare expense on the unemployed; they do not want their economic planning disrupted; and some of them are strongly racist and/or nationalist themselves. On the other hand, the governments of poor countries in Asia and Africa generally restrict immigration closely so as to protect their own labour markets. If anyone is supposed to have a natural right to freedom of movement, can the refusal of a Canadian professional, say by India, be justified?; or the refusal by one African country, with poor people of its own, to admit poor people from another African country? (It is worth noting that African countries have been far more generous to refugees over the last decade than have rich, Western democracies: they have less to give but are readier to give it. However, it is also true that many poor countries limit *ordinary* immigration strictly; a distinction is made, which Western countries have been deliberately blurring, between the special claims of the persecuted or starving and the lesser claims of an ordinary migrant.)

It is consistent with a natural law line of argument to prefer the refugee whose life is in immediate danger to other applicants for entry. The asylum-seeker has an overwhelming claim. But this is not to say that other claims are non-existent, only that their basis is different: a claim to free movement rather than a claim to life itself or freedom from torture. I think that if one is arguing on the basis of universal human rights, and asserting that one of these is a right to free movement, the only reasonable position to take is that no state can prefer one migrant to another on the grounds of skill, economic status or other consideration, save for the preservation of the individual human rights of others. A person asking at the border to come in has to be seen simply as a human being possessed of a right to move. In the world as it is today, if such a right were established, it seems likely that many millions would try to move at once. Under the United Nations definition of a refugee (a person with a well-founded fear of persecution on grounds of race, religion, political opinion, etc.) the number of refugees seeking asylum in the world rose from 4.6 million in 1978 to 13.3 million in 1988. People not coming under this definition but being, in many ways, obvious refugees (e.g. those fleeing to avoid military service in South Africa) number many millions more. Besides these groups, there is an incalculable number of people around the world who would probably move if they could, for motives ranging from the urgent to the trivial.

In practical terms, even if states were to agree on a universal right to move in principle it would probably cause chaos if all borders were instantly opened. But there are many matters on which states have agreed certain rights in principle and begun to implement these rights in a limited way, by agreement among themselves. The UN Convention on the Reduction of Statelessness (1961) represents two things: an agreement in principle that statelessness must be done away with, and a set of practical measures to *begin* to get rid of it. States party to the Convention have introduced domestic legislation to put its provisions into effect in their own territories. Some local groupings of states have taken it up: the American Convention on Human Rights 1969 binds member-states more closely to provisions preventing statelessness than does the UN Convention. An impetus towards change has been set in motion, and many individuals now possess a nationality who would not have done if this initiative had not been taken.

Could there not be similar progress towards acknowledging a human right to freedom of movement across borders? Even if the aim could not be realized at once, would it not be worthwhile to begin the process by an international agreement whereby each state party to it would accept, in addition to those it admits under its law of refugees and other migrants, a quota of people who merely apply?

The historian Marc Bloch said that in the end, the point of history, like that of any other science, was to make the world a little – just a little – better. If the same is true of political theory, an argument which takes in the world, rather than an arbitrary collection of people within one state's borders, is clearly necessary.

Notes

1. *Hansard Parliamentary Debates*, vol. 114, col. 2746 (House of Commons).
2. Richard Plender, *Human Rights of Aliens in Europe*, contribution to a Council of Europe Colloquy of the same name (Dordrecht: Martinus Nijhoff, 1985).
3. Preamble, UN Universal Declaration of Human Rights (1948).
4. This paragraph was written in August 1989, and events have confirmed a guess that was then highly speculative: people from eastern Europe have begun to emigrate. The scale of their movement has been partly concealed by German reunification and by the German state's readiness to receive immediately into citizenship not only east Germans but ethnic Germans from other states. But it is noteworthy that after the Hungarian authorities destroyed the wire fence on their side of the Austro-Hungarian border, which had been put there to stop emigration, the Austrian authorities introduced new guards and barriers on their side to stop immigration.
5. Alan Dowty, *Closed Borders: The Contemporary Assault on Freedom of Movement* (New Haven, Conn.: Yale University Press, 1987).
6. Michael Walzer, *Spheres of Justice* (Oxford: Oxford University Press, 1983).
7. Ibid., p.21.
8. Ibid., p.15.
9. In *Review of Politics*, vol. 49, no. 2 (Spring 1987).

── 13 ──

Natural law, solidarity and international justice*

Paul J. Weithman

Some of the contributors to this volume have been asked to provide moral assessment of the international movement of money from the points of view afforded by various ethical theories. The task that has fallen to me is that of discussing these questions from the point of view which natural law theory affords. Before I do so it will be helpful to say something about what I take natural law theory to be.

Natural law theory, as I shall understand it, is constituted by work in the tradition of moral thought that began with Thomas Aquinas's treatment of natural law in his *Summa Theologiae*. At the heart of this tradition are the works of Renaissance scholastics like Vitoria and Suarez, of twentieth-century neo-Thomists like Jacques Maritain and Yves Simon, and the recent work of John Finnis, Joseph Boyle and Germain Grisez. Moreover, for roughly the last century, since Leo XIII's encyclical *Aeterni Patris*,[1] Thomistic philosophy has been accorded official preeminence by the Roman Catholic Church. Natural law ethics has therefore found expression in the Catholic Church's moral and social teaching. This teaching, too, belongs to the natural law tradition.

What distinguishes these and other works of natural law ethics is not

* This paper was prepared as a contribution to a conference on the international movement of money and people sponsored by the Ethikon Institute; I am especially grateful to Philip Valera of the Institute for his gracious invitation to contribute to this discussion. Thanks are also due to Joseph Boyle and Paul Sigmund for their encouragement, and to Michael Arnold, Joseph Boyle, Kenneth Kuttner, Michael Pakaluk and Thomas Pogge for helpful discussion and correspondence.

their authors' fidelity to Aquinas's texts and intentions. It is, rather, that their authors looked to Aquinas's work for inspiration and legitimacy even when they sought to extend or reinterpret fundamental features of his moral thought. The unity of the tradition is further maintained by common appeal to fundamental values and principles and by pursuit of certain problems, the meanings and significance of which were none the less subject to change as work in the tradition continued.

As these remarks suggest, natural law ethics has long been conscious of itself *as* a tradition of moral thought with seminal texts like those of Aquinas. To that this chapter is no exception. I am attempting to extend the values and principles of the natural law tradition to the problem at hand, although few of the great philosophers of the natural law tradition gave sustained attention to questions of international distributive justice.[2] On the other hand, recent social teaching of the Catholic Church shows great interest in these questions. That teaching is to be found in documents of the Second Vatican Council, in Papal encyclicals since John XXIII's *Pacem in Terris* and in recent statements by various national Bishops' conferences. I have therefore relied heavily on these documents in what follows.

Encyclicals and episcopal letters, however, pose problems of their own, for they are primarily pastoral or homiletic in character. While they articulate values fundamental to Catholic social teaching and sometimes advocate fairly specific solutions to particular problems of international distributive justice, they are, from a philosophical point of view, regrettably unsystematic. Certainly they do not permit easy derivation of the moral principles necessary for directly assessing the international movement of money. In the discussion that follows, I therefore want to focus not on what principles of this kind can be eked out of these works, but on the possibilities they suggest for a comprehensive and systematic theory of international distributive justice.

My reasons for this focus are amplified in Section I. There I also argue that the recent documents on which I am relying imply the need for such a theory and that this theory, while superficially at odds with traditional emphases of natural law ethics, in fact accords with its deepest aims. In Section III, I argue that solidarity, civic friendship and the Thomistic principle of common use make a global version of John Rawls' Difference Principle the preferred principle of international distributive justice for natural law ethics.

Rawls' principle applies, however, to a particular subject of justice – to the operations of what he calls the 'basic structure' of domestic society – and not to acts or states of affairs. The argument of Section III therefore presupposes that a natural law theory of international distributive justice would take as its subject something sufficiently like the basic structure of domestic society for a global version of the Difference Principle to be applicable. In Section II, I discuss the primary subject of such a theory and argue that it would be the operations of the international basic structure, the productive and distributive operations of the international economy taken as a whole.

I. The movement of money and the need for theory

Money moves across national borders in a great variety of ways, as the diversity of topics addressed by chapters in this volume demonstrates. Participants in the discussion to which my chapter is intended as a contribution have taken up the moral implications of capital flight, the movement of money into a country by foreign investors, the repatriation of profits earned by multinational corporations, foreign trade and its imbalances, debt-forgiveness, lending by banks and by sovereign states, foreign aid, currency exchange and speculation in foreign currency. This variety virtually guarantees that the principles by which the justice of money's movement is to be assessed will be extremely complex and the set of such principles very large.

Ethicists of the natural law tradition could best develop these principles. I believe, as part of a natural law theory of international distributive justice which deals not just with the movement of money across national borders but all international economic relationships and their consequences. Rectifying the international movement of money is not, after all, an end in itself. The movement of money across national borders derives its moral importance from the impact that movement has on the global distribution of wealth, opportunities to participate in the economy and in various forms of community life, dignity, rights, liberties and material well-being. The movement of money is just or unjust as it promotes or impedes the just distribution of these goods. Specifying in what their just distribution consists is therefore logically prior to the principles of justice by which the movement of money is to be assessed.

Each person must have access at least to some minimum amount of these goods in order to develop and exercise the virtues the natural law tradition has traditionally recognized as constituent of a good human character. Moreover, some regulation of the inequalities of distribution are necessary if ties of community are to develop. A natural law theory of international distributive justice would specify principles production and distribution must satisfy to meet these requirements. It would do so by appealing to those values (like solidarity) and ideals (like that of a world in which all live in dignity) drawn from the natural law tradition that ideally just international economic relations realize and promote. It would show as well how consistent and conscientious adherence to principles of justice, including those that apply to the movement of money, would realize those values and ideals and it would specify criteria for determining when the movement of money satisfies these principles.

This thesis about the priority of theory has a foundation in recent Catholic social teaching. Consider its treatment of but one of the ways money moves: the extension and repayment of loans between First World creditors and Third World debtors. In his testimony on international debt before the US Congress Archbishop Weakland of Milwaukee expressed reservations about recommending solutions to the Third World debt problem 'without addressing all aspects of the international order'.[3] A coherent set of solutions to all the problems 'of the international order', however, surely requires, not just principles for assessing the justice of international lending or of the international movement of money, but also a theory of international justice which has at its heart a set of values that the international order is to realize. The USCC Administrative Board expressed similar doubts about the separability of the debt from other problems in its statement on the subject and advocated 'fundamental change in the global economic system itself'.[4] Moreover, in voicing its sentiments the USCC echoed and footnoted reminiscent remarks by the Pontifical Justice and Peace Commission.[5] In *Sollicitudo Rei Socialis*, John Paul II also asserts the inseparability of the debt question from larger issues.[6] Such fundamental changes as the USCC and the Pope have in mind must surely be guided by a theory of international distributive justice which is itself animated by values from the natural law tradition.

I have suggested that such a theory would be a theory of ideally just international institutions. Catholic social teaching has tended towards ideal theory at least since Paul VI[7] and I have tried to show how that tendency is exemplified by certain more recent pronouncements. Moreover, I shall ask later whether natural law theorists should endorse some global extension of John Rawls' Difference Principle. The Difference Principle is part of an ideal theory premised on the supposition of strict compliance;[8] extensions of that theory to international justice would presumably be similarly ideal.

This approach to the question of international justice might, however, seem fundamentally at odds with the natural law tradition. Normative ethics in that tradition is often thought to consist in the application of fundamental moral principles to the conditions in which various individual agents actually find themselves. Development of principles that would regulate an ideally just economy therefore seems at variance with this traditional task in two ways. First, the focus on institutions and their distributive operations constitutes a shift from the traditional focus on individuals and their responsibilities. Second, the focus on the ideal is a shift from the traditional application of natural law principles to the conditions in which those individuals actually find themselves.

Let me respond to the first objection first. Development of a theory of just international *institutions* is not only compatible with natural law thinkers' traditional focus, it is a necessary prelude to moral reasoning about the obligations of actually existing agents. To see this, recall that Aquinas numbered among the fundamental principles of natural law that of giving to each his due,[9] that of mutual aid[10] and that requiring that external goods be put to common use[11]. The normative ethics of natural law has among its tasks that of specifying how individuals can fulfil the duties these more general principles enjoin.

What Catholic social teaching has come to recognize with increasing clarity is that for some, because of their station, opportunity or expertise,[12] these principles impose the duty of altering or eliminating institutions which give rise to unjust distribution and replacing them with more just ones. Deliberation about how *these* duties are to be fulfilled requires a theory of international justice. Progressive transition to institutions by which the world's goods are best put to common use, for example, requires some knowledge of the goal of that transition, and therefore some knowledge of what institutions and practices satisfy the requirement of common use. That knowledge would be provided by a theory of international justice of the sort I have recommended.

The need for such a theory is all the more pressing because the responsibility to change institutions requires more than a reallocation of the goods the international economy produces. It requires that the *production* as well as the allocation of goods conform to principles of justice. This, in turn, may require that the world economy produce different goods than it currently does, that far fewer resources be devoted to the production of arms or luxury items and that participants in the world economy co-operate from different motives than they now do. Transition to a world economy so different from the current one must be guided by some conception of the goal of that transition.

But why a theory of *ideally* just institutions? To address this question, it is helpful to see in what ways the theory would and in what ways it would not be ideal. It would not be ideal in abstracting completely from the facts of human psychology and from global economic conditions. Rather, it would be premised on human physical and psychological needs and limitations. In particular, the need for incentives is presupposed, as will be clear in Section III. The theory would, moreover, be premised on salient prevailing conditions. That will become apparent in the next section, where I argue that the theory would be premised on global economic interdependence. On the other hand, the theory would be ideal in so far as it would be premised on the supposition that individuals and institutions, both private and governmental, comply perfectly with the principles of justice. The aim of the theory also makes it an ideal one. Its aim is the articulation of principles of justice to which institutions must conform if they are best to satisfy the fundamental principles of natural law and realize the values central to the natural law tradition, given global interdependence and various facts about human psychology.

This idealization, like Rawls', serves two purposes. First, the supposition of perfect compliance enables us temporarily to put aside questions of retributive justice. This is desirable because determining what distributive justice requires is difficult enough without considering problems that attend the just treatment of those who fail to comply with its requirements. But postponing questions of retributive justice is not only desirable, it is also necessary. Determining what retributive justice demands first requires determining to what extent those from whom retribution is to be exacted have violated the just claims of others. This, in turn, requires an account of those claims, and hence an account of just distribution. Second, whatever obligations of justice bind actually existing individuals, they are obligations the fulfilment of which would conduce to the justice of the international economy. I am supposing that a conception of an ideally just international economy, if laid out with sufficient specificity, can play an important role in motivating individuals to honour their obligations. Seeing a conception of an ideally just world and aspiring to live as a citizen of it, I am supposing, elicits an interest in acting on obligations of justice. Eliciting this moral motivation is the second purpose served by the conception of ideally just institutions a theory of international justice would specify.

The principles to which an ideally just international economy would conform are the most important part of a theory of just international institutions. These principles are not, of course, identical to those that express the obligations binding individual agents. But the very difficult task of determining the latter requires prior determination of the former.

II. The primary subject of a theory of international justice

A theory of just international institutions might be concerned primarily to address the allocation of wealth or material goods obtaining at a given time. The conduct of economic and political institutions would, on this view, be subject to moral assessment because it promotes or impedes states of affairs characterized by just allocations. Contemporary Catholic social teaching suggests, however, that a theory of international distributive justice would have as its primary subject the way in which the whole network of institutions and practices that sustain international economic relationships produces and distributes goods among individuals. This network includes multinational corporations, private and international banks, lending institutions of sovereign states, domestic economic institutions like the Federal Reserve whose conduct affects the international economy, etc., including the institutions by which money moves internationally. Judgements about momentary allocations of wealth will be among the criteria employed to assess the productive and distributive operations of these institutions, but will not be the primary subjects of assessment. A natural law theory of international distributive justice would therefore be a theory primarily concerned to specify what values the operations of these institutions must realize and what principles of justice they must observe in order to do so.

The distinction between these two possible subjects of international justice is an important one. In this section, I want first to show that recent Catholic social teaching does in fact imply that the primary subject of international justice is operation of the network of international institutions and practices rather than momentary states of allocation. I shall then discuss some of the implications this has for assessing the operation of the international economy's productive as well as allocative mechanisms.

The emphasis contemporary Catholic teaching places on global economic interdependence suggests that operation of the network of international economic institutions would be the subject of a natural law theory of international justice. This emphasis is well summarized and illustrated by a crucial passage from the USCC's statement on Third World debt:

> From Pope John XXIII through John Paul II, a major theme of [Catholic social teaching] has been the meaning and implications of increasing global interdependence. The *fact* of interdependence is clear to anyone aware of the economic, social and political forces at work in our world. Our concern, however, has been the *moral quality* of interdependence[.] How should the fact of interdependence be shaped to meet the demands of human dignity and human rights? The development of Catholic social teaching in the last 30 years has grown steadily in the direction of expanding the standards of justice and charity traditionally applied to domestic (national) societies, so that they also apply to relations among states and peoples across national boundaries.[13]

The Bishops' remark that they are concerned with the '*moral quality* of interdependence', with how 'the fact of interdependence [should] be shaped', suggests that in fact the institutions and practices on which international economic interdependence rests constitute the subject of justice which the Bishops are concerned to assess.

Moreover, the juxtaposition of their concern with how 'the fact of interdependence [should] be shaped' with a remark about the international turn in the last three decades of Catholic social teaching is very suggestive. It suggests the claim that *because* of international economic interdependence, international economic relations – including the international movement of money – are subject to moral assessment and, more specifically, assessment from the point of view of 'social justice'. The argument for this claim, once spelled out, supports my thesis that Catholic social teaching takes the operation of the global economic network, rather than momentary allocations of wealth, as the primary subject of international justice.

By premising their claim upon economic interdependence, the Bishops follow recent trends in political philosophy. Political philosophers have often based their theorizing on the assumption that political societies are self-contained and self-sufficient entities among which the only interaction of moral significance is war. The first task undertaken by those philosophers who want to address the morality of international economic relations has therefore been to argue for the falsity of this assumption. One finds in the work of Charles Beitz, for example, an extended argument showing the economic interdependence of contemporary nation-states and their citizens and the inadequacy of the Hobbesian model of international relations as a state of nature.[14]

Because of international economic relationships and institutions, the well-being or poverty of citizens in some countries depends upon the conduct of citizens and institutions in others, who can themselves benefit from or be harmed by the transactions. It is this interdependence of citizens of rich and poor nations that shows international economic relationships to be of moral significance. More specifically, this interdependence shows that the *justice* of those relationships can be assessed, for questions of justice can be raised when institutions or relationships generate and distribute moderately scarce necessities.[15] To demonstrate economic interdependence it suffices to demonstrate that such generation and distribution takes place.

This interdependence is amply exhibited by the consequences of the international movement of money. To take but one example of these consequences, lending policies of banks in wealthy countries like the United States influence the quality of life among the poor in debtor nations, often for the worse, for those policies determine how much money is available for development projects and how much debtor nations must divert from social programmes and the manufacture of consumer goods to service their foreign debts. Citizens of creditor countries, on the other hand, benefit from international lending: the recession in the industrialized world in the 1970s would have been far worse had it not been for the contemporaneous quadrupling of foreign debt by developing countries.[16] Moreover, the international economic interdependence in which the movement of money bulks so large exacerbates economic inequalities.

The point of these examples is not to show that the consequences of the international movement of money are unjust. Their point, rather, is to demonstrate that that movement has important implications for the well-being of many of the people of the world and is therefore a manifestation of economic interdependence. It is as a manifestation of economic interdependence that the movement of money has moral significance: because the international movement of money affects the life prospects of so many and can engender or mitigate inequalities, the movement of money plays a significant role in the international distribution of scarce necessities. As such, that movement and the mechanisms by which it moves are subject to moral assessment from the point of view of justice. And contemporary teaching in the natural law tradition insists that they must be assessed from that point of view, as the quote from the USCC document illustrates.

To appreciate the import of this line of argument, premised upon interdependence, it is important to note another argument that the Bishops might have used to establish that the international economy is subject to moral assessment. In laying out the USCC's argument, I noted that like the argument of Beitz's work, it denies the assumption traditional in political philosophy that nations are self-contained. While some philosophers may think this assumption incompatible with the moral assessment of international economic affairs, natural law tradition has within it the resources to argue for such moral assessment even if it is assumed that states *are* economically self-contained.

The argument would no doubt be very complicated and I can only sketch its main lines. It would begin from the conception of ownership found in the natural law tradition, according to which those who have a superfluity of goods are obligated to use them to promote the well-being of those in need.[17] This obligation imposes the further duty, as Joseph Boyle notes, to form communities for this purpose.[18] This further obligation implies that, if possible, even citizens of a nation whose wealth did not result from its participation in an international economic system would be obligated, as a matter of justice, to establish institutions to facilitate reallocation of their superfluous wealth. Thus even on the traditional assumption of self-contained economies, reallocation of wealth would be morally required by natural law ethics.

It is a natural corollary of this line of argument, which concedes the traditional assumption, that what is subject to moral evaluation is the allocation of wealth and other necessities at a given time. Thus, according to this line of argument, if at a given time there are some who have a superfluity of goods and others who are in want, then a reallocation of goods is demanded as a matter of justice. The line of argument is tenable given the natural law conception of ownership; it is therefore consistent with the natural law tradition to insist that momentary states of the allocation of the world's wealth are the primary subjects of justice.

This is not, however, the line of argument the USCC chose to pursue. Instead, contemporary Catholic teaching consistently rests upon what the USCC called 'the *fact* of interdependence': the denial of self-containedness and the assertion that the superfluity of goods possessed by some results from participation in international economic relationships which impoverish others. And it is a natural corollary of *this* line of argument that the subject of moral assessment is not a momentary state of allocation, but the way in which relationships and institutions effect the production and distribution of wealth and thereby distribute among individuals the benefits and burdens of economic relationships in which all nations participate. In so far as contemporary Catholic social teaching shows a consistent emphasis on interdependence, it is a consistent theme of that teaching that the operations of institutions and relationships be the primary subject of international justice.

Taking them as the primary subject fits well with purposes which I suggested a theory of international justice would advance. Some conception of ideally just institutions is, I argued, necessary to guide the determination and fulfilment of duties that fundamental principles of natural law impose. That conception, while ideal, must none the less be realizable if it is to be used for this purpose. It must not assume the mutability of conditions which cannot be changed. Prominent among obtaining economic conditions is a high degree of international interdependence. This is not a logically necessary fact about international economics. It is, however, a condition which for all practical purposes must be regarded as unchangeable since it is extremely unlikely that nations will become less interdependent in the future. A theory specifying principles to which ideally just institutions conform must therefore take 'the *fact* of interdependence' as given and the operations of institutions and relationships as the primary subject of justice. That the theory must be premised on interdependence is therefore a requirement imposed by its ultimately practical aim and by the fact that interdependence, though a historical contingency, is irreversible.

What a theory that takes institutions and relationships as its primary subject *does* regard as mutable are the institutions in virtue of which interdependence obtains. The productive and allocative functions of international economic institutons can be changed even if the increasing interdependence these institutions establish cannot be reversed. It is for this reason that such a theory is useful in guiding those whose responsibilities include changing those institutions. To see that such a theory can guide assessment of both production and allocation, it will be helpful to consider the value of participation.

Contemporary Catholic social teaching insists that an ideally just economy is one which allows for widespread and meaningful participation in economic activity.[19] A theory of international justice which has as its primary subject the distributive operations of economic institutions is better suited to provide a conception of an ideally just economy that allows for participation than is one that takes as its subject momentary states of allocation.

To see this, consider what remedies to injustice are permitted by a theory of international justice framed to assess the latter. Rectification of an unjust allocation could be accomplished by transferring money, food, construction materials and the like from one nation to another, or from citizens of one nation to citizens of another, until a just allocation is achieved. Clearly this method of rectification fits well with the assumption that states are self-contained entities, each producing a stock of goods with minimal reliance on the demands or contributions of those beyond national borders. It takes as given the stock of goods to be allocated and the needs and desires of those among whom the goods are to be shared internationally. How the goods to be distributed were produced is, from the standpoint of a theory with which this rectification is associated, irrelevant.

By contrast, consider a theory of international justice that is premised on interdependence and that takes as its primary subject the operation of institutions that affect the world economy. An important part of the operation of those institutions is their impact on how goods are produced. Such a theory therefore permits productive as well as allocative processes to be assessed from the point of view of justice. It does not interpret the problem of international justice as that of justly allocating a stock of goods taken as given. Rather, it interprets the problem to include that of arranging institutions so that goods are justly produced as well as allocated.

A theory that endorses this latter interpretation of the problem of international justice is far more congenial than is one that endorses the former to the claim that a just international economy is one which permits widespread and meaningful participation in that economy. Consider, for example, the implications of the two theories for a country whose economy is largely based on the cultivation of a small number of crops for export and for which farmers receive low prices. Suppose further that an acceptable standard of living is maintained through large-scale transfers from wealthy countries.

A theory that assesses the production of goods does not entail criticism of this reliance on transfers. It does, however, leave room for such criticism and for the requirement that wealthier nations direct their capital into the country to permit economic diversification. Capital investment leading to such diversification would be morally required if it better conduced to meaningful participation by making available more meaningful and less menial work, by permitting greater participation in the organization of the domestic economy or by lessening the sense of dependence on countries making transfer payments. And this seems to be the sort of rectification favoured by contemporary Catholic social teaching.[20] A theory that focuses only on the allocation of goods, on the other hand, can permit no such criticism. From its point of view, two states of affairs characterized by identical allocations of goods are equally just. And it therefore furnishes less guidance to those whose responsibilities include altering or eliminating institutions to permit greater participation.

Taking the global distribution of goods among individuals as the primary subject of international justice may, however, seem contrary to the importance Catholic social teaching consistently attaches to the goods of community. Local, regional, ethnic and national communities must be allowed to flourish and maintain their cultural identities.[21] But to do so, they must have material resources at their disposal. Focusing on the global distribution of goods among individuals seems to ignore the just claims of various communities. Moreover, the importance of participation seems to testify in favour of taking as primary the way the international economy distributes goods among communities rather than among individuals, since individuals participate in the international economy only via their participation in smaller organizations. What resources *these* organizations can justly claim therefore seems the most important question.

But taking as primary the question of just distribution among individuals only implies that questions about the claims of communities are logically posterior. Their posteriority follows from the fact that the functioning of these communities is itself subject to moral assessment. The maintenance and cultural identity of these communities cannot become ends in themselves; they must respect the dignity of individuals.[22] Principles of international distributive justice partially specify these constraints on what communities may do. These principles specify, in so far as is possible, what is due to human beings as such, rather than as members of one or another community. Moreover, as we shall see, observance of the principles of just distribution among individuals promotes solidarity among all people; acting contrary to the principles by denying individuals their share of goods impedes this global solidarity. But national, ethnic and local communities cannot so act as to fragment global solidarity.[23] The claims communities have are therefore constrained by the claims of individuals; determination of the latter must be primary.

It might also be objected that taking the distribution among individuals as the primary problem of justice ignores allocation of the resources necessary to promote the universal common good, which has long been an important value in Catholic social thought. Now it is not entirely clear what the universal common good includes. One important ingredient is compliance with the principles of justice; but since strict compliance is presupposed, the funding of international coercive mechanisms to ensure compliance can be safely ignored. Another is solidarity among all members of the human race. I shall argue in the next section that this requires strict regulation of economic inequalities. Seeing how this element of the universal common good is to be realized and determining what its realization might cost therefore requires that we first determine what a just distribution among individuals is.

Still another important element of the universal common good is conservation of the natural world.[24] Just allocation of the resources necessary to clean and preserve the environment and to protect endangered species might significantly complicate the problem of distribution among individuals and seems *not* to presuppose a prior solution to this problem. But whatever claims the world of nature has, it is not at all obvious that they are claims of justice: surely bodies of water, uninhabited lands, rare plants and species of insects have claims grounded very differently than are the entitlements of human beings. Even if these *are* claims of justice, it is not clear against whom such claims are held. The entitlements of lakes and ponds entirely within national borders would surely require different treatment than would claims of species, international waters, the ozone layer and other things which are commonly possessed if possessed at all. Without a very thorough analysis of these issues, it is impossible to determine their priority, parity or posteriority to the question of just distribution among individuals.[25] In any case, analysis of a just distribution among individuals is bound to clarify the demands of international distributive justice even if it should turn out that justice to nature requires its modification.

III. Solidarity and the Difference Principle

I have argued that the primary subject of a theory of international justice which continues the trend of contemporary Catholic social teaching would be the operation of institutions and relationships that effect the production and distribution of goods internationally. I have tried to show how focusing the analysis there rather than on momentary states of allocation permits criticism of the productive as well as the allocative functions of the international economy. I have not, however, defended a principle of justice with which those operations must conform.

The principles at the heart of a natural law theory of international justice will be principles derived from fundamental principles of natural law. Important among these principles is Aquinas's requirement of common use, according to which what Aquinas calls 'external goods' must be used to satisfy the needs of all.[26] Aquinas does not distinguish, in this context, between goods produced by nature and those produced by human industry; his requirement can therefore be taken to apply to wealth, income and manufactured goods, as well as to natural resources.[27] There are, however, a number of principles of justice observance of which would seem to satisfy Aquinas's requirement. I want to consider a global version of John Rawls' Difference Principle in this connection.

Rawls' second principle of justice reads: 'Social and economic inequalities are to be arranged so that they are both (a) to the greatest benefit of the least advantaged and (b) attached to offices and positions open to all under conditions of fair equality of opportunity.'[28] The Difference Principle is the first clause of this principle; it is, of course, a principle designed to regulate domestic and not international economies. Efforts have, however, been made to extend Rawls' theory to the global case. Proponents of this extension argue that the Difference Principle should be applied internationally, so that social and economic inequalities must be arranged to the greatest benefit of the world's least advantaged people.[29] I shall suppose that there are no insurmountable theoretical difficulties with extending the Principle in this way, whatever its merits when so extended.

A global version of the Difference Principle would fit well with the emphasis recent Catholic social thought attaches to interdependence. Rawls says that the primary subject of his theory of justice is 'the basic structure of society, or more exactly, the way in which major social institutions distribute fundamental rights and duties and determine the division of advantages from social cooperation'.[30] It is to the basic structure so understood, and not to momentary states of allocation in the domestic economy, that Rawls' principles of justice, including his Difference Principle, apply. A global Difference Principle would provide a criterion for assessing the justice of a global basic structure, for assessing the ways in which major institutions of the international economy 'distribute rights and duties and determine the division of advantages from social cooperation'. And it is just such a criterion that would be provided by a natural law theory of international justice that is premised on interdependence.

The question I shall be concerned with in what follows is: Should a natural law theory of international justice endorse the global Difference Principle as the principle to which an ideally just international economy would conform and against which other arrangements are to be measured? Note that I am not asking whether natural law theorists or Catholic moral teachers should endorse global extensions of Rawls' whole theory of justice. There are, no doubt, elements of Rawls' theory that are incompatible with natural law ethics or with the trends of contemporary Catholic social teaching. I am concerned only with a global version of the Difference Principle itself. I will argue for the global Difference Principle, first by arguing that the stronger principle of equal distribution is too strong, and then by arguing that weaker principles do not foster the goods of community and solidarity as well as would a global Difference Principle.

In a world that satisfied the Principle of Equality, operation of the world economy would tend towards equal division of the material necessities. This arrangement of the international economy obviously satisfies the requirement of common use. If division is exactly equal, then, if material goods meet the needs of anyone at all, they are used to meet the needs of *every* individual. But though conformity with the Principle would satisfy the common use requirement, the Principle of Equality may be less satisfactory than other principles. Conditions of equality can eliminate incentives for inventiveness, risk and economic growth. One result of compliance with the Principle of Equality might be that *all* are worse off than the worst off would be under arrangements which permit inequalities to function as incentives. Moreover, by eliminating incentive, the Principle threatens to stifle innovation, which is one form of the meaningful participation that a just economy is supposed to realize. The need for at least some economic incentives has therefore been central to the criticisms of the Principle in recent Catholic social teaching.[31]

The problem with an argument premised on the need for incentives is not that it fails against the Principle of Equality; incentive problems underlie the most common objection to radical egalitarianism. The problem is demonstrating that such arguments can be made from within the natural law tradition. At issue is not simply that the natural law tradition has often been uncongenial to entrepreneurial capitalism, and hence to the profit motive. Rather, the problem is the place that concessions to human psychology or human weakness have in determining the demands of justice. By resorting to an argument from incentive to reject the Principle of Equality, I am taking evidence that human beings cannot comply with a principle as evidence that that principle is an inadequate specification of the requirement of common use. But why not acknowledge that the Principle *is* the best specification of that requirement and take evidence of probable non-compliance as evidence that human beings are unable to sustain ideally just institutions?[32]

In response, it is important to recall *why* the just distribution and common use of goods are morally required. These are enjoined so that all can have what they need to develop and exercise the virtues and so that ties of community can develop among human beings. Deriving more specific principles of justice from the fundamental principles of natural law requires deriving principles which promote those ends. Deriving the principles that regulate an ideally just economy requires deriving principles that regulate production and distribution of income, wealth and other goods so that those ends are best realized. How they are best realized depends upon certain features of human psychology, including the way in which humans actually develop ties of friendship, the way they develop the virtue of justice and the fact that human beings need some economic incentives. These are features of human nature that must be taken into account when fundamental precepts of natural law are applied to political institutions. Evidence that human beings cannot realize the goods of justice and community under a given principle is therefore evidence that the principle is in some way deficient and does not express a demand of justice.

Aquinas's own discussion of what institutions best satisfy the requirement of common use confirms that institutions or principles can be rejected because human beings are incapable of realizing these goods under them.[33] Aquinas argues in favour of private possession with common use and against common possession. He does so on the grounds that human beings are prone to quarrel over common property and to neglect the maintenance of commonly held goods. The first of these reasons suggests that Aquinas rejects common possession because, given certain features of human nature, it impedes rather than promotes ties of community, one of the ends that property arrangements should be designed to promote. The second suggests that Aquinas has in mind an incentive argument. Human beings are better motivated to care for commonly used goods, Aquinas argues, if they possess those goods themselves. Both arguments imply that institutional arrangements can be rejected as inadequate on the grounds that they are inappropriate given certain features of human psychology. Incentive arguments against the Principle of Equality are not, therefore, inconsistent with the natural law tradition.

A global Difference Principle, while weaker than the Principle of Equality, is none the less a strongly egalitarian principle. There are a number of weaker principles that might suffice as a standard of global distributive justice: a principle that simply guarantees an acceptable minimum share of goods, one that maximizes average utility subject to a guaranteed acceptable minimum, or one that maximizes total utility subject to a guaranteed acceptable minimum, for example. All of these principles put the world's goods to common use but, because they are weaker, might be easier to sustain. Why choose a global Difference Principle over one of these weaker principles?

Other factors than the strength of a global Difference Principle make this question even more pressing. The Difference Principle is a principle designed to regulate the *inequalities* in income that a domestic economy permits. Rawls argues for the Difference Principle because unregulated or improperly regulated inequalities compromise the self-respect of citizens who are less well off, make political society less stable, and result in the unequal value of the political rights and liberties possessed by those of diverse levels of income.[34] But these reasons for endorsing the Difference Principle in the domestic case, even if sound, do not necessarily have the same force in the global one. Even if unjustified domestic inequalities *do* endanger the social bases of self-respect of citizens of the same nation, a great deal of argument is required to show that inequalities in income between people on opposite sides of the globe sufficiently undermine self-respect to justify the strict regulation a global Difference Principle would impose. Moreover, it is hard to see how a concern to protect the parity of value in political liberty could favour a global Difference Principle since there are no global political institutions to which it is important that all persons have equal access. It might be important that differences in income do not undermine equal and maximal access to the political processes of each country, but that could be guaranteed by conformity of each domestic economy to the Difference Principle. No global Difference Principle is required.

The point of the foregoing arguments is not that a global Difference Principle is unsupportable. It is, rather, that the Difference Principle relies on reasons for regulating inequalities that seem peculiar to the case of a domestic economy. Supporting the claim that a natural law theory of just international institutions would include a global Difference Principle requires finding strong reasons within the natural law tradition for using the Principle to regulate the inequalities to which the international economy can give rise. Interest in a sense of community and civic friendship, deeply rooted in the natural law tradition, provide those reasons.

Rawls' reliance on the device of the Original Position and his efforts to locate his work within the contract tradition have led many readers to overlook the communitarian implications of his work. One of the great strengths of the Difference Principle is that it arranges production and distribution to promote mutual respect and a sense of cooperation, and thus to foster a form of civic friendship. Rawls, of course, expresses this in Kantian terms. To permit lesser prospects for some to be justified by greater benefits for others would, he argues, be to permit the treatment of some as means for the well-being of others. And it would encourage a sense of competition for the benefits the economy distributes. The Difference Principle, by contrast, diminishes the sense of competition by allowing some to benefit only when all do.[35] It fosters a sense of cooperation by guaranteeing that gains realized by any one person are gains for all. And by forbidding trade-offs that result in lesser well-being for some just so that

others can have more, the Difference Principle 'rule[s] out even the tendency to regard men as means to one another's welfare'.[36] The Difference
Principle therefore, Rawls says, best realizes the Kantian dictum that
others are to be respected and treated as ends in themselves.

These considerations favour a global version of the Difference Principle
even against principles which would guarantee a minimum standard of
living. Principles that maximize average or total utility subject to a guaranteed minimum permit the sort of trade-offs the Difference Principle forbids.
In the interest of maximizing utility, they permit better prospects for some
to be secured by lessening the prospects of others. This encourages people
to regard one another as means or impediments to well-being. The possibility of such trade-offs also permits a sense of competition to develop,
since some would benefit from the operations of the world economy only
if others lose out. Of course, if the minimum guaranteed is high enough,
the level of material well-being that these other principles provide may be
satisfactory. When only material well-being is considered, the Difference
Principle may be on a par with these other principles. But because the
Difference Principle better fosters mutual respect and a sense of cooperation than do other principles, it is to be preferred.

By drawing on the conditions of civic friendship and mutual respect,
these last arguments in favour of the Difference Principle draw on
considerations that have also been prominent in the natural law tradition
from its beginnings in Aquinas. Aquinas learned from Aristotle's *Politics*
that human beings are naturally social. He took this to entail that political
society should be ordered to foster concerns for the good of others singly
and for the common good. And he took it to entail that laws should be
framed to foster a state of civic friendship.[37]

Aquinas assumed that political societies were *societates perfectae*,
relatively small, self-contained and self-sufficient communities in which
fairly strong bonds of civic friendship were possible. As I argued in
Section II, the conditions of modern life require that the natural law
political theory should reject that assumption and recognize a high degree
of international interdependence. Natural law political theory need not,
however, reject Aquinas's view that political and economic institutions,
including production relations, property arrangements and the allocation
of goods, should be so ordered that they foster bonds of civic friendship
and community that are as strong as the size of the society in question
permits.

This is exactly the approach to questions of international justice found
in contemporary Catholic social teaching. There the values of international
community and concern for the common good are asserted as proper in the
face of global economic interdependence. Thus John Paul II writes in
Sollicitudo Rei Socialis that:

When interdependence becomes recognized in this way, the correlative response as a moral and social attitude, as a 'virtue' is *solidarity*. [Solidarity] is *a firm and persevering determination* to commit oneself to the *common good*; that is to say to the good of all and of each individual, because we are *all* really responsible *for all.*[38]

Solidarity is therefore the virtue to be developed and exercised by all in so far as they participate in and are affected by the world economy. Its possession entails commitment to the good of all and of each, and it restrains the desires for profit and power. The remark about mutual responsibility suggests that it includes an attitude of cooperation rather than competition to secure the necessities of life. Another remark in the same encyclical suggests that it is a virtue which lays the basis for a sort of civic friendship or sense of universal community that extends the notion of civic friendship so important to Aquinas's political thought:

Solidarity helps us to see the 'other' – whether *person, people,* or *nation* – not just as some kind of instrument, with a work capacity and physical strength to be exploited at low cost and then discarded when no longer useful, but as our 'neighbor', a 'helper', to be made a sharer on a par with ourselves[.][39]

The problem for a natural law theory of international justice is that of stipulating an arrangement of the international economy that best fosters individuals' development of the virtue of solidarity and thereby lays the basis for civic friendship. A global version of the Difference Principle would, I have argued, better foster it than would weaker principles which guarantee a minimum, but which do not regulate inequalities as strictly. There are also, I have argued, reasons consistent with the natural law tradition for rejecting a principle stronger than the global Difference Principle, the Principle of Equality. Natural law theory should therefore endorse a global Difference Principle as a principle of international distributive justice.

If an ideally just economy would conform to a global Difference Principle, then the current international economy is gravely flawed. And certainly the international movement of money contributes significantly to the creation and perpetuation of injustice. International trade, lending and repayment, processes of production, international investment practices and the conduct of multinationals all stand in need of rectification. Unfortunately, a global Difference Principle does not entail a course to a more just world, nor does it specify what individuals must do to realize one. But I hope that by tying fundamental values and principles of natural law teaching to a principle of international distributive justice, I have given some indication of the world to which natural law ethicists think that course should lead.

Notes

1. I have used official Vatican translations of all the encyclicals to which I have referred. Latin editions of all these encyclicals, except those of Leo XIII, are published in the Vatican's *Acta Apostolicae Sedis*; those of Leo XIII can be found in the Vatican's *Leonis XIII P. M. Acta*.

2. The best known exceptions are the Renaissance scholastics who disputed the justice of Spanish conquests in the New World; see Anthony Pagden "Dispossessing the Barbarian: The Languages of Spanish Thomism and the Debate Over the Property Rights of the American Indians," *The Languages of Political Theory in Early Modern Europe*, ed. Pagden (Cambridge: Cambridge University Press, 1987) pp. 79–98.

3. Para. 44 of the testimony presented before the House Subcommittee on Foreign Operations by Archbishop Rembart Weakland, OSB on behalf of the United States Catholic Conference March 4, 1987. Archbishop Weakland was quoting a report of the Organization for Economic Cooperation and Development. His testimony can be found in *Pastoral Letters of the United States Catholic Bishops* (Washington, D.C.: US Catholic Conference, 1989) vol. 5, pp. 501–12.

4. USCC "Statement", par. 45.

5. Pontifical Justice and Peace Commission "An Ethical Approach to the International Debt Question", *Origins*, 16 (1987), 601–11 at 604.

6. John Paul II, *Sollicitudo Rei Socialis* (Boston: Daughters of St Paul, 1987), sec. 19.

7. Donal Dorr contrasts the Pauline and post-Pauline approaches with that characteristic of the documents of Vatican II, particularly *Gaudium et Spes*. Donal Dorr, "Solidarity and Integral Human Development," *The Logic of Solidarity*, ed. G. Baum and R. Ellsberg (New York: Orbis Books, 1989), pp. 143–54 at 145.

8. John Rawls, *A Theory of Justice* (Cambridge, Mass.: Harvard University Press, 1971), pp. 8–9.

9. Aquinas, *Summa Theologiae* (Madrid: Biblioteca de Autores Cristianos.) II–II,58, 1; this work will hereafter be cited *ST*.

10. Ibid., II–II, 71, 1, for example.

11. Ibid., II–II, 66, 2.

12. Cf. Ibid., II–II, 71,1 and ad 1 and 2 for the conditions on mutual aid.

13. USCC "Statement," pars 29, 31; emphasis in original. For John XXIII on interdependence, see *Pacem in Terris* (Boston: Daughters of St Paul, 1963) par. 130; for Paul VI, *Populorum Progressio* (Boston: Daughters of St Paul, 1971) par. 3; for John Paul II, *Sollicitudo Rei Socialis*, par. 38; for the National Conference of Catholic Bishops, *Economic Justice for all* in *Pastoral Letters of the United States Catholic Bishops*, ibid., pp. 371–492.

14. Charles Beitz, *Political Theory and International Relations* (Princeton, N.J.: Princeton University Press, 1979) pp. 3–66. For the rejection of the international state of nature model by the Catholic tradition of natural law see

Heinrich Rommen, *The State and Catholic Thought* (St Louis: B. Herder Book Co., 1945) p. 617.

15. For a clear discussion of the circumstances of justice, see Rawls, *A Theory of Justice*, pp. 126–30. For a source in the natural law tradition, see Aquinas *ST*, II–II,51,1 and 2. John Finnis, *Natural Law and Natural Right* (Oxford: Oxford University Press, 1980) pp. 165ff. helpfully explains these difficult passages in Aquinas.

16. See pars 15–16 of Archbishop Weakland's testimony. Archbishop Weakland was quoting a report of the Organisation for Economic Co-operation and Development.

17. The *locus classicus* of the natural law conception of ownership is Aquinas, *ST*, II–II, 66.

18. Joseph Boyle, "Natural Law, Ownership and the World's Resources," *Journal of Value Inquiry*, 23 (1989), 191–207 at p. 195. Boyle's paper was a contribution to the Ethikon Conference on Allocation and Ownership of the World's Resources; I am much indebted to it.

19. See, e.g., NCCB, *Economic Justice*, pars. 1, 77–8; John Paul II, *Sollicitudo Rei Socialis*, secs 17–18. For the relationship of participation to the tradition, see NCCB, *Economic Justice*, pars 99ff. and the sources listed at note 53.

20. USCC "Statement," par. 44; also John Paul II, *Sollicitudo Rei Socialis*, secs 15, 44–5.

21. See, e.g., John Paul II, *Sollicitudo Rei Socialis*, sec. 26.

22. See John Paul II, *Address to the XXXIV General Assembly of the United Nations*, October 2, 1979 (Daughters of St Paul, 1980) par. 5.

23. John Paul II, *Sollicitudo Rei Socialis*, sec. 33.

24. See, e.g., John Paul II's Message for the World Day of Peace, January 1, 1990 "The Ecological Crisis: A Common Responsibility".

25. The natural law tradition makes it clear that duties to nature are not entirely derivative from duties to preserve natural resources for future generations. The order of nature and the diversity of creatures are treated as goods in themselves and thus as having value independent of their use or enjoyment value to present and future human beings. For a contemporary source see ibid., par. 8; for a classical one, Aquinas, *ST*, I, 103, 2 and 3. Analysis of our responsibilities towards nature will include a discussion of justice towards future generations, but will not be exhausted by it.

26. Aquinas, *ST*, II–II, 66, 2.

27. As they are for Boyle's purposes at "Natural Law. . . ."

28. Rawls, *A Theory of Justice*, p. 83., Rawls' first principle enjoins the equal distribution of rights and liberties. In what follows I will take it for granted that natural law theory would endorse some global version of this principle; I am therefore concerned only with what that theory implies about the just distribution of 'duties and the division of advantages from social cooperation'. For remarks suggesting Catholic acceptance of some global version of the first principle, see discussion of the UN Universal Declaration of Human Rights at John XXIII, *Pacem in Terris*, pars 143–5; also Jacques Maritain, *Man and the State* (Chicago: University of Chicago Press, 1951) pp. 76ff.

29. Thomas Pogge, *Realizing Rawls* (Ithaca, N.Y.: Cornell University Press, 1989) is an excellent example; for Pogge's persuasive argument that the Difference Principle enjoins arranging inequalities for the world's least advantaged people rather than least advantaged states, see pp. 242ff.

30. Rawls, *A Theory of Justice*, p. 7.

31. John Paul II, *Sollicitudo Rei Socialis*, par. 15.

32. Thanks to Joseph Boyle for helpful correspondence on this point.

33. Aquinas, *ST*, II–II, 66, 2.

34. See Joshua Cohen, "Democratic Equality," *Ethics*, 99 (1989), 757–82.

35. If, following Rawls, we assume the chain-connection; see *A Theory of Justice*, pp. 80ff.

36. Ibid., p. 183.

37. On concern for the common good as a motive, see *ST*, II–II, 58, 6; for the good of others, *ST*, I–II, 56, 6. Aquinas discusses civic friendship in a number of places. Especially important for present purposes is *ST*, I–II, 99, 2 where Aquinas says that the principal purpose of the law is to produce (*faciat*) friendship among citizens.

38. John Paul II, *Sollicitudo Rei Socialis*, sec. 38, emphases in original.

39. John Paul II, *Sollicitudo Rei Socialis*, sec. 39.

Commentary on Dummett and Weithman

John Finnis

Because the basic goods intrinsic to human flourishing are multiple, and because each human being belongs to a number of communities (each of whose common good is an aspect of the intrinsic good of each of its members), our responsibilities are complex. Similarly complex is the theory which accurately identifies these goods, communities and responsibilities – natural law theory. The complexity of this theory is enhanced by the complexity of rational choice and action, in which ends, means, and unintended but foreseen side-effects each fall within the chooser's responsibility, but in very different ways.

Both Ann Dummett's and Paul Weithman's chapters seem to me to over-simplify the theory. Since my role is only to suggest some comments, I shall take no position on the question of what is just and what unjust in the international movement of people and funds. Nor shall I attempt to state the extent of my agreement with either of the chapters. It should not be assumed that the policies I favour involve less far-reaching reforms than theirs. I shall merely indicate some points at which I think the logic of their arguments fails.

I

Ann Dummett thinks that the Home Secretary, Mr Edward Shortt, KC, was rejecting a natural law concept of justice when he said that steps to secure national safety are just even when they result necessarily in 'the infliction of hardship upon an alien'. I think her assessment is hasty. Mr Shortt's statement is ambiguous, and although nothing in his speech itself resolves the ambiguity, neither his words nor the traditions of British public discourse they take for granted commit him to the view that the interest of a single political unit is a complete moral guide, or that aliens have no human rights valid against a nation-state.[1]

Suppose a heckler had asked whether Mr Shortt was asserting that aliens could be held hostage, tortured or killed in order to secure national safety. Nothing in the statement of this Liberal politician (and judge) would have been negated by the reply he would certainly have given: that such an assertion was far from his meaning and unacceptable both to him and to the nation. The heckler's intervention would thus have brought to the surface the ambiguity between hardship imposed *as a means* and hardship *resulting as an unintended though foreseen side-effect*. The word 'infliction' fosters this ambiguity – though probably unintentionally. If Shortt was not careful about the morally essentially distinction, nor is Ann Dummett. And her own phrase 'promote the good of citizens *at the expense of others*' trades on the same ambiguity, even more misleadingly.

Consider a statement essential to Aquinas's account of the justice of self-defence: 'One is not morally required to abstain – in order to avoid killing someone else – from an act of self-defence proportionate to the occasion; for one has a stronger obligation to preserve one's own life than the life of another.'[2] Aquinas is saying, if you like, that one may justly 'inflict' harm on another in self-defence, and that one may defend oneself 'at the expense of another'. But more precisely, he is saying that one private individual may never *choose to* inflict death or any other harm *as a means* to his safety or any other good – may never *intend* death or any other harm to anyone;[3] one may only choose to stop the attack by those measures which are available to one, are no more than sufficient for stopping the attack, and impose no unfair side-effects on the assailant or anyone else. One may not defend oneself by killing or harming hostages, even if that is the only means of self-defence likely to suffice. In that sense, one may not act 'at the expense of others', i.e. to impose on them a harm as a means to one's own gain or even one's security. (This negative norm of justice does not itself derive from the principle of fairness with which I shall later be concerned.)

Now consider a case which is like private self-defence as conceived by Aquinas in that it involves a kind of preference for one's own security (or the interests of those for whom one has a special responsibility) over the interests of others, but which differs in that it involved no application of harmful force, no 'infliction of harm'. Suppose one comes home one evening to find squatters occupying one's house; one's children have nowhere to sleep and study; so one has the squatters put out into the street. Is one promoting the good of one's children at the expense of other human beings, in defiance of human rights and natural law? No. One acts to preserve and retain the space and facilities one had justly held in possession for one's children. If there is foreseeable loss to the squatters, that is a side-effect, not a means. Perhaps there is no loss, since they are rich people who squat for fun. Perhaps there is loss, since they have nowhere else to go. In either case, their losing, precisely as such, is not a means to one's gain; and where there is loss it results from a lack (their lack of *anywhere else* to go) of which one is not oneself, as such, the cause. Does this exhaust one's responsibilities? By no means. If it is an icy night and the squatters are sick or thinly clad, one has some responsibilities . . . And if a political party credibly proposes fair means of alleviating homelessness, one has a responsibility to count that a serious reason for favouring that party.

II

Ann Dummett's next major proposition about natural law or the natural law tradition is: Since, by natural law, one's rights arise from one's being human (not from one's being a citizen), any legal or political arrangement in which citizens have rights which aliens do not have must contradict natural law and be unjust. This argument seems to me invalid and mistaken.

Some of my children's rights are predicated on no fact other than that they are human: notably, their right not to be intentionally killed or harmed in their health and bodily integrity, their right not to be lied to, their right to be considered in any sharing of the world's resources, their right not to be punished without fair trial. Some of their most important rights, however, are predicated on the combination of their being human with some further, so to speak more contingent fact(s), such as that they are mine, or that I have paid such and such a school to educate them: hence their right to be fed and clothed and educated *by me*, and their right to be cared for during school hours *by that school* and *its* responsible employees and agents (not to mention their right to attend gatherings for alumni of the school). Other important rights which they have are predicated on the fact that they have made the commitments they have, by which they undertook responsibilities and enjoy rights which fairly correspond to those responsibilities – e.g. as spouses, or as owners of property, or as members of a college. Some other rights and duties of theirs – such as their right to vote – have an intelligible correspondence to responsibilities such as their contingent liability as citizens to do military or other national service, responsibilities which they have without having voluntarily undertaken them, but which are predicated on facts which include the undertakings which others have made and maintain and the responsibilities which others respect and fulfil for the sake of benefiting members of the community as members of which my children have precisely these obligations or liabilities and corresponding rights.

Underlying the notion that such and such a right corresponds to such and such an obligation is a modality of the principle of fairness, a principle of natural law most pithily captured in the Golden Rule. This principle is fundamental to most of our specific affirmative obligations and to the correlative rights which we have (correlative to others' obligations to us). The modality in play in the last sentence of the preceding paragraph is: fairness requires that one who takes the benefits of a fair system of cooperation and mutual restraints and service should take the corresponding burdens; and that one who has assumed the burdens is entitled to the benefits. The application of this modality of fairness is, of course, conditional on the conformity of the system with all other moral norms, including fairness in its other modalities.

If Japan adopts a law like one under discussion there in mid-1990, permitting Malaysians to enter Japan for the purposes of employment on condition that no such immigrant may stay for more than two years, or be visited by any members of his or her family, must we condemn this as unjust? Suppose that such workers are paid wages ample for feeding, housing and educating their families in Malaysia but less than the wages paid to Japanese who are doing comparable work but who need wages well above the Malaysian level to pay for the housing and education in Japan which these Malaysians will never have to provide for. Must we say that this is unjust? I can think of no plausible norm of justice which compels us to. And: to say this, is not to accept the fairness and justice of every system which allows in alien migrant workers to work for long periods in conditions and for emoluments inferior to those available to citizens.

III

Ann Dummett proposes a norm of justice which would condemn the Japanese–Malaysian proposal. The norm she proposes is: Everyone has a right to enter any territory he or she chooses, with a view to living and working peacefully under the laws applicable to citizens, provided only that the exercise of this right does not coincide with its exercise by so many other people that the fundamental human rights of other human individuals are threatened – such fundamental human rights *not* including the right that the moral, demographic, economic, political or other cultural character or well-being of a national or lesser community be preserved.

Her primary argument for this norm is that it is logically or rationally entailed by the norm – whose justice is widely admitted – according to which everyone has the right to emigrate. (It is not clear to me that the exercise of this right is, in justice, as free from conditions as Western policies have asserted and Ann Dummett assumes.) But there simply is no such entailment. It is quite clear who has the duty correlative to the right to emigrate. It is quite unclear that (as Ann Dummett seems to suggest) every other community everywhere has an equivalent duty to admit unlimited numbers of foreigners whatever the foreseeable consequences for the economic, political and cultural life of its citizens (short of 'violation' of their 'recognized individual' fundamental rights defined as narrowly as Ann Dummett proposes).

It seems to me that the fundamental norms of justice which underlie the institution of property (*dominium*) are applicable, *mutatis mutandis*, to the institution of territorial dominion by politically organized communities. The first of these fundamental norms is that the world with its resources is radically common to all, for the benefit of each and every member of the human race. The second is that a system of dominion – entailing restrictions on the availability of defined parcels of land and resources – tends to result in important benefits to all and can be fair, provided that its immediate negative implications for those who remain in serious deprivation by reason of their exclusion from lands and/or resources are alleviated. Ann Dummett criticizes 'Western countries' for 'deliberately blurring' the distinction between 'the special claims of the persecuted or starving and the lesser claims of an ordinary migrant' (or would-be migrant). But the principal weakness of her own radical proposal is that it blurs to the point of eliminating that very distinction, a distinction which seems to me inherent in the norms of justice I have mentioned (all too briefly) in this paragraph.

IV

Natural law theory is a reflective account of what practical reasonableness, oriented by an integral openness to and respect for the intrinsic human goods, requires of human choosers in the various sorts of conditions in which they have to make and carry out their choices. It has no particular interest in states of affairs of a type no one is likely to encounter, such as the state of affairs in which 'individuals and institutions . . . comply perfectly with the principles of justice'.[4] Moreover, justice and injustice are not properties of any state of affairs, except in so far as it may be considered precisely *qua* exemplifying the fulfilment or neglect of responsibilities of justice by ascertainable people.

Justice, in short, is essentially a property of choices and dispositions which bear on choice. Choices and dispositions are just in so far as they satisfy all that morality requires of a choice, or other disposition of will, which impacts on other people. (I say 'people' deliberately; *pace* Weithman, one's moral responsibilities to respect and promote the sub-human realm of nature are not, I think, helpfully assimilated to responsibilities of justice in response to 'claims' e.g. of bodies of water, etc.) That is the fundamental reason why a sensible theory of justice has little or nothing to do with imagining states of affairs in which resources would be distributed according to a pattern which the theory identifies as just, under conditions which more or less guarantee that no one's choices or actions could move us from the world in which we live to that state of affairs.

Rawls' second principle of justice, as articulated in the formula quoted by Weithman, seems to me to be either a commendation of injustice, or no principle of justice/injustice at all. Who can properly define their role as 'arranging social and economic inequalities'? Anyone who undertook such a role would be undertaking to act unjustly. To say that, is not of course to say that anyone should undertake to *eliminate* all social and economic inqualities; that too would be a work of injustice. It is to say that justice has to do with fair choices, and that fairness – whose rational criteria are complex and in their application partly relative to non-rational factors such as feelings ('Do as you would *be willing* to be done by') – accepts inequalities only as a side-effect of choices concerned with other matters and not as an objective to be attained by some 'arrangement' of means to ends.

But where one's action is such that some whom one could otherwise have helped are left worse-off than if one had helped them, it can be unfair to accept such a side-effect; one can have a responsibility, in accordance with the principle of fairness, to make an alternative choice which avoids that side-effect and helps those people. So the justice of the 'Difference Principle' can be tested by asking: Can it ever be fair for anyone, in the exercise of responsibilities in and for a community (family, voluntary association, nation, church, and so on), to make a choice in such a way that the least advantaged people in the world are not benefited by that choice? Weithman's answer appears to be: No, such a choice could never be fair.

That answer seems to me very implausible, and the argument advanced in defence of it seems quite inadequate. The strong form of the argument is clearly guilty of the fallacy I have noted in section I above, of confusing means with side-effects. This is the 'Kantian' argument that: 'to *permit* lesser prospects for some to be justified by greater benefits for others would be to permit the treatment of some *as a means for* the well-being of others.' Not so. If a couple spend £100 on educating their children, thereby permitting every other child (anywhere) who could have benefited from that £100 to have lesser prospects than if they had spent in on that child, they are not thereby treating (or permitting the treatment of) any other child (let alone every other child) *as a means for* the well-being of their own children.

The weaker version of Weithman's argument for the Difference Principle is not clearly fallacious, but I see no clear reason to accept it. It asserts that accepting the principle would 'foster the goods of community' better than any other principle of justice. To me it seems highly probable that if anyone arrogated to themselves the role of 'arranging inequalities' so that those inequalities were 'to the greatest benefit of the least advantaged' anywhere in the world, there would result a far-reaching disruption of community as soon as people found all their particular commitments, undertakings, roles and communities being deflected and overridden for the sake of a single supreme objective – the bettering of the (currently?) least advantaged. But, more to the point, there would very probably be well-founded complaints, raised by many people who are poor but not of the class of 'the least advantaged' (however one may specify that vague category), that the arrangements designed to benefit the least advantaged more than any alternative arrangements were arrangements which imposed on them, the poor-but-not-poorest, burdens quite disproportionate to the burdens (if any) imposed on the really well off. Such complaints are often justly made about the politics of our own real-world societies, in which welfare policies fashioned by the rich and powerful in the interest of the poorest are financed by exactions which bear unfairly heavily on the not quite so poor, or the lower middle class. Rawls' one-dimensional Difference Principle ignores this and many other sources and forms of unfairness in distributions of benefits and burdens in communities.

The poverty of the worst off is an evil which very many people, in very many different ways, have a responsibility to do something to alleviate. The responsibility of any particular person or institution to be of service to the worst off is a responsibility which, under the general principle of fairness (and consistently with all other moral requirements), is specified in moral norms (norms of natural law) corresponding to that person or institution's resources and other responsibilities. For people *in extremis*, all the world and its resources is again common: no claim to property or dominion is, precisely as such, morally valid against them. It does not follow that particular owners, trustees or possessors have the obligation to make the service of such people the dominant end to which every use of their resources must be a means, regardless of their own opportunities of putting those resources to other good uses and of the extent to which others in their position are cooperating with, free-riding on or defecting from cooperative efforts to provide the services which the worst off need. Still less have they the obligation to harness all their resources to the service of world 'community' or 'solidarity',[5] conceived of as a dominant end, a future end state of affairs to be achieved by efficient arrangements of means.

Notes

1. Anyone minded to infer that I am naive about the morals of British statesmen and their public should first read J. Finnis, J. Boyle and G. Grisez, *Nuclear Deterrence, Morality and Realism* (Oxford: Oxford University Press, 1987), pp. 8–10, 38–44. But issues of honesty and hypocrisy are irrelevant to the point being made by Ann Dummett.

2. Aquinas, *Summa Theologiae*, II–II, 64, 7c: 'Nec est necessarium ad salutem ut homo actum moderatae tutelae praetermittat ad evitandum occisionem alterius, quia plus tenetur homo vitae suae providere quam vitae alienae.'

3. Ibid.: 'illicitum est quod homo intendat occidere hominem ut seipsum defendat . . . '.

4. Nor do I agree that the social teaching of the Popes since Vatican II has been directed towards that 'ideal' state of affairs, whose unattainability in this world is guaranteed by important Christian teachings about original sin, the transcendence of the Kingdom, and the portents which will precede the Kingdom's definitive installation. Certainly the essay of Donal Dorr which Weithman cites hugely exaggerates the methodological difference between Vatican II and Paul VI, and simply overlooks the continuity between the pre-Vatican II concept of the common good and Paul VI's concept of integral development. But since I think it unsafe to assume that Catholic social teaching is directed solely by principles knowable independently of revelation, or that recent documents of the US Catholic Conference adequately represent Catholic social teaching, I here make no arguments about or by reference to Catholic teaching, beyond saying that nothing in it seems to me inconsistent with what I say in this commentary.

5. Weithman seems to treat 'community' as synonymous with the 'solidarity' which is thematic in John Paul II's encyclical *Sollicitudo Rei Socialis*. But the word is not used by the Pope to refer to an end state which might be achieved by skilful 'selection' of principles efficient for promoting a certain future state of affairs. Instead, it is used to pick out a specific moral attitude or virtue by which individuals fulfil themselves by including the *common* good in their own *proper* (individual) good. The word thus corresponds closely to the virtue of 'general (or legal) justice' as that term was understood by Aquinas, but not as the term was used in later scholastic writing: see J. Finnis, *Natural Law and Natural Rights* (Oxford: Oxford University Press, 1980, 1989), pp. 184–6.

Political Realist Perspectives

— 15 —

Migration in law and ethics:
A realist perspective*

David C. Hendrickson

I

It is not easy to assess the contribution that the tradition of political realism might make to the ethical debate over the transnational migration of peoples. The difficulty is not only that questions of migration have traditionally lain on the periphery of concern for most realist writers. More importantly, the whole point of departure of the conference at Mont St Michel in 1989 was one which assumes the supremacy of the moral point of view, whereas realism is often identified with a radically different stance. In their works on international ethics, both Michael Walzer and Charles Beitz begin their enquiries by arguing 'against realism', a doctrine identified with Thrasymachus's teaching that 'justice is the advantage of the stronger', or the speech of the Athenian generals to the Melians.[1] In short, the doctrines often identified with a political realist perspective would seem at first glance to have very little to contribute to a debate on the ethical appropriateness of restrictions on the free transnational migration of peoples. In so far as realists subscribe to Thrasymachus's principle, they would seem hardly to have an ethical doctrine at all, much less one that might have illuminated the topic of our conference.

Such a conclusion, however, would be misleading. The tradition of political realism is a rich one, and it is by no means as bereft of ethical considerations as most of its detractors claim. Nearly all realists, on close inspection, think there is a difference between good and evil; they appear

---

* I should like to thank Terry Nardin, Robert W. Tucker, Timothy Fuller and David Mapel for their valuable comments.

normally to prefer the former to the latter; and they are often harsh critics of the exercise of state power. It is also true, however, that realists do not usually approach political questions from an exclusively moral point of view. The single-minded focus on the ethical appropriateness of restrictions on the free transnational migration of peoples, such as we have been asked to consider, is not a line of enquiry that would normally suggest itself to the realist. With Montesquieu, realists tend to think that it is 'useless to attack politics directly by showing how much its practices are in conflict with morality and reason. This sort of discourse convinces everybody, but changes nobody.' Given the world as it is, 'it is better to follow a roundabout road and to try to convey to the great a distaste for certain political practices by showing how little they yield that is at all useful.'[2]

II

Political realism is less a doctrine than a disposition. It offers an outlook and a method for addressing political issues, but not specific conclusions, which often turn on fact and circumstances. It is sceptical, pessimistic and anti-utopian. Attempts to transcend the essentially self-interested character of human beings, the realist thinks, are likely to fail save in the most exceptional of circumstances, and may lead to danger or hypocrisy. In 'the eternal dispute between those who imagine the world to suit their policy, and those who arrange their policy to suit the realities of the world', the realist takes sides with the latter.[3]

The outlook of the realist tends to be informed by a thoroughgoing consequentialism. The teaching of Kantians and Christian theologians – that justice be done, though the heavens fall – is rejected as being otherworldly. Though realists differ in their view of the circumstances in which ordinary morality may be overridden, they believe that in cases of necessity it is permissible to do so. The inveterate tendency to highlight the disparity between professed intention and actual result is by no means distinct to political realism: it is a central part of both the tragic and comic understandings of human existence, with which realism has genuine affinity. Realists are alive to the possibility that good intentions may yield evil results, and that actions contravening ordinary moral or legal rules may be necessary in bringing forth a desired good. Machiavelli's comment on Hannibal's reputation for cruelty and its utility in keeping his army disciplined nicely illustrates the latter point: 'thoughtless writers', he claimed, 'admire on the one hand [Hannibal's] actions, and on the other blame the principal cause of them.'[4]

Realists find it morally acceptable that we should prefer the interests of our own collective to those of mankind in general; and they insist that the statesman, the trustee for the community, is under a peculiar obligation to serve the interests of the state he represents. In part, this embrace of collective egoism rests on certain psychological facts (or what are taken to be such) of human nature. Alexander Hamilton, in the debate over the ratification of the Constitution, put the matter in the following way: 'The human affections, like solar heat, lose their intensity, as they depart from the center; and become languid, in proportion to the expansion of the circle, on which they act.' Thus, 'we love our families, more than our neighbours: We love our neighbours, more than our countrymen in general.'[5] As the experience of nationalism abundantly testifies, we also love our countrymen more than mankind in general. Collective egoism derives a great part of its force from social affections, and the ineffectiveness of moral doctrines which assert that the rights and interests of all are to be given an equal weight in any ethical reckoning is easily deducible from this fact: such doctrines must contend not only with the individual selfishness endemic to human nature but also with social affections that tend powerfully towards particularism.

That collective egoism is firmly rooted in human nature seems uncontestable; its moral basis, however, is far more problematic. For some realists morality and politics exist in two different realms, whose respective claims are in eternal opposition to one another. On this view, political action inherently tends toward evil deeds and dirty hands, and nothing is to be gained by pretending that politics can be anything other than the bad business it normally is. The attempt to introduce moral considerations into the alien world of politics only succeeds in muddying the waters of moral discourse.[6] Far more characteristic of the realist position, however, is the view that action on behalf of the national interest is itself an ethical imperative. The preservation of the state's security, well-being and institutional integrity is the condition for the realization of other values, without which no civilized existence is possible at all. According to the former interpretation, realism is the view that morality must give way before the necessities of the state; according to the latter, the necessities of the state are part and parcel of any ethical reckoning. This distinction is of considerable philosophical interest, though its significance with regard to any particular ethical problem is of lesser weight: in either case, the vital interests of the state serve to override otherwise binding moral and legal obligations.

In considering a problem of international ethics, the political realist is likely to place much value on the enquiry into the customary usages of states, and in this respect realism has much affinity with positivist conceptions of international law. Law and morality are no doubt two very different things, and such an enquiry into customary usage or treaty obligation cannot be determinative of the moral question. As Brierly observes, 'Every state habitually commits acts of selfishness which are often gravely injurious to other states, and yet are not contrary to international law; but we do not on that account necessarily judge them to have been "right".'[7] Still, the realist is likely to be sceptical that states will ever reach agreement on principles of justice founded in nature or reason. Under these circumstances, international law, founded on express agreement or customary usage, may play a more valuable role in regulating the relations among states than moral norms and human rights either proclaimed by the philosopher or held to be part of international law because of their conformity with the principles of natural justice. There would, at the very least, appear to be no necessary relationship between more advanced conceptions of human rights and better state conduct, as the experience of the twentieth century attests.[8]

A positivist doctrine may constitute a greater restraint on state action than critics are willing to acknowledge, but there is no denying that the consequentialist and egoistic character of realist thought is often used to justify exercises of state power that other traditions of discourse might find immoral or unethical. In the old tradition of *raison d'état*, the state's security, well-being and integrity took precedence over all other values. When the safety of the country is in question, as Machiavelli said, 'no considerations of justice or injustice, humanity or cruelty, nor of glory or of shame, should be allowed to prevail.'[9]

Writers in the realist tradition have not been uncritical of the abuses to which the doctrine of reason of state has regularly led; few would hold that the doctrine constitutes a *carte blanche* to override normal moral or legal restraints for considerations of mere advantage or convenience. At the same time, the realist rejects the notion that the statesman should conduct himself according to a system of Christian ethics. We are not obliged to love neighbouring nations as we love our own. Justice, on this view, is satisfied by doing others no wrongful injury. Beyond the claims of justice there are distinct claims of humanitarianism or charity, and realists differ in the weight to be accorded these. For some, humanitarian duties appear to be of only marginal significance, and for them it would be possible to elaborate the duties of states with hardly any reference at all to the humanitarian obligations states bear towards strangers. To others, such as Montesquieu or Vattel, social duties are of real weight, but nevertheless remain of lesser force than the 'duties to oneself'. That 'nations should do to one another in times of peace the most good possible, and in times of war the least ill possible, without harming their true interests', was the rule that Montesquieu proposed to summarize the basic principle of the law of nations.[10] It might be stretching matters to place such an enlightened principle squarely within the tradition of political realism, for the realist may object that, in a system of competitive states, it is frequently impossible to do much good for others without impairing ones's own interests. The point here is simply that, in the realist tradition, humanitarian duties do have some weight, and there is a presumption against action that does real or permanent injury to others while providing only slight or temporary advantages to oneself. There is no blanket licence to do as one pleases, quite apart from the effect that state action has on others.

III

There is nothing in the realist tradition that would hinder recognition of the idea (normally associated with liberalism) that the free movement of individuals across borders often serves important human values. There are too many instances in which such migration seems inseparable from that 'flourishing' of human communities that is a basic human good.[11] Realism, moreover, has been closely identified in European history with the defence of the state system and with the refuge from oppressive power that a system of independent states permitted. A pointed contrast was often drawn – most memorably, perhaps, by Gibbon – between the multiplicity and diversity fostered by this system and the oppressive weight of the old Roman dominion.[12] The ability to flee is an important value secured by the plurality of independent states, and has always formed one of its most compelling justifications.

If free movement across borders does serve important human values, it is also the case that such movement may pose a serious threat to the security, well-being, or institutional integrity of peoples into whose midst strangers move. Migration creates new social facts that may often be irresistible and overwhelming. One thinks here of the predicament in which Mexican officials found themselves in trying to preserve their lands against the encroachment of the Anglo-American civilization of the north. Moving alternately from policies of exclusion and assimilation, neither alternative seemed capable of offering an effective solution to the danger of territorial encroachment.[13] Arabs who attempted to keep Jewish settlers to a minimum during the period of the British mandate also trembled at the results of unrestricted Jewish immigration, and not without reason. Many other examples might be cited here, all of which go to the same effect. There are instances in human history when the migration of peoples seems indistinguishable in its effects from conquest by an invading army.

It was perhaps largely from recognition of this fact that international law has traditionally accorded the state virtually unlimited discretion in controlling the admission of individuals or peoples into its territory.

According to a widely cited maxim, every nation has the power 'as inherent in sovereignty, and essential to self-preservation, to forbid the entrance of foreigners within its dominions, or to admit them only in such cases and upon such conditions as it may see fit to prescribe'.[14] This assertion of national sovereignty, made in the late nineteenth century by the US Supreme Court and still generally accepted today in judicial decisions (though less so in scholarly commentaries), is qualified in a few important respects. Aliens that are admitted must be treated according to a minimum international standard,[15] and there are certain classes of visitors, such as diplomats, whose privileges and immunities are well defined in law and over whom the host state's discretion is limited once it has allowed entry. On the whole, however, it is fair to say that international law accords wide discretion to states to refuse admission to outsiders or otherwise restrict the enjoyment of a whole range of rights and benefits to its own national citizens. In so acting, states have justified their actions on grounds of national security, public health, domestic order, racial or ethnic affinity, and internal welfare; but the main principle on which such restrictions rest is the right of every state 'to live its life in its own way, so long as it keeps rigidly to itself, and refrains from interfering with the equal right of other states to live their life in the manner which commends itself to them'.[16]

In the traditional understanding of international law, a state need not invoke its vital interests in order to justify the exclusion of strangers. Its discretion is unbounded save by customary or treaty law relating to special classes of visitors (diplomats, students, travellers, foreign businessmen or workers). It may act solely on the basis of considerations of advantage or convenience. If it wishes to withhold residence or participation in a national community from strangers for purely self-interested reasons, it cannot be said to have acted illegally.

Whether this austere principle would satisfy the realist's moral sense is another question. As we have seen, there is no consensus among realists themselves as to the precise nature and scope of humanitarian duties to others. It would appear, however, that an ethical enquiry would have to give at least some weight both to the principle of individual liberty (of which free movement forms an important part) as well as to considerations of charity for refugees from particularly oppressive regimes, while nevertheless reserving to the state the right to preserve its own character and to otherwise guard against serious threats to its vital interests and essential institutions. At least as a point of departure, such a rule might be formulated as follows: 'A state has a duty to admit aliens if, individually or collectively, they pose no serious danger to its public safety, security, general welfare, or essential institutions';[17] it being understood that some groups will have particular claims on its sympathies, either because of their contribution to humanitarian endeavour, or because they are the victims of inhuman oppression, or because of some special tie or relationship to the receiving state. Conversely, it may exclude individuals or peoples if admission poses a serious threat to the same values.

It is not clear that all realists would in fact subscribe to such a rule. Those for whom the legal rule of state sovereignty is itself an important moral value might object that it infringes too severely on the right of every state to 'live its life in its own way', and that a showing of serious danger to national security, general welfare, or other essential institutions imposes too great a restriction on a discretion that ought properly to remain unfettered. Others will point out that the values and institutions that might indeed justify such restrictions on entry and membership are so elastic as to leave the discretion of the state virtually unbounded. The latter objection probably has the greater force, since, as we shall see, the idea of a 'serious state interest' is indeed an elastic one. Nevertheless, the rule does have the advantage of accommodating the principal values that, for the realist, appear to be of relevance in the enquiry. The principle of free movement is qualified by that of serious danger to state institutions, whereas the state's normal propensity to rely solely on considerations of mere advantage or convenience is qualified both by the value of individual freedom and by general humanitarian obligations.

One advantage of this formulation is that it accommodates, in a way that the traditional legal formulation does not, the right to travel. Minimal duties of hospitality would seem to require states to admit visitors for at least a limited period of time, especially if there is no likelihood that they will displace domestic workers from employment. Save for those who pose a threat to some important public interest (such as national security or public health), there would seem to be little justification for states to deny visitors the right to satisfy their curiosity. The acquisition of nationality is a more momentous step, and it would not be inconsistent with this formulation to hold that the state's discretion is much wider in deciding upon membership and nationality than in rejecting admission to visitors. Still, freedom of movement is too important a value to be arbitrarily dismissed without assigning any serious reason at all, as the traditional legal rule permits in theory (if not, by and large, in practice).

This rule also underscores the duties of states to provide a refuge to those individuals who have made an important contribution to human knowledge, or who have otherwise distinguished themselves by some achievement of general value to mankind. The loss to humanity of the distinguished philosophers, artists, scientists and writers who were persecuted and driven from their native lands by the totalitarian regimes of the twentieth century would have been even greater than it was had not some countries offered them a refuge.[18] Any rule which failed to create a presumptive duty to receive them would seem on its face to be deficient.

The duty of states to treat some classes of people in a preferential manner also seems evident. The least contestable basis for doing so is that of a family relationship. Husbands and wives, parents and children, have a moral claim to reunion, and it would be heartless for the state to deny them privileged status. The same considerations apply, though with less force, to other classes of relatives. This principle of preferential treatment for family members is not unbounded, and may in some circumstances be carried too far, as contemporary American immigration policy attests. Its application in the United States has, quite unexpectedly, had the effect of favouring migrants from Latin America and Asia, while penalizing potential migrants from Europe, Africa and elsewhere. As John Higham has observed: 'Just as the national origins quota system in the early 20th century suppressed variety in the interest of favored ethnic groups, so the current law does that in the interest of family chains.'[19] These consequences cannot be simply ignored in the assessment of immigration policy; at the same time, they serve only to limit the principle of family reunion, which ought to remain a major criterion in any conceivable immigration policy.

Those with whom the state has formed special ties or for whom its previous actions have given it some responsibility would also seem to enjoy a special status. Some peoples have a special claim on particular nations, usually because there was some enterprise in which both were involved that turned out badly and meant danger or displacement. In the case of the United States, the acceptance of over one million Vietnamese refugees after the collapse in 1975, or the acceptance of a large number of Hungarian refugees after the Soviet intervention of 1956, owed something to a sense of moral obligation on the part of this country.[20] Given its historic involvement in Central America, the United States may also have a particular obligation to take in greater numbers of refugees from Nicaragua or El Salvador than it would otherwise be disposed to do. At the least, they would appear to have a greater claim on our sympathy than refugees from areas of the world where the United States has had little contact and where the effects of national policy have been minimal.

In recognizing that such humanitarian claims ought to form an exception to the absolute discretion of the state in deciding upon criteria for immigration policy, no attempt is being made to convert realists into the bleeding hearts so often lampooned by hard headed representatives of the national interest. It is simply to recognize that realists are not always and absolutely concerned to elevate the interests of the state over every other human value. Such a vulgarization of realism is attractive to many critics because it offers a straw man that may easily be refuted, but it is not a proposition that would commend itself to any of the great realist writers of the past.

May states legitimately apply self-interested criteria for admitting or excluding immigrants? So far as naturalization policy (or admittance to citizenship) is concerned, the realist would almost certainly answer that they may in fact do so. It is to be expected that no state would willingly do itself an injury through its immigration policy. No state is under any obligation to receive the common criminals of another, or to admit for naturalization those who may be unwilling or unable to learn a new language, or who evidence no serious desire to assume the obligations of citizenship. Whether *purely* self-interested criteria may be employed is another question. If other states are seriously injured by the employment by another of purely self-interested criteria in admission policy (for which see the discussion below of the 'brain drain'), then there may indeed be a compelling case for taking their vital interests into account in the determination of one's own policy. Nor may refugee policy be guided solely by considerations of self-interest. The principle of asylum, which forbids returning refugees to countries to which they are unwilling to go 'owing to well-founded fear of being persecuted for reasons of race, religion, nationality . . . or political opinion', constitutes an important limitation on purely self-interested criteria, though it may work an important hardship on the states where refugees can get to. This principle is sufficiently valuable and so closely tied to the justification for a system of independent states that it is unlikely that realists would reject it save under exceptional circumstances. These two exceptions apart, however, it is to be expected that self-interested criteria will be employed by host states. It seems equally clear that the realist would not find such criteria to be immoral.

It would appear to be more difficult to sustain the claim that a host nation may deport migrants if changing circumstances which first made their inclusion beneficial to the host nation later makes their exclusion favourable to the same interests. Such a policy would, in the first instance, be limited by obligations of good faith. The state has no right to break an agreement it has made save under conditions of necessity, and it is doubtful if a showing of necessity could be made in such circumstances. Most such 'guest worker' agreements, of course, make it clear that the arrangements are of a temporary nature; the guest worker who makes a moral claim to stay put is usually the one who is going beyond the terms of his agreement. Still, the longer temporary workers have stayed in a given country the more they are likely to have put down roots, and their temporary residence comes to resemble a permanent home. Under those circumstances, it would certainly be uncharitable and probably unjust for the state to deport them, even if such a policy imposes strain on the state's resources. Such a recognition lies behind the unwillingness of Western European states to deport their guest workers during hard times, and a similar recognition lay behind the decision of the US Congress to grant membership to undocumented aliens who are able to demonstrate long-term residence in the United States.

The admission or rejection of strangers on the basis of racial, ethnic, or cultural criteria would appear to be the most contentious potential basis for different treatment. In practice, states do favour their own ethnic or racial kin above others and, in many circumstances, there would appear to be no objection to their doing so. Germany's policy of admitting for membership 'ethnic Germans' from the East, while admitting few others for citizenship, has been a reasonable and defensible practice, though in effect it has discriminated against all others without German blood. Israel accepts the duty to admit Jews from all round the world, though, as in Germany, some disagreement persists over who meets the test. In the case of both Germany and Israel, these preferential policies have adversely affected the interests of, respectively, Turkish guest workers and Palestinian Arabs, and the resentment fostered in both these groups has raised up diplomatic problems (admittedly far more severe in the Israeli case) which must be addressed by policy. Nevertheless, the right of both states to practise favouritism in their naturalization policy seems uncontestable, for both might plausibly claim compelling state interests in justification. Such discriminations in favour of particular racial, cultural, or religious groups derive their force from their family resemblance to the right of return to one's own country, a right widely recognized in international legal conventions, and this despite the fact that most such individuals never have lived on German or Israeli territory.

There are other circumstances in which the exclusion of particular racial, ethnic, or religious groups might be justifiable on grounds of national security or internal order. Given the apparently natural propensity of human beings to form themselves into conflict groups divided in one way or another, there is little question that the intermingling of such disparate groups may pose a serious danger to the maintenance of public order. Where communal strife is an ever present reality, as is the case in much of the Middle East, Asia and Africa, the security of groups separated by colour, language, or culture can often be provided for only under conditions of separation. Save in exceptional circumstances, it would be difficult to justify expulsion on such grounds: the right to stay seems of much greater force than the qualified right of entry proposed here. Still, it would be difficult to make out a blanket condemnation of the introduction of such criteria in admissions policies, which will normally be hidden in the interstices of legalese and administrative discretion. Where such communal hatreds exist, the relevant norm appears to be not relatively open admissions but the right of every people (however they define themselves) to some measure of internal autonomy.[21]

The moral reasonableness of such discrimination seems inescapably to depend on the circumstances of particular societies. Other states may consider the preservation of their ethnic, cultural, or religious uniformity to be central to the maintenance of their identity, and it is improper continually to berate them for their moral shortcomings if they wish to remain distinct. The best traditions of the United States lie in a much different direction: it celebrates the contributions that peoples from all over the world have made to its national culture; the immigrant appears as a source of perpetual renewal in virtually all spheres of national life. American realists may thus be found on all sides of the contemporary debate over immigration policy. Many favour a considerable loosening of naturalization policy (if not of border controls); others are identified with a more exclusivist or even nativist perspective.[22] Like the American conservative who wishes to preserve what has been a predominantly liberal heritage, American realists find themselves in the peculiar position of supporting the interests of a state whose distinctive self-understanding (or mission) has been the promotion of liberty against state power. The realist canon affords no explicit guidance over how this dilemma ought to be resolved. All that the realist would claim is that the collective well-being of our own state, and of the individuals who compose it, ought to have a greater weight in our moral accounting than the well-being of those outside the community. This principle is perfectly compatible with a more generous immigration policy, but it may also be employed to so qualify the duty to admit as to make it seem hardly distinguishable from the unfettered discretion international law has traditionally accorded the state in matters of entry.

IV

In the traditional understanding of international law, the right of the state to forbid entry had a parallel in its right to control exit. In the customary understanding, both were matters that lay entirely within the internal jurisdiction of individual states. There was no general right of emigration under international law, and most states clung to the idea that a subject was bound to his sovereign from birth, which conferred upon the former (either through his place of birth or his line of descent) a status that could not be renounced. That doctrine had been regularly acted upon in the course of the development of the European state system. It was used to justify restrictions on the emigration of skilled artisans and manufacturers (commonly enacted though loosely enforced in the eighteenth century);

and it might, and did, justify even more draconian measures in time of war. During the wars of the French Revolution and Napoleon, the natural right to unimpeded travel, proclaimed in the French Constitution of 1791, rapidly gave way to the necessities of war, as all the European states instituted passport controls and regimes of harsh conscription. The same phenomenon recurred in the two world wars of the twentieth century.[23]

The customary understanding of international law was, to be sure, in tension with emergent liberal conceptions of citizenship, which made allegiance depend upon consent, whether tacit or express.[24] Even in the United States, however, the government of which was explicitly founded on consensualist principles, legal authorities continued to assume that no natural right of emigration existed. As late as 1856, Attorney General Caleb Cushing observed that:

> the assumption of a natural right of emigration, without restriction in law, can be defended only by maintaining that each individual has all possible rights against the society and the society none with respect to the individual; that there is no social organization, but a mere anarchy of elements, each wholly independent of the other, and not otherwise consociated save than by their casual coexistence in the same territory.[25]

The United States had not asserted a contrary doctrine in the years leading up to the war of 1812, as is often assumed. The right of the British government to act upon its own doctrine of indefeasible allegiance was admitted; it was under no obligation to recognize the American citizenship of a British subject who, after 1783, had undergone naturalization in the United States. The American government did hold, however, that the British government had no right to search and remove British subjects from vessels flying the American flag on the high seas (which were considered to be American territory). The contested issue involved, not the right of expatriation, but contrary assumptions regarding territoriality at sea.

Only in 1868 did the US Congress declare the right of expatriation to be a 'natural and inherent right of all people, indispensable to the enjoyment of the right to life, liberty, and the pursuit of happiness'.[26] The impetus for the declaration was not so much the desire to see consensualist principles take root elsewhere in the world as the vexing problems of dual nationality in which the country, with an ever larger immigrant population, was inescapably involved. By the end of the nineteenth century, a number of states (such as Great Britain) had recognized a right of expatriation for its own nationals, and the question was regulated in a number of conventions the United States signed with a variety of European powers. But if the right of expatriation was becoming more generally recognized in practice, in theory the doctrine of indissoluble allegiance continued to hold sway. 'It may be assumed', Hall wrote, that when a state makes the recognition of a change of nationality by a subject dependent on his fulfillment of certain conditions determined by itself, or when it concedes a right of expatriation by express law, it in effect affirms the doctrine of an allegiance indissoluble except by consent of the state.[27]

The doctrine continued to enjoy general acceptance even during the inter-war period. In 1928, for instance, it was held that 'emigration is in fact entirely a matter of internal legislation of the different States . . . the Law of Nations does not, and cannot, grant a right of emigration to every individual.'[28]

From the standpoint of customary international law, then, the state's authority to regulate immigration and emigration was considered absolute, and a state committed no infraction of the law of nations if it followed a policy of the most barbarous insularity and permitted no alien to enter and no national to leave. Such regulations were 'vigorously legal, though not friendly'. Unlike the law of immigration, however, which continues to vest states with wide discretion in deciding upon the criteria for admittance to membership, the right of exit has been recognized in a number of international conventions signed since World War II. The Covenant on Civil and Political Rights, for instance, provides that 'everyone shall be free to leave any country, including his own.' It does not, however, recognise a 'general right of entry into another country of which one is not a national'. The right of exit is not absolute; but 'there must be a clear threat to a vital state interest in order to justify restricting this right.' Specifically, the right of exit may be subject to no restrictions 'except those which are provided by law, are necessary to protect national security, public order (*ordre public*), public health or morals or the rights and freedoms of others, and are consistent with the other rights recognized in the present Covenant.'[29]

The realist's moral sense is not likely to be offended by this rule. It attempts to balance, as any such rule must, the rights of the individual and the legitimate interests of the collective. It seems reasonable to think that the latter might be held to include, among others, a right to forbid exit to individuals who have not fulfilled a period of military service (if required by the laws of the state); who are genuinely in possession of state secrets; or who are criminals seeking to escape their just reward. Each of these appear to be legitimate exertions of state power necessary for the maintenance of external security or social order. It may be objected that here, too, the concession made to the right of the state is capable of an interpretation so elastic that it swallows up the right of exit almost entirely, and the objection seems to be given added force by virtue of the many notorious instances in which these limited exceptions to the right of exit have been invoked to justify sweeping restraints on free movement. In fact, however, the rule is a fairly stringent one. The requirement of a 'clear threat to a vital state interest' to justify exit restrictions is much more exacting than the requirements necessary to justify restrictions on admission and membership.

One qualification seems in order. It is difficult to judge the appropriateness of restrictions on exit without enquiring into the overall character of the states which attempt to deny free movement. The moral claim of the state, in so far as it is allowed at all, would appear to rest pre-eminently on the protection or aid it has afforded the individual from the moment of his birth; the discharge of its own duties generates a right to require the performance of social duties by the individual. If this reasoning is solid (as it is likely to be for the realist, though not necessarily for others), one is struck by a paradox: in the contemporary world, those states that have most rigorously attempted to restrict exit have normally been those that seem most destitute of all the qualities of good government, and in which the vaunted protection given by the state seems nothing better than a farce. In circumstances in which the state itself has been the agency of individual oppression or persecution, its moral right to assure the performance of social duties by the individual becomes correspondingly weaker and may indeed disappear altogether. Conversely, well governed states seem generally to allow the right of emigration. The peculiar result is that those states with the best claim to restrict exit exercise it the least, and that those states with the worst claim to restrict exit exercise it the most.

May the exceptions to the right of free exit be extended so far as to embrace restrictions on the emigration of skilled workers? In the eighteenth century, the question arose in the context of mercantilist attempts to preserve the wealth and power of the state; the answer given by the publicists was a qualified 'yes'. According to Vattel, a state might use force to prevent 'useful workmen' from emigrating, though it was obliged to offer them the opportunity for 'honest profit'.[30] Though affirming the general right of the state to restrict emigration, however, the publicists also recognized that emigration might be advantageous to the state which lost people, if only as a safety valve for social discontent; and many also appreciated that the real remedy in the prevention of such emigration was a mild government that avoided the confiscation of property or other arbitrary acts. Here, too, the diversity afforded by the existence of independent states served important values. Despots who mistreated their subjects and offered no reward for their industry had difficulty in preventing the flight of either people or capital; in a system of competitive states, the reward for internal oppression was often a loss of relative power – a phenomenon not without relevance today.

A similar argument might be advanced with respect to the contemporary dispute over the 'brain drain' from the developing states to the advanced industrialized countries. It is not clear in many circumstances that restrictions on emigration do serve the interests of the states which seek to implement them. The ability to emigrate, moreover, does operate as a restraint on the willingness of states to oppress their citizens – as it did, most recently, in East Germany. Both these considerations should make us careful in justifying restrictions on exit on the grounds that they are necessary for internal development. Having said this, however, it is difficult not to sympathize with the complaints of the developing countries, who may quite reasonably look with dismay on the tendency of professionals – in the training of which public funds have been committed – to depart for fairer horizons in the developed world. The loss of portions of the middle class may threaten to undermine seriously the fragile fabric of economic and social life in such countries. If a serious injury caused by such departures can in fact be shown, it is probably true to say that realists would be sympathetic to regulations that mitigated such dangers for countries that allow a modicum of civil and political liberty. At the least, it would appear incumbent on the countries of immigration to adjust their policy so that the gains they sought from allowing immigrants in did not impose a severe burden on the ability of other states to grow and prosper.

V

The argument developed in this chapter has been denominated as realist, but it might also be considered as constitutionalist or internationalist.[31] The latter traditions of enquiry are distinguished by their emphasis on law and by their concern to identify and balance the respective rights and duties of individuals and states. The rights of individuals, to be sure, were virtually unknown under traditional international law, where individuals as such had no rights save as they were members of a state willing to extend its protection to them. But the development of international law since 1945 has at least altered the way in which we speak about internationally recognized rights of individuals even while it has remained wedded to states for effective implementation. It seems appropriate, therefore, for the realist to adopt the language of rights and duties in weighing the ethical questions raised by the migration of peoples; such, at least, was the choice made here.

Internationalist doctrines also provide formidable support for a realist perspective in that both traditions share the assumption that mankind naturally divides itself into distinct political communities (or conflict groups). For internationalists, the ethical corollary of this empirical observation is an insistence on such values as self-determination, non-intervention and the balance of power. Such norms, though often in tension with each other, are all concerned with achieving a justly ordered relationship among largely autonomous groups. As against the assumption of liberal egalitarianism – that all individuals have an equal moral worth and should be treated as such – the internationalist would counterpoise the basic norm of the society of states, that all states or collectives, within certain broad limits, have a right to order their own internal existence in ways they are free to determine for themselves. Some natural law theorists (such as Vattel) and liberal-communitarians (such as Michael Walzer) also embrace the same norm.

It would be misleading to conflate the realist and internationalist perspectives, or to ignore the differences that may arise between the two traditions. What may be said, however, is that the ethical questions raised by the migration of peoples do not appear to set the two traditions at odds in any fundamental way. In this case, the realist has no need to justify the transgression of otherwise binding legal and moral obligations. The internationalist's norm of state sovereignty – the right of every state to 'live its life in its own way' – is perfectly adequate to justify whatever restrictions on entry or exit the realist may find necessary in any given instance. In so far as liberal communitarians and natural law theorists impute moral worth to self-determination or state sovereignty, the same may be said of them.

Nor, finally, is the realist necessarily oblivious to the humanitarian concerns that the movement of individuals and peoples across borders inevitably raises. If realists do look first and foremost to the interests of their own state, they are not doctrinally committed to acting in an inhumane manner save in exceptional circumstances. They tend, moreover, to be sharply circumscribed in their egoism by the recognition that a wanton indifference to the interests and aspirations of other peoples and states tends not in the long run to be good policy. Realists enter the topsy-turvy world of moral inversions only *in extremis*, 'when the safety of the state is in question'. Otherwise they inhabit the same moral world as the rest of us, and are not forbidden to do justice and to love mercy.

Notes

1. Michael Walzer, *Just and Unjust Wars* (New York: Basic Books, 1977); Charles Beitz, *Political Theory and International Relations* (Princeton, N.J.: Princeton University Press, 1979).
2. Cited in Albert O. Hirschman, *The Passions and the Interests* (Princeton, N.J.: Princeton University Press, 1977).
3. Albert Sorel, quoted in E. H. Carr, *The Twenty Years' Crisis*, 2nd ed. (New York: Harper and Row, 1946), p. 11.

4. Niccolo Machiavelli, *The Prince and the Discourses*, ed. Max Lerner (New York: Random House, 1950), p. 62.
5. Cited in Gerald Stourzh, *Alexander Hamilton and the Idea of Republican Government* (Stanford, Calif.: Stanford University Press, 1970), p. 81.
6. As Meinecke put it, 'every influx of unpolitical motives into the province of pure conflicts of power and interest brings with it the danger that these motives will be misused and debased by the naturally stronger motives of mere profit, of *raison d'état*. The latter resembles some mud-coloured stream that swiftly changes all the pure waters flowing into it into its own murky colour.' Friedrich Meinecke, *Machiavellism: The Doctrine of Raison D'État And Its Place in Modern History*, trans. Douglas Scott (New Haven, Conn.: Yale University Press, 1957), p. 210.
7. J. L. Brierly, *The Law of Nations: An Introduction to the International Law of Peace*, 6th ed., ed. Sir Humphrey Waldock (New York and Oxford: Oxford University Press, 1963), p. 69.
8. On this point, see Martin Wight, "Why Is There No International Theory?" *Diplomatic Investigations: Essays In the Theory of International Politics*, ed. Martin Wight and Herbert Butterfield, (Cambridge, Mass.: Harvard University Press, 1966), p. 29. 'When diplomacy is violent and unscrupulous', Wight observed, 'international law soars into the regions of natural law; when diplomacy acquires a certain habit of co-operation, international law crawls in the mud of legal positivism.'
9. Niccolo Machiavelli, *Discourses on the First Ten Books of Titus Livius*, bk. 3 of *The Prince and the Discourses*, p. 528.
10. See Montesquieu, *The Spirit of the Laws*, trans. and ed. Anne M. Cohler, Basia Carolyn Miller, and Harold Samuel Stone (Cambridge: Cambridge University Press, 1989), p. 7. Raymond Aron, normally considered a realist, used this citation as the epigraph of his *Peace and War: A Theory of International Relations* (New York: Praeger, 1968). See also Emmerich de Vattel, *The Law of Nations or the Principles of Natural Law Applied to the Conduct and to the Affairs of Nations and of Sovereigns*, trans. Charles G. Fenwick (Washington: Carnegie Endowment for International Peace, 1916), 3 vols., III, p. 114 (bk. 2, sec. 2). The 'offices of humanity, which Nations mutually owe one another,' consisted for Vattel 'in doing all in our power for the welfare and happiness of others, as far as is consistent with our duties towards ourselves.'
11. For a good statement to this effect, see Paul Johnson, *A History of the Jews* (New York: Harper and Row, 1987), p. 245.
12. Edward Gibbon, *The Decline and Fall of the Roman Empire*, chap. iii, last para., ed. J. B. Bury (London: Methuen & Co., 1930 [1776–88] 7 vols., I, pp. 81–2.
13. See Isaac Joslin Cox, *The West Florida Controversy, 1798–1813* (Baltimore: Johns Hopkins University Press, 1918), pp. 22–4, 58–9.
14. *Nishimura Ekiu v United States*, 142 US 651, 659 (1892) (citation omitted).
15. Michael Akehurst, *A Modern Introduction to International Law* (London: Allen & Unwin, 1987), 6th ed., p. 88.
16. William Edward Hall, *A Treatise on International Law* (Oxford: Oxford

University Press, 1909, 6th ed., ed. J. B. Atlay, pp. 43–4.

17. See the informative study of James A. R. Nafziger, "The General Admission of Aliens Under International Law," *American Journal of International Law*, 77 (October 1983), no. 4, p. 832.

18. See the moving account of Laura Fermi, *Illustrious Immigrants: The Intellectual Migration from Europe* (Chicago: Chicago University Press, 1968).

19. John Higham, cited in Joyce Vialet, "Immigration: Numerical limits and the preference system," *Congressional Research Service Issue Brief* (Washington, D.C.: The Library of Congress), June 15, 1989, p. 6.

20. See Michael Walzer, *Spheres of Justice: A Defense of Pluralism and Equality* (New York: Basic Books, 1983), p. 49.

21. Since realism is not to be equated with the defence of tyranny, it seems reasonable to include internal autonomy as a value that nearly all realists would embrace. 'The right of national self determination' is a more advanced formulation of the same principle, and has historically been associated with a liberal (or liberal communitarian) theory of international relations. Realists have generally taken a far more sceptical view about the consequences to which the thoroughgoing application of this principle (ambiguous as it necessarily is) might lead. Whatever the ultimate status of this 'right', realists have normally feared the potentially anarchical consequences of its thoroughgoing application and have generally considered it to be subordinate in status to the value of ensuring a stable international order.

22. Two valuables discussions of American immigration policy are: Nathan Glazer, ed., *Clamor at the Gates: The New American Immigration* (San Francisco, Calif.: Institute for Contemporary Studies 1985), and Robert W. Tucker, Charles Keeley, and Linda Wrigley, *Immigration and Foreign Policy* (Boulder, Colo.: Westview Press, 1990).

23. Among discussions of the right of exit, see particularly the recent work of Alan Dowty, *Closed Borders: The Contemporary Assault on Freedom of Movement* (New Haven, Conn.: Yale University Press, 1987).

24. See the discussion in Peter H. Schuck and Rogers M. Smith, *Citizenship Without Consent: Illegal Aliens in the American Polity* (New Haven, Conn.: Yale University Press, 1985).

25. Quoted in John Bassett Moore, *The Principles of American Diplomacy*, 2nd ed. (New York: Harper and Brothers, 1918), p. 279.

26. Cited in ibid., p. 289. See also John Bassett Moore, ed., *A Digest of International Law*, 8 vols (Washington, D.C.: Government Printing Office, 1906), III, pp, 579–80.

27. Hall, *Treatise on International Law*, p. 235.

28. Cited in Dowty, *Closed Borders*, p. 82.

29. See Stig Jagerskiold, "The Freedom of Movement," *The International Bill of Rights: The Covenant on Civil and Political Rights*, ed. Louis Henkin (New York: Columbia Univesity Press, 1981), 178; and Hurst Hannum, *The Right to Leave and Return in International Law and Practice* (Dordrecht: Martins Nijhoff, 1987), p. 19.

30. de Vattel, *Law of Nations*, bk. I, sec. 73, p. 35.

31. For discussion of the 'constitutional' tradition in diplomacy, see Martin Wight, "Western Values in International Relations," *Diplomatic Investigations*, pp. 90–1. See also Hedley Bull, *The Anarchical Society: A Study of Order in World Politics* (New York: Columbia University Press, 1977), pp. 24–7. Bull identifies a 'Grotian or internationalist' tradition that is distinguishable from a 'Hobbesian or realist tradition on the one hand, and from the Kantian or universalist tradition on the other.' According to Bull, "the Hobbesian prescription for international conduct is that the state is free to pursue its goals in relation to other states without moral or legal restrictions of any kind.' This interpretation of Hobbes' outlook is admittedly the conventional one, but it neglects to consider Hobbes' observation that the laws of nature, which command the seeking of peace as well as other virtues, 'oblige *in foro interno*'. They are, that is to say, obligatory on the conscience always, but may be violated in circumstances where there is no security that others will observe the same laws towards us. This proviso is of crucial significance, and is remarkably similar to Machiavelli's warning that those who pursue the traditional virtues risk coming to a bad end in a world where so many are not good. Neither Hobbes nor Machiavelli deprecates the traditional virtues as such; whether such virtues may be safely observed, however, will depend on circumstances.

— 16 —

Ethics and the movement of money: Realist approaches

Susan Strange

In the study of international society, the realist approach is probably the predominant one. It is distinguished from other approaches in two ways. The focus of attention, the main concern, is with power – the nature, use and consequences of power. Second, the approach accepts as given, and therefore assumes, the 'world of states', the anarchical society, or in other words, an international system composed of territorial states each acknowledging (generally speaking and for most purposes) the authority of others.[1] Both these characteristics cause problems when it comes to answering the question: What is the realist view of the justice or injustice of arrangements concerning the movement of money across territorial frontiers?

Let us take first the acceptance as given of an anarchical political system composed of individual states. It follows from this that realist writers become rather incoherent when they make moral judgements or advocate moral prescriptions for the world. They cannot easily defend the anarchical system as an ideal one; they accept it *faute de mieux*. The best they can usually suggest as an improvement on the present system is a more stable balance of power,[2] or a better method of conflict resolution,[3] or the pursuit by leading states of enlightened self-interest.[4]

By definition, most realists are more at home in writing about the foreign policies of individual states, or blocs of states, in terms of which policies would best serve the national interest and not in terms of which are morally preferable, whether alliance or neutrality, free trade or protection. The fact is there are not many global realists around. The world-system school of writers may claim to be realists, but it seems to me that most of them are rather woolly minded idealists. I would describe myself as both a structuralist and a realist. I am a structuralist in that I am more interested

232

in and concerned for the prospects and destiny of the global system than I am for the prospects and destiny of Britain. As an international political economist, I prefer to leave the weighing of competing strategies for the national interest (whether of my own or any other country) to the foreign policy analysts. (Parenthetically, though, I have to say that most of them grossly underestimate the comparative importance for the national interest of industrial policy as compared to foreign policy.) But I am an unrepentant realist when it comes to analyzing the international political economy. As such, I accept that I am limited like other realists to the advocacy of second-best solutions to its ills and problems precisely because (like them) I reject the possibility of fundamental change in the international political system, at least for the foreseeable future. Political authority over world markets may be shared with other institutions – but the lion's share remains with something called the state.

I said at the outset that realists have an overriding concern with power. They understand power and discuss it intelligently when they are referring to power derived from military capability, the ability of states to get their own way and to make their views prevail by reason of their superior armed forces. But they do not understand much about power derived from money. Understandably so, for it is not an easy question: Who has monetary power and how is it, or should it be, used? For there are different sources of monetary power. In the first place, whoever possesses money has purchasing power and, as with foreign aid donors, indirect leverage over those whom it is proposed to pay or give money. Those with purchasing power also exert power over the market as consumers or as dealers (the grain brokers in cereal markets, for example). Then, there is another kind of monetary power derived from the capacity to create money or to control access to money in the form of credit. This is shared, but unequally, by both governments and financial institutions including (but not only) banks. Even here, all is not plain sailing. For there is a balancing power – as we see today in debt rescheduling negotiations – that belongs to the debtor once the credit has been taken. The fact that there are many different kinds of monetary power, and many different sources of monetary power, means that realist attitudes to its use are apt to be highly inconsistent and even downright contradictory, as we shall see.

But first we must recognize that rapid structural change in the international political economy over the past quarter-century or so has exacerbated an old but unavoidable question for this particular discussion: What is money? And there is another question, equally unavoidable and equally difficult: How do you know when money – especially capital for investment – is moving from one territorial state to another? Both need a little explanation because the ethical implications of the answers, especially for realists, are not immediately clear.

Economists describe money as having three indispensable attributes or functions: it is a medium of exchange; it is a store of value; and it is a unit of account. Anything – whether paper, gold or an electronic record – which has all three attributes and is accepted in all three functions is considered to be money. Definitional problems, however, arise as soon as two things happen: when primitive monetary systems become sophisticated and get beyond using physical, specie money like gold or silver; and when we are dealing with money which is no longer used exclusively within a single territorially defined system but is something used in international transactions in an international economy transcending national borders.

From a political and ethical point of view, there is a big difference between primitive monetary systems in which few goods and services are exchanged by means of money and there is little use of credit, and a developed monetary system in which money is used for almost all transactions involving the production and consumption of goods and services and in which the use of credit is widespread. The major difference that concerns us is that the opportunities for political authority – the state – to cheat are enormously greater in the latter case than in the former. In a primitive system, the rulers, like Nero or Cleopatra, may debase the currency by adding lead to silver or reducing the weight of gold or silver in the coins and using the debased currency to pay for goods and services at the old prices before the swollen money supply raises their price. In an intermediate, partially developed monetary system, the rulers can (and regularly did) cheat by issuing paper promises to pay in specie which they could not or would not keep. In a fully developed monetary system, in which paper money cannot be converted into anything else but more paper, the opportunity to cheat by inflation are even greater; no promises need be broken but people holding inflated monetary assets lose wealth without being able to do anything about it. The 1947 currency reform in occupied Germany was one example of what is now a rather common form of political deception.

The relevant point for our purposes is that, while the opportunity may be equal in equally developed monetary systems, the use of that opportunity by different political authorities has been and is unequal. Some states are bigger cheats than others. That would be less complicating from an analytical point of view if national monetary systems were self-contained, impenetrable systems. But once you get trade, investment and speculative monetary movements between systems, the unequal exercise of the power to cheat becomes rather important. When you have, as we have today, a highly developed and highly integrated international monetary system and financial structure (i.e. the structure within which credit is created, traded and used) and when you also have an international political system in which authority still resides in territorially defined states, the consequences that follow from the unequal use of national currencies for international transactions combined with the unequal exercise of the power to cheat are complex, to say the least.

The answer, therefore, to the question 'What is money?' can only be that it depends where you are and who you are. Few national currencies fulfil all three functions outside the realm of their national government. Some – the Polish zloty or the Brazilian cruzado to give just two examples – do not fulfil all three functions even within their countries. Other currencies are used by foreigners outside the country as a store of value – the Dmark or the Swiss franc or (though surprisingly little) the Japanese yen. Some, like the French franc or the Dutch guilder are still used for exchange purposes and are joined as units of account by 'artificial' or basket currencies like the SDR (the IMF's Special Drawing Right) or the ECU (European Currency Unit). The Eurodollar, and other Euro (or offshore) currencies are also a medium of exchange – but only for wholesale transaction in amounts too large for most academics to buy or sell. We can only conclude, first, that because it is markets that mostly determine the unequal acceptability of currencies, markets as well as states have some authority over money; and, second, that some states have authority over money that is used outside their territory. For both reasons it is difficult, not to say impossible, to generalize about the responsibility of the state (in general) for the movement of money (in general).

A word now about the other difficult question, how to know when money is being or has been moved. It was different in the old days when money was mostly moved in a few simple forms – the letter of credit, the bill of exchange, bonds and various kinds of shares. Now there are not only complex global markets for foreign exchange and short- and medium-term credit denominated in each of the major currencies. There are also international markets in options and futures for commodities, currencies, financial assets and insurance. It was also easier to see when money was being moved because most states even in the 1950s had legal exchange controls restricting the transnational movement of money. Now, though some controls remain, they exist mostly in developing countries. The major developed countries have few if any exchange controls. Trade in goods is counted by busy officials at ports, frontier posts and airports. Trade in services and in money goes on unrecorded. And even when recorded it may mislead. Big corporations have captive insurance companies in Bermuda, financial affiliates in London or Sydney, tax-avoiding holding companies in Nassau or Luxembourg. Their money moves by roundabout routes, heavily disguised. The extent – and the seriousness – of significant administrative ignorance is growing every year with the increased complexity of finance and banking.[5]

Even more important, perhaps, is the fact that the internationalization of production by transnational corporations (TNCs) of all shapes, origins and sizes has produced a large new invisible form of transnational investment. This is so important now that anyone in global business will agree that the available statistics on foreign direct investment, solemnly compiled and used by the IMF, World Bank, OECD, etc., are utterly useless and meaningless. This is best explained by some examples. Chase Manhattan 'buys' US$200 million shares in the Brazilian car company Autolatina – a joint VW–Ford enterprise. But the sale, arranged in 1988, is financed by a debt-equity deal which merely takes cruzados held by the central bank against foreign debt liabilities and exchanges them at a substantial discount for the Autolatina shares. In fact, even without debt-equity swaps, most TNC investments in developing countries are now made with locally raised or borrowed funds, not by the transfer of funds from company headquarters; or they are made with past profits that have not been repatriated to the parent company because they are not allowed or are stringently penalized taxwise.

The extreme case of invisible investment by TNCs, though, is in the form of technology of one form or another. An example here is a General Motors (GM) venture producing car engines in Brazil. The Brazilian government, like most others, favours ventures by TNCs that use as much local content components as possible. The local suppliers do not know how to reach the quality standards demanded by GM. GM sends a large number of its engineers down from Michigan to Brazil to work alongside the local suppliers and advise them on production methods and quality controls. Some stay a month, three months, even six months. For GM it counts as 'salaries', a part of its total labour costs. Yet it is in effect an investment in Brazil of human capital necessary to the project, and of substantial benefit to Brazil, paid for at the arbitrary intra-firm price of the finished product exported to GM for the US market. The growth over the last decade in trade in services – management fees, licensing fees, consultancy fees (US investment banks advising scores of LDCs how to negotiate their debt rescheduling), royalties and franchising payments – actually reflects the growth of invisible investments. What else is R&D or management expertise in running a hotel but the capital asset of an enterprise that is then transferred to its own or someone else's foreign operations and paid for as a service?

To sum up this rather long, but necessary introduction, there are five points to be made about the realist approaches as follows:

1. A structural or global realist view of issues relating to the transnational movement of money is possible but rare; and starting from the realist assumption of the continued existence of the state in some form or other, it can only propose solutions that are relative rather than absolute.

2. For most realists, acceptance of the present international political system means that their perception of morality is bounded by perceptions of the national interest of the individual state; whatever best serves the national interest is morally approved. Action which in other circumstances would be judged immoral is acceptable when done in the name of the state, only provided – which rarely happens – that the loss of reputation does not damage the state severely in other ways.

3. Realists' concern with power means that the acquisition of power by the state is morally justified because it serves the national interest. But the complexity of monetary power means that there are likely to be severe trade-off, or swings-and-roundabout problems when it comes to choosing (a portfolio of) policies to maximize monetary power. In other words, the perception of the national interest will differ according to the monetary role of a particular state. But some, perhaps most, states will have multiple roles, so that perceptions of what is needed to serve the national interest in one role will contradict policies perceived as necessary to the state in another role. The point can best be illustrated in table form, taking as example the different views possible according to the role of the state as creditor or as debtor in the international financial system:

STATE ROLE	Creditor		Debtor	
STRATEGY	mercantilist *or* imperialist		autarkist *or* developmental	
POLICY	stop exit	allow exit	stop entry	allow entry

Similar illustrations could be drawn and elaborated to show the diverse policies likely to be advocated in the national interest according to whether a country is host or home state to transnational corporations, or according to whether it has acquired status and income as an international banking and financial market-place or is only a peripheral and dependent one.

4. The coexistence of a complex, integrated international monetary and financial system and a disaggregated international political system means that the use of national currencies (notably the US$) for international transactions even between third parties gives some states who control such currencies the asymmetric opportunity to cheat not only their own citizens but those of other countries.

5. Never mind the morality; there is a prior practical issue. Recent rapid change in the international financial system has put in doubt whether it is possible for authority to know when money is moving, by what channels, and whether such ignorance does not impair the practical capacity to check or prevent movement. In short, exchange controls often prove merely cosmetic; they catch the small fish but let the large ones go free

Questions and answers

As a direct result of the above five points, there may be as many as five different realist answers to questions about the transnational migration of money. None of these is morally superior to the others – though political rhetoric will often lay claim to moral superiority. As the table indicates, you can have a global (or structural) realist answer. This may not be too different from an enlightened imperialist answer. There is also a mercantilist realist answer; and, in developing countries, you will still hear an autarkist, or *dependencia*, decoupling answer as well as the developmentalist answer that has become more popular in recent years.

Let us take the first and most basic question, whether it is ever ethical for a state to interrupt or forbid the exit – or, conversely, the entry – of money into a country.

Realists would argue that the prior duty of the state, in the general interest of society, is to nurture and protect the national economy. Therefore it has a prior right to limit the freedom of the individual or the corporate enterprise to dispose of its capital where and how he, she or it wishes. Capital – especially liquid assets – is the sinews of war: Mussolini called on Italian wives to sacrifice their wedding rings; Churchill insisted on the sale of privately owned shares in US companies to finance the British war effort. In war, all belligerent states and even most neutrals have exercised their right to administer exchange controls over current as well as capital transactions with the rest of the world. In the interests of national economic security, European states for more than a decade after World War II prolonged these wartime controls and did so with the blessing and consent of the US administrators of Marshall Aid. Some European countries – France and Italy, for example – continue to cling to relics of exchange control even to this day, though whether the prior national interest in giving effect to the Single European Act will cause these to be dismantled by 1993 is still an open question at the time of writing.

Whether capital-rich countries, with a surplus of capital for investment, ought in peacetime to restrict the exit of money is debatable. Idealists and liberals would presumably argue that to do so is selfish and nationalistic. Realists would be less dogmatic. Under pressure of a deteriorating US balance of payments, the Kennedy Administration instituted the Interest Equalization Tax (IET) in 1963 which penalized and effectively prevented foreign governments from issuing bonds on Wall Street. But it did not stop US capital from going abroad because at the same time the US government permitted banks to conduct unregulated, untaxed business in US dollars in London, thus giving rise to the Eurodollar market in which US bank branches could freely lend dollars to other US banks and corporations or to foreign banks and corporations. Realist American writers on international political economy have never questioned, so far as I am aware, the moral right of the US government to impose the IET. Yet the global (or structural) realist might well argue that it would have been better for the world market economy, and in the long run also for the United States, if foreigners had been able to issue bonds in New York as they had in London before 1914. And if this had forced the United States at an earlier date than 1989 to cut back on its inflated and costly military spending in foreign exchange, this would have been to the moral advantage of the system,[6] as well as in the enlightened long-term interest of the United States.

The impunity with which the United States was able to run a persistent balance-of-payments deficit – to which capital exit substantially contributed – and therefore to pay its debts in IOUs was criticized by Jacques Rueff and General de Gaulle as morally reprehensible. The significant title of a contemporary book by Rueff was *The Monetary Sin of the West*.[7] In it he argued that the United States was not only acting against its own traditions and long-term interests, but that it was actually wrong to have International Monetary Fund (IMF) rules for all to which the United States need pay no heed. De Gaulle's famous 1965 press conference praising the virtues of gold (as compared, by implication, to US dollars) echoed Rueff's argument, besides striking chords in many European memories of the disastrous personal consequences of putting too much trust in governments' paper promises to pay. But the truth is that the moral tone adopted by Rueff and the General only cloaked an essentially realist objection to the asymmetric freedom which the United States as key currency country enjoyed from the IMF rule book. That freedom President Nixon exercised to the full in 1971 when he unilaterally declared the US dollar inconvertible into gold. Contemporary criticism of this step by liberal internationalists like Ed Morse or Fred Bergsten were not, significantly, based on moral grounds.[8] Bergsten only argued that the manner in which the Japanese and the Germans had been forced by market pressures released by the United States to revalue was unwise in the long-term interests of the Western alliance because such unilateralism was bound to be resented by America's best allies. His attitude was that of an enlightened imperialist, concerned for the damage Nixon had done to the US role as hegemon over the world market economy. It was a realist argument claiming loss of US reputation and credibility in other policy areas. Nixon's concerns were narrower and more short-term: to improve the US balance of trade and with it his own and the Republican party's future electoral prospects.[9]

But, it may be asked, what about the more pressing, immediate and special problem of policy towards capital flight, especially – but not exclusively – from poor countries. (Recall that there was some legal and illegal capital flight from Britain under Labour governments and a much more serious exodus from France in the early 1980s.) Robin Naylor has argued that there would hardly be a Third World debt problem if so much of the money poured in as aid and as bank loans had not leaked quickly back into numbered accounts in Swiss or Bermudan banks or real estate in Texas or Florida.[10] In face of such circumstances, realists would argue that developing countries have every reason to try and stop the haemorrhage. The economic security of the state, in view of the penalties of non-payment of debt servicing, must take precedence over the economic freedom of the owners of flight capital to seek security for their money. However, recent studies have shown that it is extremely difficult for countries suffering capital flight to do more than make it difficult and/or costly for the exporter; and that it is easier to police foreign corporations than the ministers and officials of the state acting in their personal or family interests.[11]

The converse question, though rarely asked – at least not in the United States – is whether or not there is some moral obligation to check capital flights at the receiving end as well as at the despatching end. The obligation is acknowledged in international agreements regarding drug or other criminally acquired funds. For nearly three decades central banks have practised recycling of hot short-term funds likely to destabilize exchange rates. The appeal to the principle of reciprocity so often heard in trade issues is not heard here. In matters of debt and money, the IMF and the World Bank are prone to adopt a hectoring, holier-than-thou tone of deep moral disapproval towards recalcitrant debtors. As Otto Niemeyer used to tell the Australians in the 1930s, 'Debtors must cut their coats according to their cloth!' Creditors play down the shared responsibility of the lenders who, unlike bondholders of old, carefully shifted the risk of higher interest rates onto the borrowers. Yet Latin American workers who have had their real wages cut by 25 per cent or more have had imposed on them more of the burden of adjustment than the bankers whose managers and shareholders have suffered comparatively little – at most, some belated loan loss provisions out of their ample profits. As two British commentators – one a journalist and the other a Labour politician – remarked,

> The outstanding stock of Third World debt has thus become a dead weight on economic activity, ensuring a deflationary bias to the world economy which the developed countries have so far been unprepared to lift by other means. . . . The burden of reducing those deficits fell entirely on to the Third World: once again it was the deficit countries that were forced to adjust rather than those with surpluses. . . . The debtors have paid most heavily for the crisis, but no one has gained.[12]

Or, to quote the old music-hall song about the poor girl taken up and dropped by a succession of heartless rich lovers:

> It's the rich as has the pleasure.
> It's the poor as gets the blame.
> It's the same the whole world over.
> Ain't it all a bleeding shame?

The realist answers to the debt issue and arrangements for debt service, therefore, are (as indicated above) fivefold. The mercantilist/realist who is a creditor will say, 'They borrowed the money didn't they?' and advocate solutions sufficient only to prevent damage to the major banks and the international financial system in which they operate – that is, pretty much what has happened since 1982. The debtor/autarkist will say: 'We told you so: too close integration with world capitalism allows them to screw you. Be warned, stay away from foreign banks and if possible, organize a collective default.' The debtor/developmentalist will say, 'Foreign credit allowed us to accelerate industrialization and growth. Now, foreign investors are scared. We have to keep up the interest payments – so we better do just enough but no more to keep aid and trade credit flowing. They too are vulnerable. Let's bargain hard.' The imperialist creditor will not be too dissatisfied with the *ad hoc* arrangements, which through debt–equity swaps allow foreign companies to buy cheap assets in debtor countries. The global realists will say that the worst victims of the *ad hoc* arrangements are Africans, because there are no bank loans, little foreign investment and not much aid to keep growth ahead of population. But they might add that the first step lies with the United States: to reduce its budget and payments deficits, raise savings, cut consumption and therefore lower interest rates and allow more of the Japanese surplus to go – with multilateral insurance – into the developing countries.

Trade: protectionism vs. liberalization

From the realist point of view of the national interest of the state, free trade has no intrinsic or moral superiority over protectionism. Strong traders are, and always have been, free traders; and strong traders who lose competitive advantage soon become protectionist (as the United States, hindered by an overvalued dollar, has tended to become, except for trade in services where it is still the strong trader). However, change in the international production structure has recently somewhat redrawn and redefined the costs and benefits, the risks and opportunities of free trade vs. protectionism. Realists are right to point out that the powerful latecomer arguments first put forward in favour of protectionism by Alexander Hamilton and Friedrich List worked well when put into practice by the United States, Germany or Japan. Moreover, in recent years they have still worked pretty well for South Korea, Taiwan, and in some sectors for Malaysia, Thailand, India and Indonesia. Nevertheless, the risks have recently been increased by the accelerating pace of technological change. Too long a period of protectionism, especially if the local market is small and the minimum scale of economic output in the industry is high, may leave local producers hopelessly outclassed technologically and undercut in price by their competitors in world markets. Moreover, the national economy as a whole may suffer when the protected industry's customers are other producers: they are saddled with higher costs than their foreign competitors; exports are handicapped and economic growth at home held back. Brazilian policies in the informatics sectors – computers, telecom, software, etc. – is such an example, where the 1968 'law of similars' has excluded until quite recently the global majors from the domestic market. The result – not denied even by nationalists – is that even personal computers in Brazil cost twice as much as foreign ones and are at least two years behind them, to the detriment of many Brazilian businesses, large and small, domestic and foreign. Yet the liberals would have to admit that, notwithstanding the economic costs, the market reserve policy did succeed politically in bringing an obdurate IBM to the bargaining table.[13]

Thus, there is a nice political judgement to be made as to just when the costs and risks of this kind of protection are not worth the benefits and opportunities. And it is worth noting that on such issues the clash of interest is not necessarily or always nationals vs. multinationals, but may often be protected enterprises, both domestic and foreign on one side, against other domestic and foreign interests (or joint ventures that are both domestic and foreign) that feel irked by the costs of protection on the other. Here again, there is no intrinsic morality about either posture. The liberal arguments about the higher morality of cheap T-shirts for consumers being more important than some protected adjustment for textile workers has never borne close rational examination. Moreover, the moralistic liberal argument about the higher ethical value of free trade, whether in food, manufactures or services, has always been based on a false assumption that there is a difference in principle between the mobility of capital and the mobility of labour. The true Ricardian should logically be in favour of both.

Profits

In realist perceptions the state is gatekeeper to the economy of the territory over which it rules. With this authority it is perfectly entitled to tax personal or corporate profits to whatever limit is politically practicable, and to put such restrictions on their repatriation to other states as it thinks fit. The only question, therefore, is whether it is in the national interest to restrict the freedom of investors to get their profits out of the country. On balance, the evidence of recent experience suggests that such restrictions are self-defeating. They put the goose that lays the golden eggs out of lay. Or, in other words, foreign investors become reluctant to put more money into a country which stops them repatriating profits.

Compare, for instance, the experience of Brazil and Malaysia in this respect. Malaysia has put no restrictions on the exit of profits or the withdrawal of capital. Brazil, back to 1962, has had a Profit Remittance Law under which foreign companies were allowed each year to repatriate only 10 per cent of the value of the capital invested. Until recently, any company that remitted more than 12 per cent of its annual profits was subject to heavy taxes. The result was that for much of the 1980s most visible foreign investment in Brazil, despite the promise of long-term economic growth, consisted of reinvested earnings. Brazilian managers of German chemical companies complained that their corporate headquarters back home were being short-sighted, but German banks, having been badly caught out in Poland and having large investments in such companies certainly advised caution in transferring more Dmarks to a country whose currency (given current rates of inflation) could only depreciate.

A related question for developing countries is whether restrictions should be put on the exit of insurance premiums, either by insisting that they stay in the country or – as Kenya has done – by nationalizing insurance and even reinsurance. The motivation is much the same as restricting remittance of profits – to keep capital from leaking out of the national economy. The trouble is that large industrial and business risks are too great for the nationalized insurance company to bear; they have to be laid off – just as little bookmakers lay off big racecourse bets with bigger ones. The reinsurance premiums therefore end up abroad anyway. The only difference may be an internal political one: when insurance of actuarially predictable risks – life and motor, for instance – is nationalized, the nationalization of insurance often becomes a new source of funding for the state.

Buy-outs and takeovers

This is more an issue concerning ownership than one concerning the right to move money across frontiers. As explained earlier, the internationalization of banking and the integration of capital markets means, nowadays, that company X in Britain can easily acquire company Y in the United States or Australia without moving pounds sterling out of the country. The only question for the host state is whether it wants to restrict the

ownership rights of foreigners over assets and enterprises within its territory. Japan, for instance, has had a Foreign Investment Law which functioned from the early 1950s until very recently to make it difficult for
foreigners to operate in Japan, let alone buy up Japanese companies. Many
developing countries, including India and Brazil, have constitutions which
reserve ownership of natural mineral resources, public utilities and com-
munications to nationals or to the state.

There are two practical difficulties with such exclusive policies, even
from a realist perspective which does not question the right of states to
adopt such policies. One is that the urgent need for foreign technology will
often cause the excluding state to modify its own rules. IBM, for instance,
is one of the biggest enterprises in Japan, and US companies in Japan
account for a bigger proportion of GNP than do Japanese companies in the
United States. The other is that no one can be sure any longer that they can
tell a national company from a foreign one. The 1988 Brazilian Constitution tried hard to define a Brazilian company. De Benedetti only laughed
and said he knew how to get round those rules and still control Olivetti do
Brasil. The French say Nissan (UK) is a Japanese company; the British say
it is British. The US government refuses subsidies to Northern Telecom
because it is Canadian; the Canadians retort that it does more business,
employs more people in the United States than it does in Canada. Who is
right?

Clearly, enterprises in Britain and the United States, and in small
outward-looking countries like Switzerland, the Netherlands and Sweden
have engaged in international production longer and to a greater extent
than Japanese enterprises. That is one reason for the American trade
deficit: US companies are producing offshore for the US market, and in the
statistics this looks like 'foreign' imports. But eventually the offshore
movement of Japanese car and electronics companies is going to have
exactly the same effect on Japan's import bill.

The point is only worth mentioning because there is still so much
nonsense talked about foreign investment and the 'danger' of foreigners
buying up national assets. Realists who understand the pace and nature of
change in the world economy recognize such emotional responses as
irrelevant anachronisms.

Conclusions

Equally obsolete is the social democrat/monetarist debate about whether
global economic justice requires a new international economic order, or
whether it would be better to move towards even freer markets, more
deregulated banks and more competition between currencies and between

countries. The facts – which realists at least should recognize – are that practical politicians in the developing countries have already given up on the 'New International Economic Order' (NIEO). They have recognized it as a non-starter. It is, quoting de Musset, 'chacun pour soi dans ce desert d'egoisme qu'on appele la vie', and the governments of less-developed countries (LDCs) are acting accordingly. The hopes of the old social democrats in the Brandt Commission that the principles of mutual dependence that worked to produce the national welfare state could also be made to work in an international political system divided into separate states have been disappointed – and predictably so.

Meanwhile, it is only the more theoretical ideologues of monetarist economics who still believe the system would benefit from more deregulation and from fewer controls over banks and financial markets. Those with knowledge and experience of banking and the systems which states have devised over the years to regulate it fear that deregulation and unregulated financial innovation may already have gone too far.[14] A comment typical of many was that 'In the world economy, a private supranationalism energised by the technical revolution in information and communication has overwhelmed public institutions designed for what now looks like the horse-and-buggy era.'[15] Richard Dale's recent study of international banking regulation has also pointed out the weaknesses even of the improved Basle Concordats system of central bank cooperation.[16] Six years ago, even a US congressional committee report concluded that the financial system had 'far outstripped the development of international political mechanisms capable of exercising economic management.'[17]

The realist who recognizes the significance of these changes is faced with a three-way dilemma – a 'trilemma'. The Brandt-type solutions which call for new and better international institutions have been rejected, basically because they are disruptive of the authority of the state. (It is significant that even in Europe, Mrs Thatcher's objections to a common central bank have been echoed by the comments on the Delors proposals by the Bundesbank and the German Finance Ministry.) The 'truly international bank backed by all the resources of the major nations' which Anthony Sampson said in 1981 was more necessary than ever is not even on the agenda of Summit discussions.[18] Even the Lever and Huhne (1985) proposal for a system of insurance for new capital to ease the recovery from chronic LDC debt has not found favour; the US government has trouble enough bailing out its own savings banks.

If realism recognizes the impossibility as things are of going forward, it must also recognize the probable impossibility of going back – i.e. of reverting to de-integrated monetary and financial systems under national control. This was the solution favoured by Fred Hirsch at the end of his life and by that cool veteran of the IMF, Jacques Polak. The rationale for it has been explained by my colleague Marcello de Cecco. Quoting the late Sir John Hicks's observation that capitalism, to be stable, needed a thick layer of unchanging contractual economic relations to balance the volatility of markets, de Cecco has commented that the United States and Britain by financial innovation and deregulation have thinned that layer, and at the same time have thickened that flexprice auction layer which, as always, is apt to cause 'deep and continuous fluctuations in investment and employment'.[19] He may be right, but the recent moves by the Italian government – supported by big business and taken in common with many others – towards financial deregulation strongly suggest the difficulty of resisting the trend, let alone reversing it – short, at least, of a major world economic depression.

The third horn of the trilemma is, of course, to allow the international banks and markets to continue with minimum controls. And this, as we see from listening to the experts, is a dangerous course. Not so much because of the danger of financial crash and collapse – though even after surviving 1987, that is still not inconceivable – as because the lack of control over banking systems leaves the banks free to stay away from investing in development and to compete for more profitable business in LBOs (leveraged buy outs), M&As (mergers and acquisitions) and securitization. The dangerous consequence of this is that it does nothing to stop the continued slowdown of economic growth especially in the weaker – mainly African – developing countries.

Of the three courses, the global realist who recognizes the strong concern of every modern state – including the United States – with wealth-creation as the salve for social conflict should perhaps ask what it is, more exactly, that stops progress towards the first course of action, collective regulation; towards a global Keynesian solution which would apply the Japanese surpluses to investment in development at tolerable, manageable rates of interest. Without wishing to start another, different debate, this realist would only suggest that the obstacles lie more in the domestic politics of the United States as unchallenged leader in the world market economy – even perhaps with the US Constitution itself – than in the shortcomings of mechanisms for international policy coordination. Nor am I alone in this contention.[20] The practical policy issue even for the global realist, then, is how to bring about radical change in US policies towards the management of trade and the regulation and management of money. To that end, it may be necessary for realists in Japan and in Europe to think how they might effectively combine forces with the more far-sighted and enlightened of American realists to bring about such change.

Notes

1. J. D. B. Miller, *The World of States* (London: Croom Helm, 1981); H. Bull, *The Anarchical Society* (London: Macmillan, 1977).
2. Raymond Aron, *Peace and War* (New York: Doubleday, 1966); R. Gilpin, *The Political Economy of International Relations* (Princeton, N.J.: Princeton University Press, 1987).
3. J. Burton, *World Society* (Cambridge: Cambridge University Press, 1972).
4. M. Wright, *Power Politics* (London: Oxford University Press for the Royal Institute of International Affairs, 1948); Bull, *The Anarchical Society*.
5. Susan Strange, *Casino Capitalism* (Oxford: Basil Blackwell, 1986).
6. D. Calleo, *The Imperious Economy* (Cambridge, Mass.: Harvard University Press, 1985) and *Beyond American Hegemony* (New York: Basic Books, 1988).
7. J. Reuff, *The Monetary Sin of the West* (New York: Macmillan, 1971).
8. E. Morse, "Crisis Diplomacy, Interdependence and the Politics of International Economic Relations," *World Politics*, vol. XXIV, supplement, (1972); Fred Bergsten, *The Dilemmas of the Dollar* (New York: New York University Press, 1975).
9. Susan Strange, *International Monetary Relations*, vol. 2 of *International Economic Relations of the Western World 1959–1971*, ed. A. Shonfield (Oxford: Oxford University Press, 1976).
10. Robin Naylor, *Hot Money and the Politics of Debt* (London: Unwin Hyman, 1987).
11. *Ibid.*
12. H. Lever and C. Huhne, *Debt and Danger: The World Financial Crisis* (Harmondsworth: Penguin, 1985), p. 127.
13. For details see J. Stopford and S. Strange, *Rival States, Rival Firms: Competition for World Market Shares* (Cambridge: Cambridge University Press, 1991), ch. 4.
14. R. Dale, *The Regulation of International Banking* (New York: Brooking Institute, 1987); A. Hamilton, *International Finance* (London: Macmillan, 1986).
15. H. Wachtel, *The Money Mandarins: The Making of a Supranational Economic Order* (New York: Pantheon, 1986).
16. R. Dale, *The Regulation of International Banking*.
17. U.S. Congress, *The United States in a Changing World Economy* (Washington, D.C.: 1983), p. 18.
18. Anthony Sampson, *The Moneylenders: Bankers in a Dangerous World* (London: Hodder and Stoughton, 1981).
19. M. de Cecco, *Changing Money* (Oxford: Basil Blackwell, 1988).
20. Y. Funabashi *Managing the Dollar: From the Plaza to the Louvre* (Washington D.C.: Washington Institute for International Economics, 1988).

Commentary: The political realism of free movement

Robert E. Goodin

Before commenting on how self-styled political realists assess movements of peoples or of money across international borders, I must first consider the status of political realism as a moral theory at all. The organizing premise of this volume as a whole is to see how such issues look from various different moral stances: liberal egalitarian, libertarian, Marxist, natural law or what have you. In the case of political realism, it is not clear that it constitutes a moral stance at all.

Surface appearances suggest that it is not. In the literature of international relations, realism is presented as the polar opposite to idealism; and as such it ostensibly repudiates altogether the pursuit of high moral ideals in foreign policies. That might, of course, amount to mere posturing, overstating the case for dramatic effect.[1] But at least on the face of it, political realism – like certain strands of Marxism, perhaps – would seem to amount to a flat denial of the relevance of moral standards of assessment, at least when it comes to international affairs.

Conventionally, *raisons d'état* are not thought to be first and foremost moral reasons. Indeed, the category need never have been invented if they were. The whole point of the political realists, to hear them tell it, is that the state does what it must or what it can, rather than what it necessarily ideally ought.[2]

The characteristic plea of political realism seems to take the form 'Of course we should do X (admit more boat people, or whatever); but it is politically unrealistic to expect us to do so.' The very form of the plea flouts moral authority. It concedes that X should be done. But it proceeds immediately to say that – morality notwithstanding – X is not going to be done. All that it offers by way of an explanation is the rather opaque claim that morality's demand is somehow politically unrealistic.

If that claim is to be taken seriously, morally – if it is to withstand critical philosophical scrutiny – much more needs to be said about *why* it is unrealistic to expect people to behave as morally they ought. Many such reasons would quite definitely not serve to excuse the delict. It might be unrealistic to expect mass murderers, when cornered, not to murder again; after all, they can only be hanged once. Unrealistic though it may be, however, the simple fact remains that morally they ought not. Unrealistic though it may be to expect careerists to resign in protest rather than carrying out immoral schemes close to the hearts of their evil superiors, still they should. Unrealistic though it may be to expect political leaders to lose elections rather than renege on promises, still they should.

In all those sorts of cases, the demands of morality may be 'unrealistic' – but they are none the less *morally* compelling for being so. The reason, quite simply, is that morality's demands are 'unrealistic' not in the sense that people cannot comply with them, but merely in the sense that they will not. There, what makes it 'unrealistic' to expect people to do the morally proper thing is simply the fact that morality does not figure as centrally as morally it should in those people's value systems. To say that it is 'unrealistic' to expect morality to motivate those who do not value morality highly enough is not, in any way, to say that their morality is excused. It is to say instead that they stand doubly condemned.

The immorality of the immoral or the amoral cannot itself be excused by appeals to political realism, then. To find any legitimate scope for application of the realist principle in politics, we must instead look elsewhere. That is my task in the first part of this chapter below, where I suggest that deviations from the ideal moral order made by those trying to do as much good as can be done, given the immorality of others around them, might well be excused by notions of political realism. But then realism serves as an excuse rather than as a justification for deviations from the moral ideal; and appealing to that excuse imposes a further obligation, namely, to make very certain that the constraints on doing better really are immutable.

Whereas the first part surveys various justifications, excuses and corollaries of realist principles in international politics quite generally, the second is addressed more specifically to their application to problems of the transnational movements of people and of money. My argument there will be that there is no need to be quite *so* realistic as many commentators might suggest in acquiescing to constraints on free movement of either people or of money across international borders. Not only is there no good reason, morally, to accept particularly restrictive policies. Politically, even, there may well be no particular advantage from imposing them.

The moral bearing of political realism

In so far as political realist claims aspire to moral status, they can be understood as offering either *excuses* or *justifications*. Appeals to excuses admit that what is being done is in some sense wrong; they claim merely that, for some special sorts of reasons, the wrong is an excusable or forgivable one. Even if the wrong is in this way 'excused', it is none the less morally unfortunate that it had to be committed at all. It would have been morally better for the conditions by virtue of which the wrong was excused to have been removed, so the excused wrong did not have to be committed in the first place. Appeals to justifications, in contrast, assert not only that it was 'all right, in the circumstances' for the actions in view to have been committed; they assert that it was right (good, morally desirable) for the circumstances to have been arranged in that way and for the acts to have been committed.[3]

Realism, as it is standardly understood, usually seems to appeal to excuses. Standardly contrasted to idealism, it purports to be a repudiation of moralistic politics. But some theorists, when pressed on the moral basis of their position, would take a different tack. They argue that the sorts of policies advocated by realists are not just excused, morally, but actually are justified – actually are good – morally. Morality, properly understood, requires us to take realist positions politically, they would assert. Whether such analysts are genuine realists or mere fellow-travellers is almost entirely a matter of semantics. Theirs is an important position to be considered, and rejected, before turning to more standardly realist themes.

Realist justifications: Autonomy and national self-preservation

The strongest way in which the political realists' appeal might be a genuinely moral one – a justification, rather than a mere excuse, for nationally self-serving policies – has to do with the moral importance attached to national self-determination. People enjoy the right of autonomy and self-determination, not just as individuals but as groups as well.[4] Sharing a common life, alongside others with similar histories and values, might be regarded as a morally important goal, from various different perspectives.[5] And, as discussed in Chapter 2, that might be one reason they are reluctant to permit foreign penetration.

This, arguably, is precisely the political realists' concern. They are preoccupied with 'national self-preservation', and with the ways in which it might be threatened if 'vital' national interests were undermined. Although they rarely come right out and say so, what realists seem to be saying when employing such terminology is that the existence of the nation as an independent, self-determining entity is at stake.[6]

For my own part, I am rather more sceptical about the nation-state as a source of ultimate moral value.[7] But I do not propose to enter into that larger argument here. For present purposes, I shall simply assume that there is some moral value – whether ultimate or derivative does not here matter – in national self-determination.

Even conceding the basic moral premise at stake here, political realists' claims are often badly overstated, though. Many of the developments that they resist would hardly mark (or even seriously risk) the end of our nation as we know it. Most would, at most, amount to modest alterations to ongoing practices in our community – practices which, being 'live' practices, are in any case undergoing constant evolution and alteration, anyway.

Furthermore, the moral argument here in view links together with the arguments of the political realist only in the very special case of a genuinely nation-state. What the moral argument for national self-determination requires is protection of the 'nation' – the organic community, its on-going practices and traditions. What the political realist would have us protect is the vital interests of the state as a legal entity. The two are rarely co-terminous: it is the rare state that encapsulates one and only one 'national' community. Where the two are not coterminous, it is far from clear that the best way to protect the common life of the national community is to protect the existing state system. Indeed, undermining the state in certain respects might actually be necessary in order for minority nationalities to enjoy a proper sort of common life at all, as recent events in the Soviet Union perhaps serve to remind us.[8]

Finally, and most importantly, notice that 'self-preservation' means something very different for nations and for individuals. Indeed, it is hard to think exactly what would be the equivalent in the life of a nation to death in the life of an individual.[9] Individuals die, nations merely 'change'. Of course, changes can sometimes be so great as to threaten identity itself. But assuming that for nations, even more than for natural individuals, the essence of identity consists in some collective equivalent to 'mental connectedness and continuity', few of the sorts of changes that are resisted by realists as threats to the nation's vital interests really promise seriously to undermine national identity.[10] The mere replacement of one regime or even one constitution with another almost certainly does not.[11] Even conquest by another state need not, so long as the nation's cultural traditions are preserved under alien rule.

All this is simply to say that I do not think that the stronger moral claim that might be made by proto-political realists can be sustained. Single-minded pursuit of national interest above all else in foreign policy cannot be justified by appeal to notions of national self-determination. And that seems to be about the only way anyone ever tries actually to *justify* such policies. At most, special circumstances surrounding international relations might *excuse* such policies. It is to that issue that I now turn.

Realist excuses: Impossibility

One of the most standard maxims in moral philosophy is 'ought implies can'. If it is literally impossible for you to do X, then you are standardly said to be relieved of any obligation to do X. Various slightly different analyses are offered as to why that should be so. In the end, all come down to the basic insight that the function of morality is to shape people's behaviour, and if it is impossible for them to do X it is simply pointless to tell them they should do it.[12]

Political realism sometimes seems to be appealing to precisely that principle. When those deeply immersed in the real world ask those with their heads in the clouds to 'be realistic', the implicit point often seems to be that what idealists prescribe is simply impossible; the world being as it is, what they want simply cannot be had.[13] The discourse of realists is peppered with the language of modality: 'can', 'may', 'must'; 'possibility', 'impossibility', 'necessity'. They ascribe to nations 'vital' interests, implying a necessity akin to an individual's need for food to sustain life itself. All this, and more, suggests that the political realist's appeal might be to the venerable moral doctrine that 'ought implies can' and, more to the point, its converse.

There are many things to be said about this argument. The first, perhaps, is a simple observation about the precise nature of that converse proposition to which political realists might be appealing. The negation of 'ought implies can' is *not* 'cannot implies ought not'. It would not be literally wrong to do (or try to do) what you cannot. Rather, it would merely be unnecessary for you to do so. (The proper formulation, perhaps, should be 'cannot implies not-ought': it is not morally obligatory, if it is not possible.) The good remains good, even when it lies beyond our grasp.[14]

The second thing to be said about this argument is that we generally cannot appeal to impossibilities of our own making to excuse us from our moral obligations. This is obviously true if it is still within our power to lift the constraints we imposed upon ourselves, but it is at least arguably true even if it is not. A lifeguard who slept through first aid classes might now find it impossible to resuscitate drowning swimmers but is hardly to be excused, on those grounds, from the duty to do so. A firm that has divested itself of almost all its assets in anticipation of a mass tort suit may find it impossible to recompense its victims but is hardly therefore to be excused, morally (however hard it might be to win an effective judgment, legally), from compensating those whom it has injured.[15]

The third thing to note about this argument is the peculiar sense of impossibility often involved. In the paradigmatic appeal to 'ought implies can', it is physical impossibility that is involved. But that is almost never what is actually involved in political realists' invocations of notions of 'political impossibility'. The reason that Britain cannot agree to honour all British passports held by citizens of Hong Kong is not that all 6 million of them would not fit onto the British Isles. Those who pronounce, curtly, that it is 'quite impossible' for Britain to join a single European currency do not mean, literally, that doing so would violate any economic laws of nature akin to the laws of physics.

Typically, to say that something is 'politically impossible' is merely to say that it entails unacceptable costs for certain crucial political actors.[16] That crucially transforms the matter, though. The key question then becomes not whether it is possible for them to bear the costs, but rather whether it is somehow reasonable to expect them to do so. In a very few cases, we might decide that it would be *so* unreasonable to expect people to bear such burdens that they should be excused from them, on grounds very akin to impossibility. Such sacrifices are so large as to impose a psychological strain that is too great for most people to bear. Those duties we dub 'supererogatory', the stuff of saints and heroes.[17]

Often, though, it is not a matter of its being literally impossible – physically, or even psychologically – to make the sacrifice in view. It is just a matter of whether or not it is 'reasonable' to expect people to do so. On that, there is far more scope for legitimate dissent than allowed by the blocking-move formulation of 'ought implies can'. Saying that something literally cannot be done takes it off the agenda altogether; saying that something would be very costly to do need not. What goals are worth what sacrifices is a legitimate subject for discussion, in a way that repealing the laws of physical necessity is not.

There is a further question implicit in the political formulation of the 'ought implies can' doctrines as set out above. Saying that a plan is politically impossible amounts, essentially, to saying that it entails unacceptable costs for certain crucial actors. Having considered the first component in that formula, let us now turn to the latter. What makes certain political actors 'crucial', thus giving them a virtual veto under this political version of the 'ought implies can' doctrine?

On the face of it, there is something deeply suspect in saying that foreign aid will never get properly distributed in Indonesia so long as Suharto remains in power, and Suharto refuses to budge. What makes that move look most suspicious, no doubt, is the appearance of letting Suharto validate his own excuse, excusing his refusal to promote social justice by virtue of his own refusal to do so or to make way for someone who would. But even if we set that problem to one side, under the general rule that people cannot appeal to impossibilities of their own creation, another genuine problem remains. The excuse, in this form, tends to let not only Suharto off the hook too easily but likewise others whom we might hold responsible for displacing him.

Saying that 'it is impossible to do the right thing with X in power' is typically offered as an excuse for not doing the right thing. It is, equally, an argument for getting rid of X. With a very few political leaders, and with rather more cases of ethnic groups or political factions, there might genuinely be no way of displacing them from central positions in the political life of their society. If there is literally no way around those individuals or groups, and they literally refuse ever to do what is right, then it may be genuinely politically impossible to do the right thing.[18] More often, they or their objections can be overcome, at a cost. And again, the question becomes one of what costs are worth paying, which is a discussable question in a way genuine impossibility is not.

The upshot of these last two points, especially, is that political realism appeals not so much to the notion that 'ought implies can' as it does to the notion that 'ought implies costs'. The costs of doing what is right may sometimes prove prohibitive, of course. But more often than not, costs are said to be 'prohibitive' on the grounds that people are unwilling, rather than strictly unable, to pay them.

The flavour of the political realist message is well captured by their 'ought implies can' doctrine. The realist's aim is indeed to get us to focus on the feasible set, and to put altogether out of our minds options that are utterly unrealistic.[19] It is perfectly proper that we should do so, provided those options genuinely are and inevitably will remain impossible. But if the only reason the options are unrealistic is that people are unwilling to make sacrifices that they could and arguably should in pursuit of morally important goals, then those options should be very much on the table. The proper role of politics, in such circumstances, is precisely not to 'be realistic' and accept uncritically people's unwillingness to make morally proper sacrifices. It is, rather, to persuade them that moral ideals are worth pursuing.

The consequences of realism: An ethic of second-best

Previously I have been discussing moral grounds – one a justification, the other an excuse – for political realism. What I want to discuss next, briefly, is more on the order of a moral corollary of political realism, whichever way it has been grounded. Realists need to argue not only that the ideal is out of reach but also that that fact makes a big difference to the way we should behave. Here, realists can properly appeal to the economic theory of second-best – as Keynes implicitly did, in the passages quoted in Chapter 2 above, in arguing for exchange controls.

The general theory of second best, as formulated by economists, starts by asking us to suppose the very best strategy for pursuing some complex moral end is, for one reason or another, ruled out. It tells us that in such circumstances the next-best course of action is not necessarily that one, among the remaining options, which is most similar to the very best.[20] The intuitive idea at the root of this theory is just this: in any complex system, a small change anywhere may well require systematic readjustments every-where else, too. The second option may – not 'necessarily will', but certainly 'may' – be altogether different in absolutely every dimension from the first. Should the second-best prove unattainable also, then the third-best option might be systematically different from both the others yet again. And so on down the list.

Political realists never put the point exactly like that, of course. Cer-tainly they never appeal explicitly to the economic theory of second-best, any more than they appeal explicitly to moral doctrines like 'ought implies can'. But that argument none the less captures something of the spirit of their position. They are anxious to emphasize the importance of doing the best you can in an imperfect world. They are anxious to insist upon the importance of not making a fetish of moral ideals: doing the best you can in an imperfect world may well require you to compromise any (indeed, all) of your moral ideals, at least at the margin.[21]

There is much to be said for the realist argument, thus construed. Failure to take due account of the probable reactions of others can, indeed, have consequences that are truly catastrophic, morally and otherwise. Doing the best we can in the circumstances, even where these circumstances are partly constituted by others doing less well than they could and should, is the most that we might reasonably demand of people. That we should be realistic in this sense – that we should choose our own actions with due regard to what others actually will do (or could be made to do) – is a plausible doctrine, and plausibly a moral one.[22]

Of course, that argument does not get going until one of the others – of which I have been more critical – has already established that the first-best option is unrealistic. But at least sometimes it will surely have some bite: at least sometimes, presumably, there really will be genuinely insurmount-able obstacles to doing what ideally we should. In such situations, the lesson that you cannot simply read what is the 'better' off a description of what is the 'best' may well prove an important one.

The doctrine of the second-best also poses intolerable perplexities,

though. Suppose it is the case that the second-best option really is totally
unlike the very best, that the third-best really is totally unlike either of the
others, and so on down the list. Then we cannot simply tell people to 'come
as close to the ideal as you can'; we cannot just pitch our moral demands,
prudently, just a little above people's presumed capacities, to make sure
they try as hard as they can.[23] Instead, what we ought to do depends
wholly upon where the boundaries of the feasible set lies. The disagreement between advocates of one option and advocates of another loses any
distinctively moral content and turns into a squabble of a basely empirical
sort about which options are feasible and which are not.

Now, if it genuinely is true that the next-best option all the way down
the list is totally distinctive, perhaps that is precisely as it should be. Still, I
think we are likely to be uncomfortable turning value discourse into
feasibility studies of the most crass sort. Something like this impatience
seems to be manifested in Bernard Williams' refusal to look into too many
mirrors when discussing the logic of deterrence, he refuses to go *too* far
down the track of 'we're thinking that they're thinking that we're thinking
that they're thinking that . . .'.[24] The logic of deterrence makes those
considerations properly central to strategic thinking, but Williams insists
that the morally right answer must not get too heavily involved in such
thinking.

Why not? I'm not sure, exactly. But perhaps the reason we should not
look in too many mirrors, there, is the same reason we should resist too
much infection of our moralizing by second-best thinking elsewhere.
Focusing too tightly on second- and third-best options makes us not look
closely enough to see whether and how the first-best option might actually
be pursued. It would be wrong to dismiss the very best option, just because
the second-best hunt poses problems that are technically more interesting.

The political realism of free movement of people and of money

Political realism was a doctrine classically concerned with the quest for
security, and that almost exclusively. National interests, as realists
traditionally perceived them, were national security interests almost
exclusively. The power that realists would ask us to maximize was,
traditionally, narrowly political power – and, all too often, more narrowly
still, purely military might.[25] Even a nation's international economic
interests were explicitly ruled out of the realist's court, in many of the most
influential original statements of the realist position; and they are still
struggling to gain entry into neo-realist accounts today.[26] Any interest the
nation might be thought to have in its national culture, ethnic composition

or genetic pool was so far outside the scope of classically realist concerns that the Founding Fathers of this school did not even bother pronouncing on the subject.

If, however, we consider 'national power' – much less 'national interest' – more broadly, it is of course true that nations take a strong interest in, and derive considerable international influence from, various attributes of their economies and their populations. Even at the crudest *realpolitik* level, a strong economic base is required to sustain a massive military effort; and nations populated either too sparsely or by groupings too diverse to sustain loyalty to the state are incapable of generating adequate cannon fodder. Less crassly, power is just a means to other ends; and the national interest that national power is meant to serve might well, and often will, include promoting material well-being and cultural values for the nation as a whole. It was, then, just plain silly – even within their own terms – for classical realists to have ignored questions of economics or demographics.

A revisionist realism, of the sort here represented by Hendrickson and Strange, would see both economics and demographics as sources of realist concern. What makes the concern indisputably 'realist', however revisionary, is the conjunction of two facts: 1) the maximizing agent in such discussions is seen to be the state, and 2) the maximand in such discussions is seen to be 'national interest' of a sort that is at least first cousin to 'national power'.

The revisionist realist, unlike many other sorts of commentators perhaps, at least displays the virtue of consistency in addressing questions of the transnational migration of people or of money. Both issues are judged by the same standard of 'national interest'. A state should allow foreigners or their money in (or nationals or their money out) if and only if it is in the interests of the state to do so.

Of course, different states are differently situated in the world economy, and states differ in their demographic mix. So what is right, by this standard, for one state is not necessarily right for all others. Furthermore, realism thus construed is a doctrine that relies more heavily than most moral theories upon empirical facts about what really will promote the national interest. Thus, there is plenty of scope for immanent critiques of ostensibly realist policies as being counterproductive of their own long-term ends.

Those facts combine to ensure that there is no agreed line among all realists worldwide on the general desirability of free movement of either people or of money across international boundaries. It all depends upon whose national interests you internalize and upon what you suppose the ultimate consequences of alternative policies actually to be.

What I suppose all realists are generally agreed upon, though, are the twin propositions that 1) a state may restrict either sort of movement, if it is genuinely in its interests to do so, and 2) it turns out to be genuinely in states' interests to do so often enough for that first proposition to be of more than purely academic interest. Here I propose to mount a minimalist challenge to political realism, taking the first proposition as given and (building upon Hendrickson and Strange's comments) merely challenging the second, and secondary, proposition.

Free trade, much less free flow of capital, may not strictly be in every state's interests at every moment in time. But given the plain truths Strange sets out about contemporary international monetary arrangements – facts that may be unfortunate, but that cannot now realistically be altered – there is little chance of restricting free capital flows; furthermore, given what she says about free movement being the only stable international regime, it may not ultimately be in anyone's long-term interests to try. Short-term advantages might be obtained by some, at the margin; but no one can seize, and confidently expect to hold, any substantial long-term advantages from such restrictions. Or at least that is how I interpret Strange's slightly elliptical remarks about the 'global realism' of free movement regimes.[27]

Free movement of peoples is less straightforward, perhaps. But let us build here upon the discussion of international law in Hendrickson's paper. Now, both customary international law and more especially international treaty law are obviously outgrowths of a process of states negotiating with other states, seeking arrangements that they see as best for promoting their own long-term interests. Hendrickson calls this an 'international morality'; but if so, it is one which is of a peculiarly Hobbesian kind, and only the most hard-bitten realist would suppose that the requirements of international morality are limited to what states might agree upon in this way.[28]

What remains interesting, however, is the extent to which those provisions of international law contain so many requirements for allowing free movement of peoples across international frontiers. What that proves is a point, not about morality, but rather about national interests. That so many states have, over so many years, been prepared to agree to such general rules of international conduct only goes to show the extent to which free movement of peoples so very rarely threatens most states' long-term interests.[29]

All that is simply to say, in line with what I take both Hendrickson and Strange to be saying, that realists for realist reasons ought to allow substantially free movement of both people and money around the world. Let me just add a pair of even more subversive thoughts.

The first is just this: perhaps the classical exponents of political realism in international relations were right not to worry about economics or demographics – still less capital or population shifts – at all. If their arguments really were about protecting vital national interests and ensuring national self-preservation, literally understood, then it may well have been right for them to focus upon national security policy almost exclusively. Unless you adopt a very attenuated sense of the 'national self' (so that, for example, Australia would cease to be Australia were it to cease to be a nation of almost exclusively rich whites), then almost no conceivable shifts of either people or of money across international borders could threaten vital national interests and national self-preservation. Physical destruction of the national fabric by an occupying force really is about the only thing that could do that. Few population movements could plausibly be represented as the functional equivalent of invasions by an occupying army.[30] And even fewer capital flows could be so construed.

A second thought which would similarly undermine restrictions rationalized in terms of realism is just this: in so far as realism is offered as an excuse rather than as a justification for the policies defended in its name, the argument is that that is the best policy that we can pursue, given the immoral proclivities of others around us. That proposition, in turn, presupposes (roughly) that one bad apple spoils the barrel, and forces all others to be equally bad.

But the strategic structure of international games is rarely like that. Much more typically, we can afford quite a few bad apples: the rich countries of the world can pretty well solve international refugee problems, merely by absorbing all those prepared to move, even if the poorest half of the world kept its doors firmly closed to refugees, for example.[31] Indeed, the strategic structure of international games is sometimes such that a single significant player can, by breaking ranks with the cartel and refusing to collude in policies of immorality, force all the rest to follow suit and pursue more honourable paths. So those wanting to argue that we cannot be good because others are behaving badly often ignore the very real possibilities that, by behaving better, we might force them to behave better, too.

Conclusion

Realists work in terms of notions of national interest. That is what, at root, makes us wonder whether it is genuinely a moral theory at all. Morality, after all, is standardly counterposed to notions of pure self-interest.

Whatever its moral standing, though, interest certainly is capable of moving people to action. It is motivationally potent. Hence the force of saying that, even from a realist perspective, there is much to be said for (and little to be said against) a regime of free movement. That is just another way of saying that such a regime is usually in the long-term self-interest of most international actors.[32]

But here the critique closes back on itself. Interest is not the only motive. There is morality on the one side, and prejudice on the other, that can also move people to action. While the first and the second – interest and morality – may converge on a regime of free movement, prejudice might still stand in its way. People may have to pay dearly for indulging their prejudices, if the interest-based argument for free movement is valid. But prejudices can be powerful, and pay they may.

All that is just to say that even if people have no good reason to close their borders to foreigners, they might none the less have lots of bad ones; motivationally, they may be compelling for being rationally groundless.

Notes

1. When rejecting the starry-eyed idealism of naive moralists, political realists are not necessarily rejecting the pursuit of moral goals in foreign policy altogether. They might just be insisting that that pursuit be properly adapted to circumstances and constraints. Marshall Cohen, "Moral Skepticism and International Relations," *Philosophy & Public Affairs*, 13 (1984), 299–346 makes much of this point. Sometimes even Hans J. Morgenthau himself talks this way: 'Realism maintains that universal moral principles cannot be applied to the actions of states in their abstract universal formulation, but that they must be filtered through the concrete circumstances of time and place', he writes at one point in *Politics Among Nations*, 3rd ed. (New York: Knopf, 1963), p. 10.

2. I take as axiomatic the 'six principles of political realism' set out in Morgenthau's *Politics Among Nations*, pp. 4–15. See also Hans J. Morgenthau, "The Twilight of International Morality," *Ethics*, 58 (1948), 79–99; "National Interest and Moral Principles in Foreign Policy," *The American Scholar*, 18 (1949), 207–12; and "Another 'Great Debate': The National Interest of the United States," *American Political Science Review*, 46 (1952), 961–88. For recent restatements, see the sources listed in footnote 25 below. For philosophically oriented critiques, see Charles R. Beitz, *Political Theory and International Relations* (Princeton, N.J.: Princeton University Press, 1979), pt. 1, esp. pp. 15–27 and Marshall Cohen, "Moral Skepticism and International Relations."

3. J. L. Austin, "A Plea for Excuses," *Proceedings of the Aristotelian Society*, 57 (1956–7), 1–30.

4. Certainly in so far as individually they so chOose, at least. It is not always clear whether advocates of 'group rights' mean to be claiming more. See, e.g., James Crawford, ed., *Rights of Peoples* (Oxford: Clarendon Press, 1988).

5. Brian Barry, "Self-Government Revisited," *The Nature of Political Theory*,

ed. D. Miller and L. Siedentop (Oxford: Clarendon Press, 1983), pp. 121–54. Michael Walzer, *Just and Unjust Wars* (New York: Basic Books, 1977) and "The Moral Standing of States," *Philosophy & Public Affairs*, 9 (1980), 209–30. David Miller, "The Ethical Significance of Nationality," *Ethics*, 98 (1988), 647–62. Will Kymlicka, *Liberalism, Community & Culture* (Oxford: Clarendon Press, 1989). Stanley French and Andres Gutman, "The Principle of National Self-Determination," *Philosophy, Morality, and International Affairs*, eds. V. Held, S. Morgenbesser and T. Nagel (New York: Oxford University Press, 1974), pp. 138–53.

6. Although talking in terms of 'national survival' as a 'moral principle', Morgenthau seems to be thinking more in terms of what the state may and must do 'in the name of those who are in its care' (*Politics Among Nations*, p. 10). The moral principles at stake for Morgenthau thus seem to be fiduciary duties rather than any independent moral value attaching to national self-determination. Indeed, earlier on that same page, in a rather different connection, Morgenthau writes,

   Nothing in the realist position militates against the assumption that the present division of the political world into nation states will be replaced by larger units of a quite different character, more in keeping with the technical potentialities and the moral requirements of the contemporary world.

   That does not sound much like a friend of national self-determination talking. On this score, perhaps the most distinguished near-contemporary practitioner of political realism in foreign policy was even more clear: in a 1964 speech at Amherst College on 'Ethics in international relations today' Dean Acheson complained that 'what passes for ethical standards . . . in foreign affairs is a collection of moralisms, maxims and slogans, which neither help nor guide, but only confuse decision . . . on complicated matters', adding that 'one of the most often invoked and delusive of these maxims is the so-called principle of self-determination'. See excerpts of this speech printed in the *New York Times*, December 10, 1964, p. 16.

7. Robert E. Goodin, "What Is So Special About Our Fellow Countrymen?" *Ethics*, 98 (1988), 663–86. See similarly Henry Shue, "Mediating Duties," *Ethics*, 98 (1988), 687–704.

8. Or, indeed, in Canada. See Kymlicka, *Liberalism, Community and Culture*, chaps. 7–13.

9. Physical or cultural genocide – the destruction of a whole culture, or the destruction physically of its carriers – would be about what it would take. On what (if anything) is awful about individuals' deaths, see: Thomas Nagel, *Mortal Questions* (Cambridge: Cambridge University Press, 1979); Robert Nozick, *Philosophical Explanations* (Cambridge, Mass.: Harvard University Press, 1981), pp. 579–85; and Michael S. Slote, "Existentialism and the Fear of Dying," *American Philosophical Quarterly*, 12 (1975), 17–28. At almost nowhere in those discussions could you substitute the word 'nation' (or still less 'state') for the word 'person' without rendering the argument nonsensical.

10. This, of course, is Derek Parfit's standard of personal identity, offered in *Reasons and Persons* (Oxford: Clarendon Press, 1984), pt. 3. On conditions governing the 'identity' and 'continuity' and 'extinction' of states – which, as I have said, are not necessarily equivalent to nations – see James Crawford, *The Creation of States in International Law* (Oxford: Clarendon Press, 1979), chaps. 16 and 17.

11. As Richard Rose and Guy Peters say in *Can Government Go Bankrupt?* (London: Macmillan, 1979), pp. 115, 263, De Gaulle's new constitution for the French Fifth Republic 'did not repudiate spending commitments embodied in the social security legislation of previous French regimes', and indeed 'the Federal Republic of Germany still pays benefits to the families of soldiers who fought for the Third Reich.' See further Robert E. Goodin, *Political Theory and Public Policy* (Chicago: University of Chicago Press, 1982), chap. 11.

12. R. M. Hare, "Freedom of the Will," *Proceedings of the Aristotelian Society* (Supplement), 25 (1951), 201–16. Alan Montefiore, " 'Ought' and 'Can' " *Philosophical Quarterly*, 8 (1958), 24–40.

13. In Stanley Hoffmann's gloss, the realist position maintains that

> One must . . . be prepared to delete those ends for which power is missing, or those ends that simply cannot be reached, either with the power that one is able to produce or with the power at one's disposal that is actually usable – for, in the nuclear age especially, not all power is rationally usable. (Hoffman, "Realism and Its Discontents," *Atlantic Monthly*, 256, no. 5 (November 1985), 131–2, 134, 136 at 134)

14. L. L. Heintz, "Excuses and 'Ought' Implies 'Can'," *Canadian Journal of Philosophy*, 5 (1976), 449–62; cf. H. A. Pritchard, "Duty and Ignorance of Fact," *Moral Obligation* (Oxford: Clarendon Press, 1949), 18–39.

15. Jeremy Bentham is characteristically, and rightly, blistering on this point in his attack on the common law of his day:

> True it is that under this system of yours it is impossible, without exception impossible, ever to do justice. Nothing was ever more true. But the impossibility, whence comes it? From yourselves. First you make the impossibility, and then you plead it. And wherefore was it made, but that it might be pleaded? (Bentham, "Rational of Judicial Evidence: Fiction," *Works*, ed. J. Bowring (Edinburgh: Tait, 1843), vol. 7, pp. 283–7 at 285)

This, presumably, is why Morgenthau, *Politics Among Nations*, p. 4 is too anxious to trace what he sees as immutable constraints on moralizing in international relations to 'the result of forces inherent in human nature'.

16. That is to say, 'possibility' – like 'liberty' on Hillel Steiner's analysis in *Proceedings of the Aristotelian Society*, 75 (1974–5), 33–50 – is essentially a matter of opportunity costs. It is not a matter of whether it is possible *tout court* for you to do X; it is rather a matter of whether it is possible for you to do 'X and Y', i.e. a matter of what else you have to give up, if you do X.

17. J. O. Urmson, "Saints and Heroes," *Essays in Moral Philosophy*, ed. A. I.

Melden (Seattle: University of Washington Press, 1958), pp. 198–216. James S. Fishkin, *The Limits of Obligation* (New Haven, Conn.: Yale University Press, 1982). These arguments have recently been uncomfortably extended by Susan Wolf, "Moral Saints," *Journal of Philosophy*, 79 (1982), 419–39 beyond cases of psychological impossibility into an argument that it is desirable that people do not always go around maximizing morally good deeds; but I take it that the arguments given for that would not translate very effectively from the level of the individual to that of the state, which is our present concern.

18. See further Robert E. Goodin, "Rights and Regimes," *The Challenge of Human Rights After Forty Years*, Proceedings of the 1988 Nobel Symposium, ed. Bernt Hagtvet and Asbjorn Eide (Oxford: Blackwell, forthcoming).

19. For further analysis of the political manoeuvre or rigging perceptions of possibility to keep certain options off the political agenda illegitimately, see Goodin, *Political Theory and Public Policy*, chap. 7.

20. R. G. Lipsey and K. Lancaster, "The General Theory of Second Best," *Review of Economic Studies*, 24 (1956), 11–33.

21. Thus, in his Amherst address on 'Ethics in international relations today' Dean Acheson asked, 'Is it moral to deny ourselves the use of force in all circumstances, when our adversaries employ it . . .? It seems to me not only a bad bargain but a stupid one. I would almost say an immoral one.' Acheson's point, presumably, was that it would undeniably be a better world where no one threatened the use of force, but in a world where at least one would then it is a better (because, through deterrence, a more peaceful) world in which everyone makes matching threats.

22. It is also at least arguably what Morgenthau was talking about all along. In *Politics Among Nations*, p. 7, he writes, 'Political realism does not require, nor does it condone, indifference to political ideals and moral principles, but it requires indeed a sharp distinction between the desirable and the possible – between what is desirable everywhere at all times and what is possible under the concrete circumstances of time and place.' For a fascinating analogue drawn from US domestic politics, consider John M. Mendeloff, *The Dilemma of Toxic Substance Regulation: How Overregulation Causes Underregulation at OSHA* (Cambridge, Mass.: MIT Press, 1988), arguing that tough regulations stir up employer resistance to implementation of existing regulations and political opposition to enactment of new ones. Mendeloff concludes that a regulatory regime that does not try to be quite so tough might actually manage to do more, by way of regulating the whole range of hazards that should be regulated.

23. George Cornewall Lewis, *A Treatise on the Methods of Observation and Reasoning in Politics* (London: Parker, 1852), vol. 2, chap. 22, sec. 25 recommends we pitch political goals just out of reach, on the grounds that otherwise 'we may, from want of energy, or of self-reliance, or of imaginative power, underrate our own capacity and overstate the difficulties of the case.'

24. Bernard Williams, "How to Think Sceptically About the Bomb," *New Society*, vol. 62, no. 1044 (November 18, 1982), pp. 288–90 at 290.

25. Morgenthau, *Politics among Nations*, pp. 9, 11. For important modern restatements, see: Kenneth N. Waltz, *Theory of International Politics* (Reading, Mass.: Addison-Wesley, 1979); and Robert Jervis, "Realism, Game Theory and Cooperation," *World Politics*, 40 (1988), 317–49.

26. Morgenthau, *Politics Among Nations*, pp. 10–11. For the contemporary debate, see Robert O. Keohane, ed., *Neorealism and Its Critics* (New York: Columbia University Press, 1986) and Joseph S. Nye, Jr., "Review Article: Neorealism and Neoliberalism," *World Politics*, 40 (1988), 235–51.

27. Similar themes are developed in really rather different ways by, e.g., Robert Gilpin, *The Political Economy of International Relations* (Princeton, N.J.: Princeton University Press, 1987) and John A. C. Conybeare, *Trade Wars* (New York: Columbia University Press, 1987). I regard Strange's references to 'global realism' as elliptical because it is unclear, in them, who the maximizing agent is supposed to be (the globe?) and what the maximand (the global interest?). But presumably she is being realistic enough to take as given something rather like the present state system, rather than postulating some world government or all-powerful global hegemon; and if so, she presumably means something rather like the proposition set out in the text.

28. Cf. Cohen, "Moral Skepticism and International Relations" and Beitz, *Political Theory and International Relations*, pt. 1.

29. Of course, international law is typically honoured in the breach, as realist writers never cease pointing out. Still, the point remains that the state in question agreed to the rule (in the case of a treaty obligation) or most other states have long agreed to it (in the case of customary international law), and most other states still agree to it (in both cases), or else the rule would not be a rule of international law at all. Breaches are the exception that prove the rule of a broad convergence of interests in rules of free movement of peoples across all countries of the world.

30. That which founded White Australia might, perhaps.

31. This is a specific application of a point made by Michael Taylor and Hugh Ward, "Whales, Chickens and Collective Action," *Political Studies*, 30 (1982), 350–70. For an earlier, less formal application to environmental policy, see George F. Kennan, "To Prevent a World Wasteland," *Foreign Affairs*, 48 (1970), 401–13.

32. Let us here join realists in glossing over the difference between the collective national interest and the individual interests of citizens of that nation. They can justify ignoring familiar problems of collective action only where there is some maximizing agent – supposed, typically, to be 'political leaders', however chosen – who completely control a nation's political decisions and whose own rewards are wholly determined by how well or ill their choices serve the national interest. Obviously, those conditions are rarely satisfied – or even approximated.

Concluding Perspectives

—— 18 ——

Alternative ethical perspectives on transnational migration

Terry Nardin

The ethical perspectives represented in this volume rest on different premises, yet the contributors often reach surprisingly similar conclusions. Most defend some kind of compromise between the opposing values of free movement and free association, between free markets and the regulation of economic activity for the common good. Even those who argue that borders should be open to the free movement of people and money, as a matter of principle, are prepared to accept restrictions on free movement under certain conditions. And this suggests that there is no absolute right to travel or reside, or to buy or sell, wherever one pleases. There may be a presumption in favour of unlimited freedom, but this presumption can be challenged on a variety of grounds.

Are there nevertheless irreducible differences of principle that make one's starting-point important? The chapters of this volume suggest that there are indeed such differences. The kinds of restrictions that may be imposed on freedom of movement make a difference, as do the reasons for these restrictions. My aim in this commentary is to clarify how the premises that define each perspective influence its characteristic approach to the practical issues raised by the transnational movement of people and money.

Underlying our judgements on these issues are assumptions concerning the moral significance of national boundaries. What gives governments the right to keep people in or out, or to regulate the movement of money from one country to another? What is the moral standing or legitimacy of the state as an institution? These questions are linked in turn to more general questions about the moral standing of social institutions.

A central issue for each perspective, therefore, is how it handles the question of existing institutions. Does it have a theory of social institutions and, if so, what is the character of this theory? What assumptions does it make about *de facto* power relations? In particular, to what extent does the perspective ascribe moral legitimacy to existing institutions, especially the state? It might be helpful to consider briefly how each perspective deals with these questions before discussing its approach to transnational migration.

Marxism is disinclined in principle to accept the legitimacy of existing institutions. For Marx, the family, property and the state are part of the superstructure of bourgeois society. They are institutions reflecting the economic requirements of a historically transient epoch and are ethically defensible, if at all, only in instrumental terms as necessary stages in the journey towards socialism.

Realist discourse usually takes the legitimacy of the state for granted; only when pressed does it take the trouble to justify the state as a condition of order and of morality itself. Realists argue about whether particular policies are or are not in the national interest, not whether the national interest should be promoted.

Libertarianism recognizes the legitimacy of the elementary institutions of contract, property and inheritance, but questions that of other institutions unless they can be constructed from these elements. Although this stripped-down theory of entitlement might in principle justify some existing arrangements, it is in fact subversive of most. Libertarians, like others committed to principles starkly at variance with existing thought and practice, tend to respond either by sticking to their guns and ignoring the degree to which this distances them from practical policy debates, or by amending these principles to make them more palatable to conventional tastes. The austere libertarianism described by Hillel Steiner, by imagining away most of the facts that actually shape the issues of transnational migration, bars itself from throwing much light on these issues. The more pragmatic libertarianism defended by Deepak Lal accepts existing entitlements as given. In doing so, however, it positions libertarianism for participation in the migration debate at the cost of jettisoning the very postulate that most clearly distinguishes it from other traditions.

Liberal egalitarianism incorporates an even wider diversity of views. On one side it shades into libertarianism, regarding equality as a premise rather than a substantive goal. On the other it approaches the Marxist perspective, for the more one emphasizes the egalitarian half of liberal egalitarianism the closer one moves towards collectivism and economic redistribution. Nor is liberty versus equality the only tension within this tradition. Liberal egalitarians often espouse a cosmopolitanism that attaches little independent significance to national boundaries. But there is also a significant communitarian strand in liberal egalitarian thinking, according to which the political community is the significant unit within which liberty and equality must be defined and guaranteed. This argument pushes the communitarian branch of liberal egalitarianism towards the proposition that the political community must be preserved as a condition for the realization of these values – that is, towards political realism.

Natural law has the most fully articulated theory of social institutions for it rests on the Aristotelian premise that human existence is intrinsically social. Human beings require membership in some kind of society. But one cannot live in society without participating in morally deficient institutions. Laws are necessary for the settlement of disputes according to known rules, and therefore one must obey even unjust laws while doing what one can to repair the injustice. Disobedience is warranted only in extreme cases. Natural law thus recognizes both the contingency and the moral legitimacy of institutions like contract, property, the family and civil society. At the same time, it does not assume that the forms these institutions take in particular societies are necessarily just. Morality, however, is universally binding – it is not just another social institution with its own particular rules.

Each of the perspectives, then, rests on a theory of social institutions in general and of the state in particular. These theories shape, though they do not necessarily determine, how each perspective approaches the issues of transnational migration. I would like therefore to look more closely at each of the perspectives, focusing on the way its theory of the state affects its approach to migration.

The Marxist critique of existing institutions as oppressive, and its attack on morality as one more form of institutionalized oppression, make it hard for Marxists to develop a consistent position on the migration issue. Marxists cannot argue about migration in terms of duties and rights. By rejecting morality, Marxists are in effect committed to an ethic of consequences according to which we ought to do whatever promotes the outcomes identified by Marxist science as best for humanity. But, given its hostility to morality as bourgeois ideology, it is far easier for Marxism to abandon its cosmopolitanism than its consequentialism, and therefore it tends to favour or oppose free movement on tactical grounds. Thus, as Chris Brown reports, Engels supported Irish immigration (it would strengthen the British working class) whereas Marx subsequently opposed it (it was dividing the proletariat). Notwithstanding Marxism's cosmopolitan premises, twentieth-century socialist regimes have typically presided over closed societies in which both internal and external movement is tightly controlled.

A similar temptation to abandon cosmopolitan values has distorted many Marxist discussions of international trade and investment. Marxist economic theory must deal with many contradictions, not least with the fact that its view of economic change as transnational sits uneasily with its commitment to economic planning. A planned economy requires frontiers, an organized society within which economic goals can be pursued by directing economic activity, yet Marxists argue (as do other economists) that nations cannot be insulated from developments in the world economy. When the discrepancy between national goals and economic realities becomes too great, economic and political systems collapse, as occurred in Eastern Europe during 1989.

The paradox of labour and capital mobility for Marxism, then, is that, whatever its long-run consequences, in the short run it undermines socialism within countries. Marxist writing on international affairs has in the past fallen all too easily into the pattern of justifying almost any foreign policy advantageous to the interests of progressive states, on the grounds that whatever advances 'socialism in one country' will in the long run advance socialism everywhere. Such arguments have been used to license whatever policies appeared most favourable to the survival of socialist states, themselves instruments for promoting the ultimate victory of communism. Under the conditions of state socialism during much of the twentieth century, this has usually meant putting severe restrictions on the movement of both people and money. But it is worth emphasizing that even a global socialism would be committed to a command economy, and therefore to imposing limits on free movement whenever the achievement of economic goals required it.

There are, of course, other Marxist positions on the issue of free movement. Indeed, the range of concepts and arguments open to Marxists is so wide that one can argue a Marxist case for almost any position, especially if one is allowed to add to the traditional stock of materialist concepts. Neo-Marxist theorists often argue in ways that are in considerable tension with Marx's own historical materialism. These theorists, not unreasonably, want to use and improve Marxism in a critical way, and, as Philippe van Parijs suggests, this may well mean substituting new ideas for old, more authentically Marxist, but nevertheless inadequate notions. This process cannot proceed very far, however, before it starts to eat away at the premises that have historically defined the Marxist viewpoint and distinguished it from its rivals. For example, the theoretical tension generated by certain recent accounts of exploitation arises because the concept of inequality cannot really generate the concept of exploitation without smuggling in a moral premise that defines exploitation as unjust inequality. What we have here, then, is a case of neo-Marxism borrowing from the superstructure to repair the crumbling foundations of historical materialism. But other traditions, on examination, also turn out to be ramshackle constructions. Perhaps making repairs and additions to keep one's inheritance from collapsing altogether is what it means to work within a tradition.

There are remarkable similarities between classical Marxism and political realism, notwithstanding their different attitudes towards the state. Marxists may slide, for tactical reasons, from *raison de classe* to *raison d'état*, but realists, when pressed, are also likely to offer universalist reasons for advancing national interests. The state, they argue, is if not the source at least the condition of value. Realism presupposes both the existence and moral legitimacy of the state and, by extension, the international system. That system is seldom defended as ideal, but as David Hendrickson's contribution makes clear, its permanence is fundamental to the realist outlook. Political realism is therefore the most unambiguously state-oriented of the perspectives considered here.

If realism is concerned in the first instance with what is good for the political community in an environment constrained by the alleged necessities of power, then, as Susan Strange argues, there will be different kinds of realism depending on what kind of political community we are talking about. Speaking only of economics, we get five: imperialist, mercantilist, autarkist, and developmental realism, each reflecting the interests of different kinds of creditor or debtor states, plus global or structural realism, which is concerned with the interests of the system as a whole. But do we really have five distinct kinds of realism? Political realism, as a logical construct, always takes the form of a community-oriented consequentialism, though the community whose interests are taken as paramount can be defined more or less inclusively.

Realism focuses on the interests of a given community, not on what it is right to do even if it harms those interests. Realist discourse therefore gets caught up with the consequences of policies, with empirical claims, and with measuring and comparing costs and benefits. Realists, like Marxists and utilitarians, find it hard to keep moral considerations distinct from other concerns; ethics merges into economics. As with economic arguments, realist arguments often turn on empirical considerations because ethical judgement, for realism, is ultimately tied to reasoning about consequences, that is, to judgements about contingent facts and causal relations. Migration, for example, may strengthen the state by expanding the economy and creating wealth, but at the same time it may weaken it by undermining cultural unity. The dependence of realist analysis on empirical arguments of this kind suggests its essential indeterminacy, morally speaking.

Political realism is not committed to the blanket rejection of moral concerns in international affairs, but includes a wide range of views that accept the force of moral arguments while limiting the full application of those arguments where the vital interests of a political community are at stake. How these limits are defended is less significant in this context than the belief, firmly held by all who are properly labelled realists, that any defensible moral system must include a consequentialist escape clause.

Some realists would invoke this escape clause at an early stage, while others argue that it must be confined to situations of supreme emergency. Just when moral principle should give way to consequentialist reason of state is the core issue that shapes realist ethical discourse. Realists are quite prepared to tolerate liberal policies on the transnational movement of people and money, provided they do not threaten important national values or interests.

It is now less puzzling why David Hendrickson keeps alluding to international law. Both realism and international law take the existence of the state and the states system as given, and assign it a certain legitimacy. This is also true of the 'morality of states' defended by moralists who reason from broadly internationalist premises. Here, the state has, as least, international legitimacy as a member of the society of states, whatever its internal legitimacy may be; in other words, as members of the society of states, tyrannies are as legitimate as democracies. Moreover, realists prefer positive law to morality as a guide to state conduct because it is based on agreement and practice, and not, as in the case of natural law, on pure (and from the realist perspective, fallible) reason. Realism exhibits a disposition to be practical – and being practical is taken to require paying attention to the consequences of what you are doing. Many realists are, as Henrickson suggests, liberal constitutionalists, possibly pessimistic liberal egalitarians; it is a mistake to say that they are not authentic realists. In our discussions at the Mont St Michel Conference, there was a lot of talk about 'hard' (amoral nationalist) realists and 'cuddly' (moral constitutionalist) realists, as if the latter did not merit the title of realist; a sounder view is that it is the constitutionalists who best represent the tradition, the 'hard' realists merely reflecting the tradition's vulgar side.

Libertarianism reverses the subordination of principles to consequences that characterize both Marxism and realism. For libertarians, outcome-oriented considerations are secondary to considerations of principle. Property rights must be respected, however uneven the distribution of wealth within and between societies, provided that the property has been legitimately acquired, either through original appropriation of unowned things or through legitimate transfers of title. In practice, however, the gap between libertarianism and other perspectives is not nearly so wide as these principles suggest, for few libertarians are prepared to defend an unqualified commitment to them. Many would introduce the egalitarian principle that 'natural resources . . . belong to all persons equally', as Hillel Steiner puts it, thereby encumbering property rights with entitlements in favour of equal individual shares to natural resources, regardless of the location and current ownership of these resources. Because this qualification really generates a kind of liberal egalitarianism, it may be useful to look at the implications of a purer, less constrained libertarianism for the issues of free movement.

This unconstrained libertarianism is both rationalist and radical. Individuals face few restrictions on what they do with themselves and their property, except for restrictions they impose on themselves through contract. They are presumably free to move anywhere they wish and to take what they own with them. And since they cannot take land with them, some libertarians hold that landowners have a right to secede from any association (such as a state) within whose jurisdiction this land is located. Laws and policies that interfere with legitimate property rights are morally indefensible. It is obvious that few existing titles of ownership would bear scrutiny if held to the standard of original appropriation from nature plus continuous lawful transfer down to the present time. Nor, since the kind of property right of most interest to libertarians has been the right to own land, could territorial states exist where landowners possessed the right of secession.

As Onora O'Neill argues in her comments on Hillel Steiner's chapter, rationalist libertarianism is handicapped in its efforts to address substantive policy questions by its minimalist theory of social institutions. Libertarianism in fact undermines its own position by postulating individuals so abstracted from any institutional or cultural context as to be virtually featureless: useful place-holders in abstract economic theory, but less useful for ethics. Ethics is about real people and real people are socially constructed. It is not clear that this minimalist theory is essential to libertarianism, however. If we regard classical liberalism as a kind of libertarianism, we encounter libertarians who are working with a much richer model of social institutions.

One of the attractions of libertarianism is its willingness to think through the implications of taking individual liberty seriously as a political principle. Classical liberalism approaches this task by arguing that the state is best regarded as a regime for regulating the relations of free individuals under known and enforceable rules, that is, the rule of law. On this view, there are no substantive purposes that government should favour or try to force on those who do not share them – no stable end-state patterns which it is the office of government to maintain. Government is the custodian of the laws, not the manager of an enterprise for the advancement of which laws are instrumental.

F. A. Hayek has argued this view vigorously, but Deepak Lal's argument is not helped by his reliance on Hayek. Hayek mistakes the possible causal connection between the market and the rule of law for a conceptual connection. He suggests that the kind of order constituted by the rule of law must, like the market, be a spontaneous order. But such a legal order can be constituted by agreement as well as emerge spontaneously through custom; a community can even agree that it will be governed by custom, that is, by common law. The political theorist who has most cogently analyzed the idea of the rule of law is not Hayek but Michael Oakeshott.

Lal's case against limiting international capital flows does not in fact rest on a Hayekian foundation, however, for he argues that such limitations impair economic efficiency, not that they violate the rule of law. Presumably if controls could be shown to increase economic efficiency, Lal would have no principled objection to them. That being the case, it is hard to see on what grounds his view can be called libertarian.

The kind of libertarianism embodied in classical liberalism, then, does not depend on theories about the contractual origins of the state, nor need it assume that any particular unit – local, national, or supranational – is the only level at which the rule of law may exist. Any association governed by the rule of law is a legitimate association, regardless of how it was established. And, despite its anti-consequentialist stance, libertarianism does not necessarily challenge views, like political realism, that permit morality or the rule of law to be overriden for the public good. A libertarian might well argue, as many have, that the minimal state could properly be concerned with security or public order as a condition for the realization of a liberal regime governed by the rule of law. Such an argument could also be used to support the extremity thesis of political realism, according to which the rule of law may be suspended, temporarily, if necessary to deal with emergencies.

This is not the place to explore the implications of what might be called 'rule of law liberalism' or answer objections to it, but it seems more attractive than the libertarianism of either Steiner or Lal, perhaps because it comes closer to the outlook of realism and natural law, each of which also, though in different ways, tries to resolve the tension between morality and necessity while acknowledging the force of each. I shall return to this point in discussing natural law.

Liberal egalitarianism offers another middle position between an ethic of rights and principles, on the one hand, and an ethic of consequences, on the other. But it is a highly eclectic compromise. Liberal egalitarianism comprises a family of viewpoints within which various liberal and egalitarian considerations receive different weights. Because the trade-offs between rights and consequences can be made in so many different ways, the liberal egalitarian position not only covers a wide range of perspectives but generates a certain incoherence. This incoherence is compounded by its attempts to combine both libertarian and welfarist theories of that state.

Ian Little and Joseph Carens are certainly aware of this incoherence. As Little suggests, liberal egalitarianism is a mixture of liberalism and egalitarianism in which either liberty comes first or equality does, or else there is some compromise. And Carens acknowledges that liberal egalitarianism contains conflicting arguments. Can these conflicts be overcome through a compromise that is not itself internally inconsistent?

The most common compromise is to restrict some but not all liberties for the sake of equality. But equality for whom? As in the case of realism, we need to specify the community within which these trade-offs are computed. Usually, this community is the state. Moreover, as Little suggests, practically speaking a concern with 'equality' often becomes a concern for aggregate welfare. Some liberal egalitarians take the idea of substantive equality seriously, but others do not. Many global egalitarians (such as defenders of the 'New International Economic Order' during the 1960s and 70s) have been concerned with redistribution among but not within states: they have argued for more equality between rich and poor states but have not been particularly concerned with the often immense disparities of individual wealth within countries.

The difficulty in articulating a consistent liberal egalitarian ethic goes deeper than the tension between liberty and equality. The liberal half of liberal egalitarianism is concerned with moral principles as constraints on conduct. This is a view of morality it shares with natural law. The egalitarian or welfarist half of liberal egalitarianism, however, is consequentialist; in this respect it resembles Marxism and political realism. The other perspectives seem able to resolve the tension between morality and consequences more consistently than does liberal egalitarianism. Realism and Marxism are ultimately instrumental viewpoints, for it is the survival of the political community or the well-being of humanity as a species-being that provides the decisive criterion for determining when to obey and when to ignore normal moral and legal constraints. Libertarianism and natural law, in contrast, are inclined to put morality first, as the slogans associated with these views suggest: that 'it is better to suffer wrong than to do it', that 'evil may not be done for the sake of good', that we should 'let justice be done, though the world perish', or, more prosaically in our own time, that 'rights are trumps'.

Joseph Carens' chapter illustrates the tension in liberal egalitarianism between principles and consequences, as well as between universal and communitarian values. He suggests that liberal egalitarianism favours freedom of movement, tolerating restrictions only if they are likely to promote liberty and equality in the long run, or are necessary to preserve a distinct way of life. But of course Marxists too want to promote liberty and equality (in the long run), while realists want to preserve communal liberty and distinct ways of life. One comes away from his discussion (and from Jim Woodward's reaction to it) with the impression that it is all too easy to combine a variety of incompatible concerns into liberal egalitarianism. The Rawlsian version of the original contract, on which many liberal egalitarian theorists rely in order to discipline this combination, has in practice generated a startling profusion of interpretations. The disagreement between Rawls and Beitz over whether the foundational contract is a communal or a global one is just one example suggesting the essentially arbitrary and indeterminate character of Rawlsian theory. In short, liberal egalitarianism sometimes looks like little more than a vehicle for whatever opinions happen currently to be in favour in democratic societies. Perhaps this eclecticsm is an advantage: philosophically purer viewpoints, like libertarianism, may not be politically sound.

Both of Carens' arguments for restrictions on movement – that such restrictions are justified when they serve to promote liberty and equality or to preserve distinct ways of life – are consequentialist ones. Carens recognizes this, suggesting that these arguments can lead to abuses of the sort that have given utilitarianism a bad name. He therefore acknowledges the essential point that promoting liberty is not the same thing as respecting it. But he also puts his finger on the utilitarian character of liberal egalitarianism, in so far as it understands liberty and equality to be substantive ends rather than formal constraints.

Ian Little agrees. For Little, the liberal egalitarian ethic is a weighted, constrained utilitarianism: it permits us to give more weight to the interests of fellow nationals than to those of foreigners, yet it is constrained by a prohibition against treating foreigners purely as instruments. Provided we avoid doing that, liberal egalitarianism permits restrictions on capital movements that increase the welfare of the restricting state. Often, however, such restrictions are counterproductive. On the whole, Little suggests, free trade benefits all countries and it benefits poor countries the most. There is no conflict here between liberalism and egalitarianism.

But we can imagine situations in which liberty and equality are not so easily reconciled, as well as versions of liberal egalitarianism with constraints on utility maximization strong enough to drive one rapidly out of the utilitarian camp. Little is sceptical of the idea of natural justice, believing all justice to depend on the conventions of existing communities, yet his definition of liberal egalitarianism leaves room for an ethical outlook that does not differ radically from that of natural law. There is not a huge difference between a utilitarianism constrained by the duty to respect human rights and a natural law ethic in which duties of beneficence are governed by principles that rule out certain ways of acting beneficently, namely those that sacrifice the rights of some for the good of others.

From the perspective of natural law, the central issue is whether the free movement of people and money is morally required. Ann Dummett has chosen to frame the issue, so far as the movement of people is concerned, in the language of human rights. She thus makes the rather large assumption that the idea of human rights belongs to natural law. Whether the idea of natural or human rights is an authentic expression of natural law, or whether human rights and natural law are conceptions essentially at odds with one another is an issue we cannot get into here. But whatever the outcome of that debate, there are grounds for doubting the claim that the free movement of peoples is something that may be asserted, within the natural law tradition, as a matter of right. In particular, the assertion of such a right would appear to run contrary to the natural law understanding of political society, which allows and may even require various kinds of closure. Certainly there will be circumstances in which both public officials and citizens ought to provide aid or refuge to those who need it, regardless of nationality. This is not the same thing as a duty to provide aid or refuge in the form of citizenship to *all* persons who may *desire* it.

Natural law, like political realism, sharply distinguishes moral principle and practical expediency. In this respect, at least, the two are in fact natural allies, despite their obvious differences. According to realism, a concern for order and welfare can override moral duties; according to natural law, moral duties limit the pursuit of order and welfare. To put it differently, in realism respect for moral principles is limited by considerations of prudence, whereas in natural law the prudential pursuit of individual and collective goals is always constrained by moral principles. But as this way of putting it suggests, both realism and natural law understand morality and prudence to be analytically distinct considerations. Each sees morality as a matter of respecting constraints, not achieving good ends, and recognizes that the prudential pursuit of order and welfare, as good ends, may necessitate but cannot justify violating moral prohibitions. In both the realist and natural law traditions, there is a strong commitment to the old view that morality concerns the intrinsic relation between an act and a principle, whereas bringing about good ends concerns the causal relation between an act and its consequences.

Both traditions are wary of compromise and incline towards an extreme solution of the tension between morality and prudence, though of course they resolve this tension in different ways. Realism does it by siding with morality in normal circumstances and with consequentialist prudence in circumstances affecting the public safety, while natural law achieves consistency by ruling out consequentialism entirely (where consequentialism is understood as an ethic driven by outcome-oriented considerations, and not merely the proposition that one should pay attention to consequences within the domain governed by moral principles). Disputes within the morality of natural law are resolved by a casuistry of principles, not through the calculation and comparison of consequences.

Despite their differences, then, both realism and natural law support the conclusion that the realm of morality is one thing and the realm of prudence another. And this has the virtue of helping them keep the issues clear, even if they reach different conclusions regarding action. This is not to say that either tradition is immune from confusion, only that their incoherences are accidental rather than necessary. Both acknowledge the importance of law and political authority in realizing the common good of the community, and both permit communities to govern the movement of people and money for the common good, provided they do this in ways that are consistent with the principles of morality and law, which are themselves part of that common good. They diverge chiefly on the issue of necessity, realists condoning violations of morality and law for the sake of the community that natural lawyers must condemn as unjust even in cases of supposed necessity.

We might conclude by asking what is involved by identifying arguments on free movement and other issues of international affairs as belonging to or reflecting an ethical 'viewpoint' or 'perspective'. Are we talking about historical traditions or analytical constructs? If the former, then we are concerned with historically specific languages of ethical debate. The various traditions may then converge because a wide range of views can be expressed in each of these languages (whether authentically or not is a matter of controversy), and because it may be hard for those working in a tradition to insulate themselves from prevailing opinion (hence the marked liberal egalitarian spin given to natural law by Ann Dummett and Paul Weithman). There is also a tendency for the traditions to converge because reasonable people within each tradition see the force of good arguments coming from the other camps. For all these reasons, one might almost say that each tradition reproduces the full range of positions on any given issue, expressing each position in its own terms. If we understand the viewpoints to be analytical constructs, however, then their essential differences come more sharply into view.

── 19 ──

The quest for consistency:
A sceptical view

Brian Barry

In Chapter 2, Robert Goodin articulates three propositions which recur a number of times in the rest of this book. These are as follows: 1) in an ideal world there would be no legal impediments to migration; 2) there is some sort of hypocrisy involved in a country's proclaiming a universal right of emigration while itself running a restrictive policy with regard to immigration; and 3) there is at any rate a prima facie moral inconsistency in having different rules for the transfer of money and the migration of people. At the risk of giving the book the appearance of an ill-coordinated pantomime horse, I should like in these concluding remarks to cast some doubt on all three propositions.

1. Would open borders be ideal?

If we say that in an ideal world borders would be open, the significance of this claim depends entirely on what we build into the specification of an ideal world. Thus, we might say that an ideal world would be one in which the vast majority of people were content with conditions in their own countries. Migration would then occur only for idiosyncratic reasons. People would still, presumably, fall in love across frontiers, and we could still expect to find British optical astronomers drawn to Southern California. But there would be no systematic quality to such migration. I believe that such a world would indeed be ideal and that much could as a practical matter be done to bring it far closer to being realized than it is now.

If that is our conception of an ideal world, it is hard to see how anyone could deny that freedom of emigration and immigration would be desirable. Now it may be said (and it appears that Goodin would be one to say it) that there is something morally obnoxious about proclaiming a right whose existence depends upon not too many people exercising it. I suggest, however, that any activity subject to congestion is liable to exactly the same phenomenon. Access to a freeway is normally unrestricted but those with mature freeway systems (as in Los Angeles) control access at peak hours with traffic lights. Unrestricted access to wilderness areas becomes self-defeating if so many people avail themselves of it to destroy the very quality of wilderness that attracted them in the first place. A system of permits is the only solution. If the same conclusion has not been drawn about jewels such as Yosemite and the English Lake District this does not mean it should not be. Nobody demands that the Bayreuth Festival should move its operations to a football stadium to accommodate the numbers who would like to attend. But the same essential connection between the quality of the experience and the limited number of participants holds far more widely than just in the arts.

A minimalist conception of an ideal world, in contrast with the one just considered, would be one that was identical with the existing one with the one exception (admittedly a big one) that states were motivated entirely by moral considerations. To claim that under these conditions there would be open borders is to say, in effect, that the only reason why there are not open borders now is that states are motivated by self-interest or other non-moral motives (such as, for example, racism). I believe that this conclusion could not possibly be endorsed on the basis of any moral outlook that paid any attention to consequences. (If the kind of libertarian theory employed by Hillel Steiner is not concerned with consequences, that is one reason, though not the only one, for rejecting it.)

Nobody can claim to know in any detail what would be the consequences of a worldwide system of open borders sustained over a number of decades. We know that millions of people already have an active wish to migrate to North America and Western Europe. But we also know that mass migration snowballs. A few pioneers emigrate to a certain place, send back advice, encouragement and money, are then joined by more, and so on.[1] As in some of the remoter parts of Norway and Sweden in the second half of the nineteenth century, this process can continue until an area becomes depopulated completely.

We might approach the question in an a priori spirit and postulate that in equilibrium under the regime of unrestricted migration all parts of the world would be equally attractive to live in. Migrants would therefore continue to flow until a state of what one might call preferential entropy obtained. This idea helps to focus thought, but it clearly oversimplifies by presupposing that everyone in the world shares, and always will share, a common set of preferences with regard to places in which to live.

It may well be that (barring man-made catastrophes such as Chernobyl) Lapps are happy to live in Lappland, but hardly anybody else wishes to join them. If so, this would show not that everybody has identical preferences and ranks Lappland equally with the rest of the world but that Lapps have a preference for a certain kind of physical environment that is not shared by others.

The point is far more general than this example might suggest. What people have preferences for is not simply the climate and the terrain but a way of life. Although not very different in climate or terrain, Germany and Britain are linguistically and culturally different in ways that make each more attractive to some people and less attractive to others. Thus, Irish people continue to flow into mainland Britain rather than take up the option of moving to wealthier EEC countries such as West Germany. Conversely, the conditions for mass migration were extremely conducive when the border between East and West Germany was opened, because the cultural deterrent was negligible; indeed, the adjustment experienced by those who moved may be no greater than that inflicted on those who stayed behind.

We might therefore formulate a rule that people will migrate from a place so long as there is at least one other place with a material standard of living higher enough to offset the cultural differences between the two places. This is, however, less of a modification than might appear of the original proposition. For mass migration obviously has the effect of changing the recipient area, as I have already observed in passing. Immigrants of similar background will almost inevitably cluster together, forming first enclaves then substantial minorities in the major cities. If we are prepared to stick with the wildly counterfactual stipulation that borders would continue to be maintained beyond this point, there will be nothing to check this process before immigrants have a majority within major units of government or indeed countries.

This is, of course, precisely what happened to the native populations of countries of European settlement, but there is no reason why it should not happen in turn to North America, Australasia and Western Europe. Especially in the light of the projections of Third World population growth in the next fifty years, a billion migrants (roughly two for every one of the current population of the developed countries just mentioned) would surely be quite a conservative estimate. Since there would be majorities from the Third World in every country of mass immigration, with culturally similar groups clustered together, the cultural barrier to further migration would disappear, and the only thing stopping its continuation would be that conditions would be no better in these countries than in the rest of the world.

If this uniform condition represented a substantial improvement over the *status quo* for the great majority of the human race, it would be hard to deny its justice, at any rate on cosmopolitan liberal premises. But this seems extraordinarily improbable. The main benefit of migration to those who stay behind is remittances sent back by emigrants. This is in itself, however, a flow of money rather than of people, and the same effects, or better ones, could clearly be achieved by systematic transfers from rich countries to poor ones. (In any case, there would be no remittances eventually because those who had left would be no better off than those who had stayed.) Apart from that, there would be some relief of population pressure on land and other resources, but a flow of a billion people over twenty or thirty years would do no more than slow the projected rise of population in the Third World. And against this very limited gain has to be offset the tendency for the population loss to be concentrated within the better-educated and most highly motivated section of the working-age population.

Within the recipient countries, immigration on the scale envisaged would inevitably cause gross overcrowding and loss of every kind of amenity. It would also result in the collapse of the medical and educational services. There is no reason to suppose that the productive capacities of these economies could survive an influx of people unaccustomed to the ways of an industrial society at a rate far too great for any kind of acculturation to be possible. Nor should we expect liberal democracy to survive, especially since uncontrolled immigration would create any number of situations of potential ethnic conflict. The countries of immigration would have all the problems of Cyprus, Sri Lanka, Northern Ireland, the Balkans and Azerbaijan.

Equilibration would come about, then, by a decline in conditions within the better-off countries to something like those of the bottom half of the world's population. Even this, however, understates the case, since it omits any consideration of the effects of open borders on world population growth and on measures to combat global warming, depletion of the ozone layer and other long-run threats to the carrying capacity of the planet. The existing regime of virtually closed borders creates pressure on governments (whether they respond to it or not) to introduce policies to control population growth. This pressure would be weakened if faster population growth in a country could be offset by faster emigration. Of course, this would be a bit worse for everyone, but a given country's increase in population spread over the world would obviously have less of an impact on those in the country than the same increase concentrated within it. Again, it seems clear that, faltering as the response of the industrial countries to 'green' issues has been, they are the only ones with the money and technology to act effectively, and will have to bankroll the rest of the world to do what has to be done. In the dystopia of open borders there would be no countries with the capacity to act. Nor, even if they had the capacity, would any have the will, since all would have the same desperation-driven short-run view understandably characteristic of present Third World governments. *De facto* the rich countries are the trustees for the planet. They are not very honest trustees – they help themselves far too much – but they are all we have.

It may perhaps be said that there is little point in belabouring the horrors of a world of open borders when it is perfectly apparent that there is never going to be such a world or one remotely approximating it. However, what makes it worth it is the consensus among the contributors that morality ideally mandates open borders. I leave out of account here the theory called realism in international relations, which bases its recommendations on national interest, and also Marxism, which is perhaps best thought of as a form of realism in which the interest of the working class replaces the interest of the nation. Natural law, liberal egalitarianism and libertarianism would all, it appears, regard open borders as the ideal. It should be admitted that Joseph Carens and Ann Dummett allow for limitations.[2] But they do not, it seems to me, confront the question: would not a regime satisfying the limitations they allow be more like the present one than like one of open borders? If it would, in what sense can we say that open borders are the ideal? I am not saying the present system could not be modified to be more humane. But I see no advantage in regarding any liberalization as a tiny move towards a supposed ideal that would in fact be a nightmare.

2. Should emigration and immigration policies be symmetrical?

The second proposition that I want to consider is that prima facie a country's policies on inflow of people should be symmetrical with its policies on outflow, so that if a country supports freedom of emigration it is under some logical pressure to adopt freedom of immigration. Both Robert Goodin and Joseph Carens toy with this idea and both endorse the view that there is something hypocritical about proclaiming a right to emigrate if under the actually existing conditions most would-be emigrants have nowhere to go. I think that what they really mean is 'nowhere to go that they want to go'. There might be several desperately poor countries with open immigration, but I doubt if Goodin or Carens would regard that as solving the problem. It is countries such as the United States that they suggest should be feeling guilt. In my view neither the general proposition nor the specific application has the slightest plausibility. Whether or not countries such as the United States ought to have more generous immigration policies, they are not committed to it by their support for freedom of emigration.

It is a general characteristic of associations that people are free to leave them but not free to join them. People can leave jobs by giving reasonable notice; they cannot get jobs by simply indicating a wish to have them. Most countries allow marriages to be dissolved unilaterally; none permits people to marry another against his or her will. As a member of the Athenaeum Club, I would have supported the wish of any member of White's to resign if he so wished, but I would never have supposed that that committed me to the view that clubs should not be free to elect their own members. Residence in a country is, of course, far more important than membership in any of these associations. But I cannot see that this affects the issue. The general point is that almost all associations operate with an asymmetry between entrance and exit, and that in all of these cases it is quite uncontroversial. So far, therefore, from there being a presumption in favour of symmetry one has to say that there is a presumption in favour of asymmetry.

In saying this I do not in the least wish to minimize the genuine hardship inflicted on somebody who wishes to migrate from one country to another and is prevented from doing so by the restrictive immigration policies of the second country. But I do not believe that anything is added – and in fact I suggest that something is subtracted – if it is argued that the hardship is somehow exacerbated and turned into a justified sense of grievance if this second country supports a right of free emigration.

Before moving on, let me briefly notice another argument from symmetry in favour of free immigration which is advanced by Joseph Carens. He points out that few countries have restrictions on internal travel and suggests that this calls for a special justification for restrictions on immigration. The first thing to be said here is that mere travel is not the issue: the parallel to travelling within one's own country is tourism within another country. If we focus on the genuine issue, which is one of residence, my comment is that governments have indeed been slow to recognize the potentially destructive effects of internal migration and should have been prepared before now to act so as to mitigate them by imposing restrictions on change of residence. Thus, it would be an excellent idea if in rural areas (especially culturally distinct ones such as Wales) nobody were allowed to buy or rent long-term accommodation who did not live or work locally. And can anyone familiar with Chicago or New York honestly say that the uncontrolled Black migration from the South between the 1930s and the 1950s has been anything but a disaster – for the inhabitants of the ghetto even more than those they displaced? A counterfactual America combining state-level controls over immigration and strong federal policies to bring economic development to the South while ensuring legal and political rights to the Blacks would surely be a better one than that which actually exists. And that is, in broad terms, the formula that I advocate for the world as a whole.

3. Should policies for people and money be similar?

The third proposition that I draw from Goodin's introductory chapter is that there is some strong suspicion of ethical inconsistency if a country has one kind of policy for movements of money and a different policy for movements of people. The aspect of this claim that he concentrates on is that most countries are pretty open to inflows of foreign capital yet all countries are relatively very restrictive about immigration. I do not believe that the suspicion of inconsistency is justified. People and money have such different characteristics that there is really no reason for expecting them to be treated in the same way.

There are, I suggest, two main differences between people and money that fully account for the widespread difference in their treatment. The first is that with a transfer of money there is a presumption that the people on both ends benefit, whereas with the migration of a person across a frontier no such presumption is in order. Provided there is no coercion involved – provided, in other words, that we are not talking about a forced borrowing or a forced loan – the lender and the borrower both presumably believe they are better off with a loan than without it. Similarly, the seller and the buyer of land or a capital asset presumably both believe that they stand to gain. There is therefore no reason for the government to intervene unless it is claimed that there is a conflict between the interest of the individual or firm engaging in the transaction and the wider interest of the collectivity. In the case of taking in capital, which is the side of the transaction we are most concerned with here, there are indeed sometimes very good reasons for preventing a person or firm from engaging in a transaction. No country would wish its defence industry to be owned by foreigners, and similar sensitivity is quite reasonable in the case of newspapers and television stations. Sales of real estate to foreigners are also sometimes restricted (in the case of Luxembourg, prohibited) and it is again easy to see why citizens of a country should take a collective view on this. It would, indeed, be quite consistent to vote for a prohibition on a kind of sale one would wish to undertake if it were not prohibited. For what we have here is a straightforward collective action problem.

Under a regime of free immigration, no such presumption of mutual advantage can be maintained. We can deduce that the immigrant must regard his or her move as on balance a good idea, but there is absolutely no reason for making the presumption that anybody in the host country thinks so. Immigration therefore fails the test, passed by financial movements, of presumptive Pareto optimality.

The situation, is of course, different in a country such as Switzerland which admits immigrants only if they have jobs and expels them when they lose them. Immigration is here simply a by-product of the workings of the labour market. The presumption is here that at any rate the employer expects to benefit from the movement across the border of the migrant. However, exactly the same potential for conflict between the interests of the individual importer (here of labour) and those of the collectivity arises here. This was made evident in Switzerland by the very strong popular support generated by proposed initiatives aimed at drastically restricting the number and concentration of immigrants.

The second point, which is so obvious that I almost feel like apologizing for making it, is that immigrants are people and societies are made up of people. Adding new people, especially if they are culturally distinctive, will inevitably change the society. (It is worth pointing out, as a sidelight on Section 2, that emigration does not change a society in the same way.) If permanent immigrants can gain citizenship after a certain time, as those who regard open borders as the ideal normally assume, this will mean that they get the vote. But even if they do not become citizens or the society is not a democracy anyway, it will inevitably have to alter its character in the process of accommodating to the presence of immigrants. And the currently wealthy countries would, obviously, be changed out of recognition if open borders meant (as I believe) that the existing populations would be greatly outnumbered by immigrants.

By contrast, foreign capital has far less effect on the everyday life of a country, especially if it is kept out of the areas I mentioned earlier. In a capitalist economy, the ownership of a firm by nationals of the country in which it is situated does nothing to guarantee that those running it will not engage in stock exchange fraud, degrade the environment, endanger the health and safety of its workforce, engage in misleading advertising, or attempt to sell shoddy goods. Checking that is the job of the unions, consumer groups and environmental groups, and above all the state. Foreign-owned firms can be caught in the same net, and may actually be easier to regulate if they are prohibited from contributing to the funds of political parties.

No doubt there is some point (in spite of Deepak Lal's complacency on the question) at which the sheer extent of foreign ownership should quite rightly become an issue. The criterion for intervention is, we may say, the same for both money and people: that the existing inhabitants of a country ought to retain control of its destiny. But precisely because of the difference between money and people, it may be quite consistent with this criterion to run a very open policy with regard to inflows of money and a very restrictive policy with regard to immigrants. If we want consistency in the policies of countries we should look for it at the level of principle and objective. To look for it at the level of policy instruments is a form of fetishism. On that basis, I could be accused of inconsistency by keeping the door closed and the window open, even though both contribute to my objective of combining ventilation with security.

Notes

1. We can analyze the process using a model developed to explain the build up of mass demonstrations, such as those that toppled the regimes of East Germany and Czechoslovakia and earlier that of the Shah of Iran. According to this, the population is divided into a number of groups differentiated by their propensity to join in a demonstration. There are some hardy souls who will demonstrate whatever the risks of injury or punishment. Once these have taken to the streets the next group, somewhat less hardy, is activated because the risk is now lower. The next group now joins in because the risk is yet lower; and so on. If the thresholds come in the right place, this model can generate a cascade effect so that the whole population eventually joins in, even if the last contingent are really quite timid. Similarly, we may suppose that a few people in an area, fuelled by some combination of desperation, ambition and restlessness, emigrate. This lowers the barriers to the group with the next highest propensity to emigrate, so they go. There are now people to live with initially who can help them get jobs, etc. Eventually there will be in the country of migration community associations, friendly societies, marriage brokers, schools, churches, lobbies and the whole panoply of social institutions. At this point going may appear to entail less discontinuity with the past than staying.
2. Robert Goodin also allows for some deviation from open borders, but his concession does not go very far. Open borders would prevail in an ideal world, but controls are permissible as a second best in an imperfect world. However, the only imperfection he admits is that of societies having less than ideal economic institutions – e.g. that some have a well-developed welfare state while others do not. However, even if all states had the same ideal economic institutions (whatever they are) the main reason for migrating – gross differences in per capita income – would still exist, and open borders would still have all the consequences I described above.

Suggested further reading

Anon., "Developments in the Law: Immigration Policy and the Rights of Aliens," *Harvard Law Review*, 96 (1983), 1286–465.

Brian Barry and Robert E. Goodin, eds., "Symposium on Duties Beyond Borders," *Ethics*, 98 (1988), 647–756.

Charles Beitz, *Political Theory and International Relations* (Princeton, N.J.: Princeton University Press, 1979).

Charles Beitz, "Cosmopolitan Ideals and National Sentiment," *Journal of Philosophy*, 80 (1983), 591–600.

Charles R. Beitz, Marshall Cohen, Thomas Scanlon and A. John Simmons, eds, *International Ethics* (Princeton, N.J.: Princeton University Press, 1985).

George J. Borjas, *Friends or Strangers: The Impact of Immigration on the U.S. Economy* (New York: Basic Books, 1990).

Peter G. Brown and Henry Shue, eds, *Boundaries: National Autonomy and Its Limits* (Totowa, N.J.: Rowman & Littlefield, 1981).

Peter G. Brown and Henry Shue, eds, *The Border that Joins: Mexican Migrants and U.S. Responsibility* (Totowa, N.J.: Rowman & Littlefield, 1983).

William Rogers Brubaker, ed., *Immigration and the Politics of Citizenship in Europe and North America* (Lanham, Md.: German Marshall Fund of America and University Press of America, 1989).

W. M. Corden, *The Theory of Protection* (Oxford: Clarendon Press, 1977).

J. R. Crotty, "On Keynes and Capital Flight," *Journal of Economic Literature*, 21 (1983), 59–65.

Alan Dowty, *Closed Borders: The Contemporary Assault on Freedom of Movement* (New Haven, Conn.: Yale University Press, 1987).

Ann Dummett and Andrew Nichol, *Subjects, Citizens, Aliens and Others: Nationality and Immigration Law* (London: Weidenfeld and Nicolson, 1990).

James Fallows, *More Like Us* (Boston, Mass.: Houghton Mifflin, 1989).

Mark Gibney, ed., *Open Borders? Closed Societies? The Ethical and Political Issues* (Westport, Conn.: Greenwood Press, 1988).

Guy S. Goodwin-Gill, *International Law and the Movement of Persons* (Oxford: Clarendon Press, 1978).

John Maynard Keynes, "National Self-Sufficiency," *Collected Writings*, ed. Donald Moggridge (London: Macmillan, 1982), vol. 21, pp. 233–46.

H. I. London, *Non-white Immigration and the "White Australia" Policy* (New York: New York University Press, 1970).

James E. Meade, "The Exchange Policy of a Socialist Government," *Collected Papers*, ed. Susan Howson (London: Unwin Hyman, 1988), vol. 3, pp. 11–26.

Terry Nardin, *Law, Morality and the Relations of States* (Princeton, N.J.: Princeton University Press, 1983).

Henry Shue, "The Burdens of Justice," *Journal of Philosophy*, 80 (1983), 600–8.

Julian Simon, *The Economic Consequences of Migration* (Oxford: Basil Blackwell, 1990).

Michael Teitelbaum, "Right versus Right: Immigration and Refugee Policy in the United States," *Foreign Affairs*, 59 (1980), 21–59.

Brinley Thomas, *International Migration and Economic Development* (Paris: UNESCO, 1961).

Karel Vasak and Sidney Liskofsky, eds, *The Right to Leave and to Return* (New York: American Jewish Commission, 1976).

Frederick G. Whelan, "Citizenship and the Right to Leave," *American Political Science Review*, 75 (1981), 53–63.

Index